*Mistress*
# PEACHUM'S
# PLEASURE

# *Mistress* PEACHUM'S PLEASURE

## Lisa Hilton

Weidenfeld & Nicolson
LONDON

First published in Great Britain in 2005
by Weidenfeld & Nicolson, a division of
the Orion Publishing Group Ltd
Orion House
5 Upper Saint Martin's Lane
London
WC2H 9EA

A CIP catalogue record for this book is
available from the British Library.

ISBN 0 297 84768 6

Typeset, printed and bound in Great Britain by
Butler and Tanner Ltd, Frome and London

www.orionbooks.co.uk

*For Michèle*

# CONTENTS

# LIST OF ILLUSTRATIONS

# $\mathcal{A}$CKNOWLEDGEMENTS

I should like to thank the Marquis of Winchester, whose thoughtful letter set me on Lavinia's trail, and to express my gratitude to Lord and Lady Bolton, who allowed me to visit Bolton Hall and were most generous with their time and knowledge. The unrolling of Will Godson's map was unforgettable. The Dowager Lady Bolton was also extremely kind in sharing her books and pictures with me

Thank you to the Garrick Club for permission to read in what must be the most elegant library in London, and particularly to Ms Enid Forster, who was both welcoming and wonderfully informative. Ms Sue Daley at the Sotheby's Archive, the staffs of the Heinz Archive, British Library, Bodleian Library, Courtauld Institute, London Theatre Museum, Blackheath Library, House of Lords Records Office, Hampshire Records Office and of the Archives Départementales at Montauban were all very helpful. The Reverend Canon Giles Harcourt provided an enchanting late-night tour of St Alphege's Church, Greenwich – many thanks.

Christopher Hamilton provided essential musical insights, and Mia Bengtsson tremendous technical help. Fosco Bianchetti and Michèle Dunstan both gave me much-needed spaces to write, without which this book could not have been completed. I should like to thank Sally Connolly and Professor Rosemary Ashton of University College London for allowing me to rehearse some of the book in lecture form. Lady Antonia Fraser was a source of encouragement and inspiring advice for which I am also very grateful.

Thank you to Michael Alcock, of Johnson and Alcock, for having such faith and patience, and to Alan Samson of Weidenfeld & Nicolson for his enduring belief in the book. I am greatly indebted to Caroline North for her wonderfully thorough editing, and for an unexpected familiarity with the mysteries of bloodstock terminology, and to Tom Graves for researching the illustrations.

My warmest thanks to Anna Hilton, for helping in too many ways to number, and to Professor Anthony Nuttall, of New College, Oxford, who first taught me that the Scriblerians were nothing to be afraid of.

Lisa Hilton
Spring 2005

'... by preserving their VARTUE, some maids had taken so with their masters that they had married them, and kept them coaches, and lived vastly grand and happy, and some, mayhap, came to be duchesses.'

John Cleland, *Memoirs of a Woman of Pleasure*

'There is no observation more frequently made by such as employ themselves in surveying the conduct of mankind that Marriage, though the dictate of Nature, and the institution of Providence, is yet very often the cause of Misery.'

Samuel Johnson, *The Rambler*

'Marry you? God, no! But I'll love you.'

Congreve, *All for Love*

# PROLOGUE

## The Duchess and the Irish Surgeon

Passion is a surprising thing to come upon a person at the age of forty-seven, particularly in Tunbridge Wells. George Kelly had tender hands and dancing Irish eyes, a soft manner with the ladies and a firm grasp on the main chance. Widowed for four years, rich and independent, a little heavier, perhaps, in the face and hips than in the days when she was the most famous woman in London, but handsome yet, the Duchess of Bolton found him irresistible. All her life, Lavinia had been prudent. Pleasure had never been permitted to take the place of profit. But now she was free of the Duke and his gouty petulance, her boys were grown, she bore a great aristocratic name and her peevish relations by marriage, the Paulets, could go hang. Years ago, her stage father in *The Beggar's Opera*, Mr Peachum, had consoled her for her stage lover's death: 'Set your heart at rest, Polly. Your husband is to die today. Therefore, if you are not already provided, it's high time to look about for another. There's comfort for you, you slut.' Handsome Tom Walker was dead himself by now, along with her old stage mates Mr Hippisley and Mr Hall, Mrs Clarke and Mrs Egleton, but there was something of the celebrated Polly Peachum in Lavinia still, of the woman who had made the town weep, so convincingly had she pleaded for the man she loved, and who had other ideas for herself beyond the world's intentions. The Duchess of Bolton had suffered enough from the scandals of the world, and now she decided to disgrace herself upon her own terms, and took George Kelly as her lover.

Charming Mr Kelly attended the Duchess in her illnesses, caught her eye meaningfully at the assembly rooms, barred to her for so long, where at last she was free to mingle with other women of her rank. Wondered in a whisper, over a hand caught briefly, discreetly, at cards or across the pages of a shared volume of poetry, whether he might dare, might presume . . . How pleasant it was, at last, to be pleased instead of pleasing, to be whimsical, a touch capricious even, to be cajoled from imaginary little sulks and petted into good humour, to take a drive, or a box at the play, with no one's pleasure to consult but one's own. Mr Kelly was so obliging, so eager that she should not feel lonely, that she could depend, slowly, slowly, solely upon him.

Surprisingly, nobody was very interested in what Horace Walpole called Lavinia's 'last lapse into Pollyhood'.[1] Her celebrity was little more than a memory, and for those who did recall that the Duchess of Bolton had once been an actress, her behaviour was only to be expected. Living quietly at Tunbridge, Lavinia enjoyed her first, brief, love affair with remarkably little interference from a society which had once clamoured for the least detail of her existence. If the world considered it at all, the world concurred, rightly, that the Duchess of Bolton was making a very great fool of herself. Mr Kelly, dancing Irish eyes or no, was clearly an adventurer, prepared to take up with an ailing middle-aged woman and play the romantic swain, to squire her about in public and to do the necessary in her bed with his imagination elsewhere and his dancing eyes on a settlement. If Lavinia knew so herself, she wouldn't care, despite the remonstrations of her watchful sons. She was perfectly accustomed to the agreement of bargains, to a life in which love was a commodity to be purchased, at best a polite gloss on a successful sale. Like John Gay, Lavinia was familiar with the milieu of trade, and like Gay, she perceived the similarities it held with the aristocratic society that assumed itself superior. Recalling Hogarth's famous picture of *The Beggar's Opera*, she was aware it was no accident after all that among the audience John Rich, the theatre manager, had been painted in next to Mr Cook the auctioneer, while Mr Gay the writer and His Grace the Duke of Bolton, the lover, looked on. Hogarth's arrangement showed those who cared to look that all the world was for sale, however fine its costume.

Mr Kelly, then, was no different from the other scramblers through Vanity Fair, no different from Lavinia, who had herself obtained the means to buy him by keeping a cool head and a just assessment of her own value. So if the Duchess indulged herself in a delusion of her surgeon's affections, she played him fair and had her money's worth. Ever since her first fame, Lavinia had lived with vicious slurs on her character and her conduct, accused of selling herself from the day she had first come to notice as Polly Peachum, shunned by society until her marriage finally entitled her to a place within it, and even then beset by the grasping prejudice of her husband's relations. She had endured loneliness, insecurity and boredom, the loss of her friends and of her successful career. So when she eventually became what the world had accused her of being all along, it was at least after a manner of her own choosing. The Duchess of Bolton skipped gaily and wilfully down to posterity hand in hand with her lover, as careless at the end as poor bedraggled Moll Hackabout, out on the spree with her highwayman beau.

Lavinia Fenton, Duchess of Bolton, died in her house at Westcombe, Greenwich on 24 January 1760. She was buried at her favourite church of St Alfege's, in a coffin inscribed:

> The Most Illustrious
> Lady Lavinia Duchess of Bolton
> Dowager of the most High
> Puissant and Nobel Prince
> Charles Powlett late Duke of Bolton
> Marquis of Winchester, Earl of Wiltshire & co.
> Died 24th January 1760
> Aged forty nine years.

'The last century has not produced', wrote William Cooke of Lavinia, 'perhaps a greater instance of the change of fortune in an individual than in the character before us ... nobody's daughter, bred up, in the early part of her life, at the bar of a public coffee house; afterwards introduced upon the stage, with a handsome person and attractive accomplishments, and yet with all these links to seduction, conducting herself with that propriety and conduct so as to attain the first rank in the country, with the esteem and approbation of the public.'[2] An article in the *British Magazine* of 1760 confidently attested that the Duke of Bolton had never regretted marrying Lavinia 'as she filled every duty of that high station with becoming dignity, as duchess, wife and mother. Admired by all, she enjoyed her envied laurels for many years, as the Bolton family can testify.' Whether this was an attempt by the disgruntled Paulets to put a good face on matters now that Lavinia was no longer a trouble is unclear, but even Lavinia's ambitious mother Mrs Beswick might have been satisfied with that. If it were true.

Four days after Lavinia's death, Horace Walpole had written to George Montague: 'There has been cruel havoc among the ladies, my Lady Granby is dead, and the famous Polly, Duchess of Bolton, and my Lady Bessborough.'[3] Lavinia might have passed away in elevated company, but Walpole, bearing in mind her association with the slights endured by his father, the former Prime Minister Robert Walpole, was keen to the last to undermine any pretensions she may have had to virtue. 'Two years ago,' he gossiped gleefully, 'ill at Tunbridge, she picked up an Irish surgeon. When she was dying the fellow sent for a lawyer to make her will, but the man, finding who was to be her heir instead of her children, refused to draw it. The Court of Chancery did furnish one other not quite so scrupulous, and her sons have but a thousand pounds apiece, the surgeon about nine thousand.' No one was at all surprised that such a scandalous story about Lavinia Fenton should prove, for once, to be correct. The day after Horace Walpole wrote his letter the *Public Advertiser* confirmed that the Duchess of Bolton had indeed left the bulk of her fortune to her Irish surgeon.

George Kelly's role in Lavinia Fenton's last years is one of the few events of her existence which have been chronicled with any accuracy. Hers was an Augustan life in terms not only of its chronology, but in its resemblance to those literary works with which its span coincides. The writings of the period are fascinating not only because of the dazzling dexterity of their scholarship and linguistic audacity, but in their ever-mutating elusiveness, a playful refusal ever to succumb, quite, to the intentionalist demands of critic or historian. Augustan literature is a gallimaufry of complex interplay between its creators and their audiences, heaping aliases upon anonymities, interweaving jokes and disguises, melding vicious criticism and exquisitely cool classicism into structures which, though they initially appear as solid, permanent and formal as the neo-classical architecture through which Lavinia's London was being transformed, are as unstable as the chaotic, swarming back-drops which topple through Hogarth's art. The works are full of oppos-itions, of course, between ancients and moderns, urban and pastoral, classical metre and contemporary language, but such apparent dichoto-mies are never fixed. Their exuberance is generated by their attempts to encompass the world which made them, with all its ambivalence and contradictions, and their recognition (sometimes joyful, sometimes despairing) that truth is an uncertain element, a mirage-like glimmer which can never be entirely apprehended. So urgent has been the desire of some critics to contain this exuberance, to force it into a neatly comprehensible form, that fact has too often been made subservient to the desire for narrative.

Such fabrication pursued Lavinia Fenton throughout her life and persisted long after her death. Hers is a contrary self, tripping between the numerous illogicalities of 'true lives' of Polly Peachum, around the ballads and pamphlets and portraits, nimble and teasing as Pope's Belinda behind her fan. Like a reader of an Augustan poem, Lavinia herself is caught in a maze of ellipses and reversals, the sense of her most evasive, to the unwary, when she makes herself most apparent. To find her story is to discover a world, still present yet impossibly distant, a world which appears to surrender its secrecies with Georgian politeness and clarity, and yet which constantly shifts out of view, so sparkling, at times, in its brightness, that we believe, mistakenly, that we see also into its shadows.

# 1

## A SUCCESSFUL EXECUTION

The precise moment of a life's definition is almost never found where we initially imagine we locate it. Cause and effect are safeguards against contingency, against the terrifyingly inaccurate mutability of chance. Dramatic events, quarrels, battles, illness, murder, devolve like a shattered glass into splinters of possibility and the connections of a story hide within the refractions of its tiniest shards. Here the future is made plain, though we are deaf to the sharp vibration of determination which appears crystalline only long after the fact. Choices are made before explanations, whether or not we care to know it.

In the summer of 1727, the writer John Gay stayed with his friends and fellow authors Alexander Pope and Jonathan Swift at Pope's villa at Twickenham. In contrast with more ostentatious country seats, like Prime Minister Walpole's vulgar pile at Houghton, the house had been designed as a place for retirement and contemplation, rather than as a demonstration of status. Pope declared archly that he was never happier than when 'piddling' amongst his 'cabbidges' at Twickenham, and indeed his Palladian house, with its lawn sloping down to the River Thames and its miniature park behind, was an enchanted place for the three writers. Dr Johnson, morosely practical as ever, pronounced Twickenham mighty diverting, but uncomfortable for the damp English climate, yet John Gay loved it. From a mere five acres of land, a pocket handkerchief of an estate, Pope had created a captivating retreat, with trees, beehives, a vineyard, kitchen gardens, orchards, quincunxes, ornamental mounts and statuary, 'packed as full and patterned as intricately, with as many quiet little mirrorings, reversals and surprises as compete for our attention in his best couplets'.[1] Gay, whose ever-expanding girth was a lifelong joke among his circle, would have enjoyed feasting on the exotic artichokes, pineapples and figs his friend conjured from the garden, as well as the more prosaic broccoli, fennel, salads and legumes. As Pope had written in his 'Farewell' to the 'Dear, dam'd, distracting Town' of London, the three companions were always content to exchange the 'laborious Lobster nights' of the capital for the rustic 'Sallads, Tarts and Pease'.

A more poetic feature of Twickenham was Pope's 'grotto', connecting the basement of the house to the park opposite. Together, the villa and the grotto were correlative to the man and his work, the clean classical lines of the Augustan house subverted beneath by whimsical caprice, the stern lines of the architecture and the order of the park linked by an anarchic space 'finished with Shells interspers'd with Pieces of Looking glass in angular forms.[2] Pope's wretched body, miserably afflicted by an apothecary's dictionary of ailments, may have been propped upright by boning and laces, just as his verse is carried by disciplined metre, but his strength is drawn from a magical, internal darkness where goblins chatter in Grub Street and fairies flirt on the rims of teacups. Perhaps, in the grotto, Swift and Gay discussed once again their old idea for a 'Newgate pastoral', a work which would overturn the conventions of classical poetry by removing its nymphs and shepherds from the placid glades of an idealised pagan Golden Age and relocate them in the real, corrupt and squalid world of eighteenth-century London. Above their heads, on the road from town to Hampton Court, the coaches of the quality rattled to the business of places and preferment, but that summer was a happy, optimistic time for the friends; places and preferment would surely come their way in other forms. Pope wrote to Swift afterwards, in mention of a collection in which their work had been included, 'I am particularly pleased with this volume, in which methinks we look like friends ... walking down hand in hand to posterity.'[3] Cosy and shady in the grotto, they were confident enough to dream of greatness while their futures bumped along the rough road above. Perhaps the heavily laden coach of Prime Minister Walpole rolled atop Gay as he worked on his satires; perhaps the road was occupied by Pope's future enemy Lord Hervey, or the Duke of Bolton, off to report on his governorship of the Isle of Wight.

The 'Newgate pastoral' which Gay had been discussing with Swift since 1716 finally had its première as *The Beggar's Opera* on 29 January 1728. Gay's nineteenth-century biographer reported wildly that during the inaugural performance 'strange glances were exchanged between Pope's bright eyes and Swift's lowering front', which contrasted with the 'quiet, thoughtful physiognomy' of their old colleague Addison.[4] The fact that Swift was at the time in Ireland and Addison had been dead nine years demonstrates the urge for grand narrative which seeks to reassemble those splinters of causality into a crooked replica of the truth. Still, the description would have pleased both Addison and Swift immensely. It was the kind of joke they most enjoyed.

Little Mr Pope, however, is very much there at the theatre in Lincoln's Inn Fields, straining forward in his seat, the cruel canvas corset that stiffens his puny spine creaking with enthusiasm. He holds his handkerchief before his face, distracted from both the drama on the stage and that which continues relentlessly beneath his coat. The smell really is appalling.

On 23 March 1728, the *London Stage* reports that 1,341 people crammed into Lincoln's Inn theatre to watch *The Beggar's Opera*, 238 in the boxes, 98 on the stage itself, 302 in the pit, 65 in the extensions of the boxes known as the slips, 440 compressed into the first gallery, 196 in the second and two unfortunates in 'pigeon holes'. The first-night audience is not so exuberantly crowded, but the accumulated odours of even a few hundred patrons are enough to try Mr Pope's fastidious nose. Too many adjectives have been heaped up in definition of London's aroma, piled like the ordure in the city's famously noisome gutters.

> Sweepings from butchers' stalls, dung, guts and blood,
> Drown'd puppies, stinking sprats all drench'd in mud,
> Dead cats and turnip tops,[5]

as Swift described. London air is popularly believed to be poisonous: everybody smells of sweat and unwashed clothes and worse, and no amount of Hungary-water or essence of violets soaked into a handkerchief can quite keep out the stench of those descriptions. Disloyally, Mr Pope catches himself dreaming of the soft sweet airs of Twickenham. But for nineteen-year-old Lavinia Fenton, kneeling onstage as Polly

Peachum on the first night of her first starring role, a handkerchief is much more than a barrier against the stink of her audience. It is the point of fission, enclosing the moment between life and death. Though Lavinia, in her short career, has never played Desdemona, she may well, like thousands of other Londoners, have enjoyed a Tyburn Holiday, and therefore might well be struck by the coincidence of the handkerchief's importance. For doomed Desdemona, the handkerchief becomes a proxy self, its loss the sign that her life must end. So too, finally, was the life of the actor at Tyburn gallows distilled into the soft movement of a pale square of linen.

The road to Tyburn, where hangings had taken place since the fourteenth century, was as established a London spectacle as the annual procession of the Lord Mayor through the city. It traversed the town in a grisly choreography from Newgate prison, where the prisoner's iron fetters would be hammered off and he was ceremoniously given into the keeping of the under-sherrif, to the yard, where the knight of the halter wound the rope around his breast, to the creeping trundle of the cart as it paused at the church of St Sepulchre, where the bellman urged the Lord to have pity on the soul of the condemned, then along Snow Hill to the reeking Fleet Ditch, down to Holborn and west along the Oxford road, across the Edgware road to skirt the wall of Hyde Park, to the arrival at the waiting gallows signalled by a pigeon released to fly back to Newgate. Another would fly east as the prisoner swung. If the condemned was famous, like Jack Sheppard, the folk-hero thief, or Claud Duval, the highwayman, then pretty girls would throw flowers into the cart as he rode by.

Lavinia's character in *The Beggar's Opera*, Polly Peachum, is aware of the grisly romanticism of hangings, a romanticism which made them a popular entertainment even for fashionable ladies. Polly's imagining of her highwayman lover's end flutters breathily with the language of a modish sentimental novel: 'Methinks I see him already in the cart, sweeter and more lovely than the nosegay in his hand! I hear the crowd extolling his resolution and intrepidity! What volleys of sighs are sent forth from the windows of Holborn, that so comely a youth should be brought to disgrace! I see him at the tree! The whole circle are in tears! Even butchers weep! Jack Ketch himself hesitates to perform his duty, and would be glad to lose his fee by a reprieve!' For Polly, the gallows

4

is a theatre, with the house brought to sobs and swoonings by the pathetic gallantry of its charmed, doomed hero.

This curiously engaging image is belied by one description of the rabble who attended executions as 'a sordid assemblage of the lowest among the vulgar',[6] though Dr Johnson considered the theatricality of public executions as a fair exchange. 'Executions are intended to draw spectators. If they do not draw spectators they do not answer their purpose. The old method was most satisfactory to all parties: the public was gratified by a procession, the criminal is supported by it.'[7] Nevertheless, the Tyburn crowd as depicted in Plate 11 of Hogarth's didactic series *Industry and Idleness* is hardly an edifying sight. As the prisoner arrives, the pigeon is released from behind the tier of pricey benches known as Mother Proctor's Pews. Proctor, a farmer's widow, did a roaring trade in seating the gentry for executions, clearing £500 when the Earl of Ferrers was hanged in his white and silver wedding clothes in 1760. In the picture, the gallows, despite the bulk required for the simultaneous dispatch of up to twenty criminals at one time, is barely visible in the swell of the crowd, who are swilling gin and stealing cakes, fighting and tumbling and upsetting the oranges which were also sold as refreshments at more conventional theatrical entertainments. An invalid hoists himself on his crutches for a better view; a baby is dropped in the excitement; Mother Douglas, the well-known Covent Garden procuress, rolls her eyes piously to heaven, at the same time keeping a firm grip on her glass; a ragged ballad-seller hawks the prisoner's 'true confession' before his neck is even in the noose, while the chaplain of Newgate, known as the ordinary, who had the perquisite on the sale of the official story (what Alexander Pope, in his poem 'The Dunciad', called the 'Tyburn Elegy'), is buried in the mob, the white clerical bands at his neck prefiguring what the rope has in store for the prisoner. There is an excess of life in the picture, an abundant vivacity which reduces the queasy-faced prisoner to a puppet, a marionette brought to jerk and dance for the amusement of a crowd whose pleasure is as savage as the law that has sent him there. No sentiment there, no compassion or privacy or dignity, except in the promise of the handkerchief bound about the prisoner's head.

Repetition makes ritual makes theatre. The handkerchief is the caesura. The hangman steps back, the spectators are silenced, their expectant stillness directed at the little cloth, and the moment when the prisoner raises his hands is the elision between life and death. The prisoner drops the handkerchief. The cart moves, the rope snaps, tighter, tighter. The audience roars the release that the gesture suffers them and launches into the afterpiece, the pantomime, scrabbling to touch the twitching body, which is believed to have magical properties, hurling bricks and bottles at the surgeon's cart come to collect the corpse for scientific dissection. Sometimes the hangman, who is often drunk, has to be forcibly restrained from hanging the chaplain as a finale, or he is eager to strip the corpse, whose clothes he can sell, along with the rope, which fetches sixpence an inch. Consumptive invalids might be helped to the scaffold, where it is thought a touch of the dead man's hand can purge the contagion from their lungs. The ordinary grabs a chair for the dash to the printer's.

So Lavinia Fenton is well aware of the symbolism of the scrap of fabric she clutches in her hand. As she pleads with her stage father, Mr Peachum, for the life of her lover, Macheath, it rises with her breath against her bosom, wringing pity from the audience, who are reminded of the handkerchief which will cover Macheath's face if Polly fails to persuade; thus it makes hangmen of the pit and the boxes, who can choose for the play, for Mr Gay's fortune, for Lavinia's future, life or death. Until this moment, the tenth scene of Act 1, the mood of the audience has been so hostile that without the appearance of Lavinia and her white flag of appeasement, the play might never have been permitted to reach its end.

The first night of the 'Beggar's Opera' was played at the Lincoln's Inn Theatre, the audience not being then much acquainted with the nature of operas, expected the usual music before the drawing up of the curtain – finding themselves (as they imagined) likely to be bilked out of their first and second music, they expressed great disapprobation, insomuch that Jack Hall (Lockit) was sent on to apologise for the omission, by explaining that it was a rule to have no music prior to the overture. Jack made his obeisance with tolerable grace, but being confounded by the general silence which so suddenly ensued on his appearance, blundered out, 'Ladies and gentlemen, we beg you not to call for first and second music, because you all know, there is never any music at all in an opera. This bull put the house in a good humour, and the piece proceeded.'[8]

Jack Hall was a seasoned actor, and his nerves betrayed more than first-night uncertainty. Rioting was a generally popular pastime for Londoners. In 1719, when Lavinia was eleven years old, she had witnessed the 4,000 Spitalfields weavers who took to the streets in protest at the undermining of their trade by imported fabrics, attacking women wearing Indian linen and spoiling their treacherous gowns with ink. Nearly any cause – gin, corn, an election, the Church – was an excuse for a riot, and the theatre was as good a place as any. Drury Lane was completely wrecked six times by violent audiences between 1743 and 1776.

In 1721, during a performance of *Macbeth*, four gentlemen, Mr Berkly, Mr Cornwallis, Mr Fielding and another, had caused 'a Disturbance . . . with intent to take off one of the Actresses, but being disarmed and committed to the Roundhouse, they are under Prosecution for a Riot.'[9] John Rich, the manager of the Lincoln's Inn Fields theatre at the time Lavinia made her debut as Polly, took issue on another occasion with a drunken earl, who insisted on his right to wander about the stage during a performance.

'I hope your Lordship will not take it ill [said Rich], if I give orders to the Stage Door-Keeper not to admit you any more. On his saying that, my Lord saluted Mr Rich with a slap on the face, which he immediately returned; and his Lordship's face being round and fat made his Cheek ring with the force of it. Upon this spirited return, my Lord's drunken Companions collected themselves directly, and Mr Rich was to be put to death.'[10] Luckily for Rich, the male actors in the company rallied valiantly and drove the gentlemen from the stage and into the pit, but the gentlemen were undaunted and proceed to climb into the boxes, slashing the curtains with their swords and smashing the sconces. After a 'grand scuffle', the actors managed to chase them out by the stage door, but this 'battle of the beaux' alerted the authorities, and subsequent performances were attended by armed guards, stationed outside the theatres by royal command.

The actor and playwright Colley Cibber (who eventually, much to the disgust of Pope, Swift and Gay, who despised him for the meretricious snob he was, became poet laureate), was disgusted by the boisterousness of English theatre audiences in comparison with their more refined French counterparts. The French, Cibber claimed, would never have stooped to duelling on the stage like Mr Dering and Mr Vaughan who, having quarrelled in the pit, the usual seating place for young unaccompanied men and therefore the usual place for the start of rowdy behaviour, hoisted themselves on to the stage to settle the matter in an honourable fashion. Mr Vaughan pleaded in his defence that, having found the seats too cramped for their sword arms, the two had done so 'for the greater comfort of the audience', who were delighted at the improvement in their view. Mr Dering was carried away by the actors with a hole in his ribs, and his assailant was carted off to Bridewell prison.

In 1737, eighteen footmen were sent to prison after a riot at Drury Lane theatre over the abolition of place-saving, in which twenty-five people were seriously injured. Traditionally, wealthy theatre patrons had sent their footmen to the house in advance to save seats, and advertise by their liveries that their masters would be present, after which they would be permitted to watch the performance for nothing from the upper gallery. This scheme had been devised by John Rich's father Christopher, who considered that the free below-stairs publicity thus gained in the houses of the quality was a fair exchange for the noise and pelting which issued from their servants. It was considered a perquisite by these 'savage spectators', as Cibber called them, so when the managements decided to charge, the footmen armed themselves with sticks and clubs fashioned from the theatre's woodwork, beat the attendants and invaded the stage, smashing the instruments in the orchestra on the way. Curiously, of the damage that frequent theatrical riots caused, it always seemed to be the harpsichord that had the worst of it. In the wake of the rampage of the footmen, John Rich introduced 'bouncers' to his theatre.

Mr Pope starts back to the stage, back to Lavinia. He has been apprehensive for his friend Gay's strange new play, commenting to fellow writer Congreve that 'whether it succeeds or not it will make a great noise, but whether of claps or hisses I know not. At worst, it is a thing which he can lose no reputation by, since he lays none upon it.' Congreve replied that 'it would either take greatly, or be damned confoundedly'.[11] But now Mr Pope overhears the Duke of Argyll, who, like most of the audience, is in tears of sympathy with Polly, whisper loudly, 'It will do, it must do! I see it in the eyes of 'em.' Mr Pope writes to a friend that the evening ended in 'a clamour of applause'. Lavinia Fenton has won over her hostile spectators so thoroughly that by the time Dr Johnson's biographer, James Boswell, hears the story (from Mr Cambridge, who has it from the actor Mr Quin), the moment, and the actress, have become a theatrical legend.

## 2

# *T*HE *C*ELEBRATED *M*ISS *F*ENTON

*F*rom the first, some London writers were less than kind about Lavinia Fenton's new-found celebrity. Despite the claim that it was her 'innocent looks' that had impressed the public, the poet Young, for one, was determined to present her as a harlot. 'Polly, a wench that acts in "The Beggar's Opera" is the publica cura of our noble youth. She plays her Newgate part well, and shows the great advantage of being born and bred in the mint, which really was the case. She, tis said, has raised her price from one guinea to one hundred, tho' she cannot be a greater whore than she was before, nor, I suppose, a younger.'

Elizabeth Beswick would have been disgusted by the charge that her daughter was born in the Mint, though her ambition might have been flattered by Young's estimate of her Lavinia's earning power, as she had always had plans for that. Lavinia, after all, was an optimistic choice of name. No Mollys or Susans or Marys for Mrs Beswick, no daughter with a coarse complexion who scoured and sweated and heaved, carried slops and stacked coals. Lavinia, the extravagance of the syllables filling the mouth like a sugar plum, the sweep of the tongue across the palate a promising whisper, like the rustle of a lady's silk sack. Lavinia, thought Mrs Beswick, was a name for steaming chocolate from delicate china, warm rooms, fine linen, who knows, a coach? 'Mrs Beswick', it must be said, was an equally hopeful title, since frankly the lieutenant had not had time to solemnise a marriage before his man o' war sailed, but he promised to return if the French spared his life, and rallied Mrs Beswick by insisting on Proteus for a boy and Lavinia for a girl, which implied an encouraging interest in his offspring. Practically, to spare any blushes over the little matter of the banns, Lieutenant Beswick supposedly suggested that his lover lie in 'like a citizen's daughter, twenty or forty miles off in the country, and then come up and rejoice with your friends, that you have recovered from a fit of sickness'. In fact, poor Mrs Beswick had little to rejoice over when her daughter was born since, true to nautical form, the lieutenant never did come back.

Having once failed in the role of a respectable married woman, Mrs Beswick determined on another attempt, and about 1708 returned to London with her new-born child and set her cap firmly at Mr Fenton, who was less likely to be mislaid as a husband, being the keeper of a land-locked coffee house in the Charing Cross Road. However, she was soon dissatisfied with the life of grinding chocolate and coffee beans. As Lavinia's stage father, Mr Peachum, was to observe in *The Beggar's Opera*, a 'handsome wench' could be profitable 'at the bar of a Temple coffee house', and the new Mrs Fenton turned her dashing dreams upon her daughter.

Admittedly, the immediate circumstances were not highly promising. In the strictly hierarchical society of eighteenth-century London, it was tremendously difficult for a girl from a modest background to move beyond her social class. The writer and traveller Lady Wortley Montagu was hardly more flattering than Young about the backdrop for Mrs Fenton's ambitions. 'My poor friend the Duchess of Bolton was educated in solitude, with some choice of books, by a saint-like governess, she thought it impossible not to find gratitude, though she failed to give passion; and upon this plan threw away her estate, was despised by her husband, and laughed at by the public. Polly, bred in an ale house, and produced on the stage, has obtained wealth and title, and found the way to be esteemed. So useful is early experience.'[1] Lady Mary, too old and too ugly when she wrote this description to create a scandal herself, and too cross for anyone to care if she did, since she had quarrelled with Mr Pope as well as nearly everyone else who mattered to her, naturally resented Lavinia's eventual *succès de scandale*, though she was a great deal less surprised by it than Mrs Fenton.

In *The Beggar's Opera*, Polly Peachum, who has been bred among thieves, contravenes her parents' code of honour by daring to marry her lover, the highwayman Macheath. Not only that, but she has the audacity to declare that she loves him, and has not married 'deliberately, for honour or money'. In the topsy-turvy underworld of the criminals, Polly has 'ruined' herself and, as her mother warns, 'Why, thou foolish jade, thou wilt be as ill-used, and as much neglected, as if thou hadst married a lord!' Better an honest whore than an impoverished wife, thinks Mrs Peachum, and Mrs Fenton agreed, Lavinia, though, who as Polly pleaded so movingly for her beloved Macheath's life, was an equally disobedient daughter. Like Polly, she had other ideas.

'Consider my dear girls, that you have no portions, and endeavour to supply the deficiencies of fortune by mind. You cannot expect to marry in such a manner as neither of you shall have occasion to work, and none but a fool will take a wife whose bread must be earned solely by his labour and who will contribute nothing towards it herself.' Thus counselled the conduct manual *A Present for a Servant Maid*, one of a popular genre of advisory tomes designed to teach servants and apprentices to mind their betters and know their place. Lavinia Fenton may have had no better hope of an inheritance than a part share in a coffee shop, but even as a girl she aimed higher than hard-working respectability as the wife of a footman or shopkeeper. Being a child of 'vivacious and lively spirit and of promising Beauty',[2] she became as much a pet of her stepfather's customers in Charing Cross as ever Lady Mary Wortley Montagu had been as the toast of the Whig grandees of the more illustrious Kit-Kat club. Aged just seven or eight, Lavinia, or 'Vinnie', as she was known, was practising her charm with some success on the fops who assembled to slurp their coffee and chocolate, exchange the current gossip and browse through the newspapers in the shop, and they took pleasure in teaching her the latest songs picked up from the theatre. She had a remarkable ability to imitate any tune having heard it just once, and though her singing voice was not the grandiose instrument of an opera diva like Faustina or Cuzzoni, it was sweet and true. Her talent attracted the attention of one customer in particular, a retired actor from the 'Old House', the theatre at Drury Lane, who took it upon himself to tutor her in singing and elocution, and 'having a lively imagination, joined with a good memory, clear voice and graceful mien, [she] seemed as if Nature had designed her for the pleasure of Mankind in such performances as are exhibited in our theatres'.[3]

Lavinia's 'graceful mien' was captured by Hogarth, George Knapton, Allan Ramsay and Thomas Bardwell. It was reproduced on fans, painted on china, engraved on pewter, pictured on screens and displayed on innumerable cheap prints, pamphlets and even playing cards well into the nineteenth century.

> While crowds attentive sit to Polly's voice
> And in their native harmony rejoice
> Th' admiring throng no vain subscription draws
> Nor affectation prompts a false applause
> Nature untaught each pleasing strain supply's
> Artless as her unbidden Blushes rise
> And charming as the Mischief in her Eyes,

cooed one accompaniment to a reproduction of 1813.[4] In 1728, however, Lavinia's is not a particularly fashionable beauty. Her hair is fairish, her large eyes grey, her nose, in her portraits, rather insistently nose-like. She is firmly built, not possessed of the modish sloping shoulders, so flattering to the drape of a gown, displayed by Pope's friend Mr Jervas's 1730 portrait of Lady Elizabeth and Lady Henrietta Finch. At least her bust, strapped high by ruthless English stays at a time when the ideal figure owed more to engineering than to nature, inspires the admiration of those who remember the luscious, overabundant charms of Lely's Restoration beauties, although this vogue too will give way to a more sylph-like effect produced by higher lacing at the front. Slimming has not yet became a craze, but Lavinia's figure is perhaps already too luscious for strictly fashionable tastes.

The best portrait of Lavinia Fenton is by John Ellys, who also captured her co-star Tom Walker. She seems much prettier here, with a slightly feline cast to her features, a teasing tilt to the eyes, but rather too much placidity about the chin. Altogether, her own century is rather hard on her appearance, but by 19 April this no longer matters, for Lavinia is a star.

Mr Gay, describing 'a mezzotint published today of Polly, the heroine of "The Beggar's Opera"', peevishly doubted whether the fame of this previously unknown actress did not now surpass the vogue for his opera itself. Nevertheless, the *Daily Journal* unkindly decides that it is her celebrity, rather than her looks, which commands homage:

All mankind agree to own,
That when they praise ye most,
They know not whence the rapture flows,
Or why thy name's their toast,

So Coarse a Voice, so Stiff a mien,
A Face so poor in Charms!
Can ne'er demand a just applause
Or lure us to thy Arms.

Perhaps Lavinia inherited her mother's capacity for making the best of a bad job, since she never seemed to doubt her own allure. She was certainly 'soon ripe' (though one biographer considerately noted that he hoped the proverb 'soon ripe, soon rotten' would not be true in her case).[5] Mrs Fenton had seemed to agree, and determining that the pleasures her nubile daughter might afford mankind were not to be quite of a theatrical nature, she set about putting her Upon the Town.

Not that a more respectable solution had not already been tried. In Lavinia's early teens, Mr Fenton had been prevailed upon to find the fees to send his stepdaughter to a boarding school, where she might have been expected to add to her natural talents with those accomplishments deemed so essential to the making of a good marriage. Dancing, music, sketching, elocution and a smattering of Italian and French, it was hoped, might prove sufficient enticements for a young lawyer who Mrs Fenton had in mind to overlook Lavinia's lack of fortune. Initially, the plan appeared to be working as predictably as the plot of a sensational novel, with the lawyer bribing a servant at the school to gain access to the garden, where he might moon like Romeo in a bag-wig over his fourteen-year-old love. Lavinia kept her head and refused to succumb to his advances until he was quite seriously prepared to consider marriage. Unfortunately, an inquiry into her social circumstances, concealed by her status as a pupil at an elegant school, soon put him off. Lavinia was, it has been said, so upset by this demeaning reminder that sweet-scented garden romance could not overcome the tang of coffee beans that she had to leave the school, but it seems more likely that Mrs Fenton thought her daughter, having failed at trapping a fortune honestly, might as well go profitably to the bad, in which case there was no sense in wasting any more money on harpsichord lessons.

Back behind the counter, polishing dishes, wiping tables and serving brandy, punch, chocolate and wine as well as the offending coffee, Lavinia was peeved that her young lady's education had come to so little. Now grown up, she was no longer amused by the affectionate petting of Mr Fenton's customers, and couldn't even console herself with the thought that her family's shop was at least distinguished. Other coffee houses, capitalising on the rage for the exotic, spicy beverage which had begun a few years before Lavinia was born, had made reputations for themselves: near to the Fentons' establishment at Charing Cross are Will's and the Bedford, where poets and writers gather; artists like Hogarth and Hayman gossip at Old Slaughter's along the road in St Martin's Lane, while the luminaries of both major political parties, Tory and Whig, divide themselves between the Cocoa Tree and Arthur's as strictly as they do along the benches in the House. Fenton's, however, is just Fenton's. In a sense, though, Lavinia was already rehearsing. Coffee houses are the nexus of cultural, social and political life: 'Books, plays and pictures were spirited through the air, sucked into the coffee house, and drawn into snug booths and corners by the animated warmth of conversation.'[6] The rich, pungent fumes carry a thrilling air of disobedience, of wraith-like, steamy dreams that might yet become possibilities. Like theatres, coffee houses are promiscuous places, not in the more traditional sense embodied by the bold-eyed orange girls of Drury Lane, but in that they allow anyone, of any class, to read a newspaper and express an opinion for the price of a stimulating drink. Attending a coffee house could be an education, a taste of the distilled sophistication and savoir faire of the metropolis, as Prior observed in his poem 'The Chameleon': 'So the young Squire, when first he comes / From Country school to Will's or Tom's . . .' The French visitor César de Saussure remarked on the freedom of the coffee houses when he saw a street porter roll up his sleeves and call for his coffee and newspaper as easily as a lord. Opposition to government and Crown, to the idea that the world is as the powerful make it, is absorbed by Lavinia with the heat of the dishes that open the pores on her face and make her fear for her complexion. At the Smyrna, a short walk away in Pall Mall, Mr Pope and Mr Gay, along with their friends Swift and Arburthnot, are making a city in words, a new city peopled by grotesques and absurdities, corrupted and dark as the tides of the filthy

Thames, as the coffee that swirls in their bowls. There are few women in the coffee houses, so Lavinia is lucky, quietly going about her tasks with her head down and her ears open, learning that wit forms a currency of its own, so that she will be surprised when she meets Mr Pope, whose words have been laughed at and respectfully repeated by Fenton's customers, to see that he is a little squiggle of a man, with no grave air of the oracle at all.

Presently, though, on the stage, Polly Peachum is explaining to her father that, in defiance of the sensible advice of servants' conduct manuals, she intends to live 'like other women, sir, upon the industry of my husband'. In the word of the 'Opera', where the mores of polite society are satirised by being placed in the criminal community, Polly has transgressed against the realistic artistocratic code of marrying for interest, insisting she has taken Macheath for love. 'Worse and worse!' exclaims Mrs Peachum wryly. 'I thought the girl had been better bred.' Her ironic pretensions to grandeur are endorsed by Lady Mary Wortley Montagu, who was explicit in her view that the high-society marriage was a matter of profit, claiming that women of her class were sold like slaves. Marriage settlements were of great popular interest, with publications such as the *Gentleman's Magazine* publishing the latest matches for the entertainment, or envy, of its readers. The bride's name is often conspicuously absent in such announcements, those of the groom and her father sufficing to indicate the exchange of goods. Miss Orell's father was clearly proud enough to mention her, since her £30,000 netted her the Lord Bishop of St Asaph in 1735, but Mr Roger Waind, aged twenty-six, preferred his beloved to remain anonymous. She was a splendid catch, providing £8,000 down, £300 per annum, with her coach and four at Mr Waind's disposal during her lifetime. Whether he enjoyed his carriage for long is doubtful, since the blushing maiden was over eighty. Lady Mary's husband, in a note eventually used in the *Tatler*, objected to this settlement system, whereby the spouses' families hammered out a financial agreement, as rendering marriage a 'sale', in which a woman 'makes a kind of auction of herself'. In aristocratic circles like those Mrs Peachum laughably wishes to emulate, a love match usually meant a *mésalliance*. About 1728, one Lady Bell Tufton, with a fortune of £2,000, fell in love with a younger son of the second Duke of Bolton, who had £2,000 a year. Yet Bell's ambitious father forbade the match on the grounds that the prospective bridegroom was too poor. Since, according to Lord Hervey, there 'is no getting a wife bespoke', romantic marriage was a mistake, and it was better to be certain of the fortune and take a chance on the ready-made woman. Mrs Fenton, like Mrs Peachum, saw no sense in her daughter submitting to the slavery of marriage unless the rewards were right.

After the debacle of Lavinia's schoolroom romance with the lawyer, rumour had it that a silk mercer's apprentice, humble but honest, proposed to make an honest woman of Lavinia. But Mrs Fenton was having none of it, whatever Lavinia might have thought. As Mr Peachum says, 'If the wench does not know her own profit, sure she knows her own pleasure better than to make herself a property.' The theatre, after all, is the very place to turn a profit from pleasure.

## A DIGRESSION ON WHORES

'Of late the playhouses are so extremely pestered with vizard masks and their trade ... that many of the more civilised parts of the town are uneasy in the company and shun the theatre as they would a house of scandal.'[7]

More than half a century after the Puritans had closed the London playhouses, the theatre was still tantalisingly tainted with a thrilling whiff of vice. In the previous century the theatre had been perceived as connected with corrupt Catholicism – the play and the Mass were similar forms of idolatry. 'The actors and spectators must all be damned, the playhouse is the porch of Hell, the place of the Devil's abode, where he holds his filthy court of evil spirits; a play is the Devil's triumph, a sacrifice performed to his glory,'[8] thundered the clergyman William Law. The play did not lose its seductive powers, but the detractors of the theatre now concentrated on condemning the real harlots who swayed enticingly across the pit rather than the Whore of Rome, their objections becoming moral rather than doctrinal.

London was alive with prostitutes. They were an essential part of the iconography of a city through which Swift's Corinnas, the toasts of the theatre district around Drury Lane, marched 'bright, battered, rolling' and defiant in their draggled finery from Smithfield to St James's, as they had done since the Restoration. John Gay, in his early poem 'Trivia', made the link between the theatre district of London and the hunting ground of the whores:

> O may thy virtue guide thee through the roads
> Of Drury'd mazy courts and dark abodes,
> The harlot's guileful path who nightly stand
> Where Catherine Street descends into the Strand.

Between December 1719 and November 1720, the Societies for Promoting a Reformation of Manners prosecuted 1,181 (mainly female) prostitutes and a further fourteen persons for keeping bawdy houses, and by 1738, the societies had obtained 101,683 such convictions. It is almost impossible to ascertain how many prostitutes were working in London at any given point, but given that the societies' figures represent only a small fraction of those who were actually apprehended, it is clear that their numbers were significant. In 1725, 107 brothels were counted around Drury Lane alone, and in Covent Garden the ladies graphically showed off their wares in broad daylight, to the prurient horror of passers-by. There were such crowds of whores that the magistrate Sir John Fielding estimated gloomily there would be enough to fill a colony (it has been estimated that as many as 25,000 women, about one-eighth of the adult female population of London, were working as prostitutes by 1796, while 1,700 lodgings in the Marylebone district alone were inhabited by whores). As Boswell observed, there was a girl for every wallet, 'free-hearted ladies of all kinds, from the splendid Madam at fifty guineas a night down to the civil nymph with white thread stockings who tramps along the Strand and will resign her engaging person to your honour for a pint of wine and a shilling'.[9]

The amiability of Boswell's description belies the wretchedness and squalor which characterised the lives of many London prostitutes. For every Nell Gwynn, there were thousands of desperate women who saw no alternative but whoring to the creeping, terrifying poverty that was a constant in the life of the London poor. In Daniel Defoe's novel *Roxana* (whose satirical double time scheme locates his heroine simultaneously in the Restoration and the period of George I), Roxana's maid Amy presents her mistress with what must have been many women's consideration of their position: 'Your Choice is fair and plain; here you may have a handsome, charming gentleman, be rich, live pleasantly, and in Plenty; or refuse him, and want a Dinner, go in Rags, live in Tears; in short, beg and starve. You know this is the Case ... I wonder how you can say you do not know what to do.' The gentlemen, though, were rarely handsome, and subsistence, rather than splendour, was the lot of most prostitutes.

Yet it was still a trade like any other, as Gay observes in *The Beggar's Opera* when he has the female members of Macheath's gang, the band of 'civil nymphs', converse on their business with ladylike delicacy:

'Pray, madam, were you ever in keeping?'

'I hope, madam, I ha'nt been so long upon the town, but I have met with some good fortune as well as my neighbours.'

The women discuss their preferences in clients – Jews are reputedly good to their girls, despite their unfortunate religion – and Mrs Vixen recommends the profligacy of apprentices, who will turn to crime when their funds are exhausted, so she has sent two or three dozen of them most satisfactorily to the colonies. Suky Tawdry hints at the contempt the whores feel for the vanity of their customers. 'I own I like an old fellow, for we always make them pay for what they can't do.'

London's sexual market was a sophisticated one, catering to the most diverse of peccadillos. Although the great age of public schools had not yet begun, the 'English vice', flagellation, was popular, and many brothels or 'academies' claimed to be 'disciplinary establishments' where young ladies were available for correction, or to give lessons to their gentlemen clients. Other prostitutes offered themselves as 'posture women', such as the famous act at the Rose tavern, which featured a naked woman on a giant silver salver, knees drawn up to her chest, who would be exhibited to the audience and then perform a predictable trick with a lighted candle. Homosexual distractions were also available in the 'molly houses' such as the transvestite tavern at Holborn. In one such, the 'thief-taker' Jonathan Wild claimed to have heard of the 'he-whores' calling one another "my dear" and hugging, kissing and tickling one another, as if they were a mixture of wanton males and females, and assuming effeminate voices and airs. Some telling others that they ought to be whipped for not coming more often to school.'[10] Whatever the customer's desire, there was a body willing to satisfy it if the price was right.

Jack Harris, an entrepreneurial waiter, began selling a handwritten guide for customers who liked to be precise about their pleasures, and by the time of his death in 1765 *Harris's List of Covent Garden Ladies* had reached sales of 8,000 copies a year. Harris took a 20 per cent fee from women for their inclusion in the list, as well as, it was rumoured, a free trial of the goods to be advertised, but his descriptions obviously drew in custom, since many whores were willing to use him as an agent. The list detailed the women's addresses, age, appearance and specialities, and Harris also attempted to inject a little poetry into the proceedings. This is his description of Miss Devonshire of Queen Anne Street: 'Many a man of war has been her willing prisoner, and paid a proper ransom; her port is said to be well-guarded by a light brown chevaux-de-frieze ... the entry is rather strait, but once in there is very good riding.' To Miss Wilkinson of Bull and Mouth Street was ascribed a pair of 'semi snowballs, that want not the support of stays; whose truly elastic state never suffers the pressure, however severe, to remain but boldly recovers its tempting smoothness'. Harris's guide was at once forthright and teasing, portraying a world where pleasure was cleanly bought and sold with a frankness surprising to those who confound the pruderies of a later century with the less hypocritical openness of an earlier age.

For all such pragmatism, though, there were two ever-present dangers which affected successful and unsuccessful whores alike: the prison and the pox. Swift's 'Beautiful Young Nymph Going To Bed' writhes through her dreams in her filthy garret, haunted by the lash of Bridewell on her shoulders. If charged with prostitution, women were flogged in Bridewell prison, and often left raw and senseless. The hypocrisy of an authority which thus tortured the bodies it was prepared to pay to use was made hideously apparent in the loose flaps of bleeding flesh which hung from women's backs like their tattered gowns. Bridewell was 'more than an image of a prostitute's decline or a sadist's delight. It was the incarnation of domination, the body subdued and beaten for punishment and profit, not enjoyed for pleasure.'[11] It could be added that those ordering the beatings were often the same men who had paid for the pleasure.

Again, it is Swift whose vicious adjectives best capture the other scourge of prostitutes: venereal disease. The mercury cure was as deadly as the illness, and in 'The Progress of Beauty', the Dean's 'rotting Celia' strolls the street, mourning that 'No painting can restore a nose / Nor will her teeth return again.' Mr Peachum in *The Beggar's Opera* reflects that thief-takers and surgeons are equally indebted to women for their profits, since men will steal to buy whores and pay doctors to cure them of what they thereby acquire. In Hogarth's *Harlot's Progress*, Moll dies of the pox while undergoing the 'sweating cure', wrapped in blankets to steam the disease from her pores, her mouth swollen and her teeth collected in a little handkerchief marked with the name of Dr Rock, the real-life quack inventor of the famous, and utterly useless, 'Anti-Venereal, Grand, Specifick Pill'.

For many commentators, the playwright Sheridan among them, there was little to choose between the lax morals of the women who appeared professionally on the stage and those who plied their profession in the pit or the boxes. 'To play the Coquet, the Wanton, to retail loose innuendoes on comedy or glow with warm descriptions in Tragedy; and in both to be hauled about, squeez'd and kiss'd by beastly pimping Actors! ... everything around them is unchaste, their Studies are Lessons of Vice and Passion. Like Wretches who work in unwholesome Mines, Their senses are corrupted in the operation of their Trade.'[12]

Not only was the sexual status of actresses dubious, their social position presented an equally disturbing ambiguity. The social hierarchy of the eighteenth century was arranged as strictly within the theatre as without: the top gallery was occupied by the common people, the middle gallery by the merchant-class citizens, the boxes were for the 'quality', mostly women, and the pit for gentlemen and those ladies who set to make their fortunes from them. But what of the mysterious creatures on the stage?

> A Pimping, Spunging, Idle, Impious Race,
> A Nest of lechers worse than Sodom bore
> Diseas'd, in Debt, and evr'y moment dun'd;
> By all good Christians Loath'd, and their own Kindred shun'd.

Robert Gould's 1709 *The Play-House: A Satyr* makes out the actors' to have been a wretched position indeed. As late as 1757, *The Players' Scourge* was prepared to go even further: 'Play actors are the most

profligate wretches, and the vilest vermin that hell ever vomited out . . .
they are the filth and garbage of the earth, the scum and stain of human
nature, the excrements and refuse of all humankind, the pests
and plagues of human society, the debauchees of men's minds and
morals.'[13]

Such an unequivocal view might seem exaggerated, but until the end
of the century, actors were often classed as no more socially worthy
than gypsies or vagabonds, which technically they still were. Until the
Licensing Act of 1737, all players not attached to one of the companies
warranted by royalty could be subject to arrest on the charge of vagrancy.
In 1735, following the arrest of one unfortunate Mr Hooper on just such
a charge, a bill was instituted to enforce the law on non-patented players,
in response to which 'Tony Aston's Petition' protested that 'if all
Country Players must promiscuously suffer by this Act, I doubt there is
Wood enough in England to hang them all on: What Recourse for their
Bread must most of them take, who for many Years, have addicted
themselves solely to Acting? Aston is attempting a defence, but his
suggestion is that despairing actors might easily fulfil their essential
nature and become criminals in the truest sense. The most it was considered an actor might hope for, early in the century, was to make a
living and perhaps be admitted 'into a nobleman's butlery'. Despite the
fact that an actor's fame was his theatre's fortune, the respectability
of the theatre remained paradoxically contingent on his ever-dubious
reputation. Even after David Garrick had transformed the status of
actors into gentlemen celebrities in the forty years that followed, the
snobbish Earl of Chesterfield refused to receive him.

Socially, then, the actress is a double outlaw, a member of a profession
which is at best tolerated, at worst scorned, and considered by her
membership of that profession to be unfit to keep company with decent
women. Peering behind the scenes at Nell Gwynn in her shift, Pepys
had commented on the actress with his usual self-righteous prurience:
'Lord! To see how [they] were painted would make a man mad and did
make me loathe them; and what base company of men come among
them and how lewdly they talk.' Even Dr Johnson was not immune to
the actress's disturbing allure, stating to Garrick: 'I'll come no more
behind your scenes, David, for the silk stockings and white bosoms of
your actresses excite my amorous propensities.'[14] (He was probably

quite safe, since it is doubtful whether shambling, smelly, pock-marked Dr Johnson produced a similar effect on the ladies.) In the eyes of the pamphlets and the prints and the conduct manuals, then, the actress in her satin train and plumed headdress and Moll Hackabout in her Bridewell smock are sisters under their saleable skin.

Pleasure and profit are the two poles between which London dances on a tightrope of luxury. Below is the morass of ruin, of the King's Bench and Newgate, where the debtors loll in mouldering silks and the divines shake their heads over where this craze for grandeur will end. Yet London is dizzy for pleasure, for balls and masquerades, for china and chocolate and chocolate-skinned Negro pages, for dancing masters and hairdressers, exquisite furniture, delicate perfumes, for everything that is novel and fine. Addison observes how every corner of the nascent Empire is racked to produce the fashionable dress and accessories of a single grand lady. Greedy London bursts its boundaries, swelling westwards from the confines of the old city to the elegant squares and stucco facades of the new homes of the rich. Great draughts of luxury flow into London's maw; the city bulges, but seems insatiable. And if there is no ready money to supply its wants, London can satisfy its cravings on credit. Ladies and gentlemen find the silversmith or the milliner to be most accommodating, so why resist the new silk bonnet or the latest watch, and what matter if the coal merchant is unpaid or the butcher's children go hungry, so long as one can appear in splendour at the play?

The theatre is the nexus for London's profligacy and dissipation, warn the moralists, encouraging the city's pretensions to grandeur while distracting it from the honest business of getting and spending. There is no substance to the theatre: it is a flimsy, transient reality where apprentices who should be at their benches lord it in the gallery and ladies who should be minding their families coquette from the boxes like the whores who tout for custom beneath. In 1734, Samuel Richardson, creator of the century's most famous sentimental heroine, Pamela, had devoted ten pages in his *Apprentice's Vade Mecum* to the 'shameful depravity' of the stage. It was as well for the theatre that John Gay had abandoned his own apprenticeship in favour of the dramatic muse, though the location he chose for his most successful work, Newgate prison, was seen by the moralists as the inevitable resort of those who attached themselves to the wickedness of the theatre.

Newgate was as much a place of entertainment for Londoners as the playhouses themselves. 'You cannot conceive the ridiculous rage there is for going to Newgate, the prints that are published of the malefactors and the memoirs of their lives set forth with as much parade as Marshal Turenne's.'[15] The prison's press yard, attached to the house of the governor, was the focus for curious sightseers, as here the most respectable prisoners, officially those who had committed crimes against the state, were herded. Twenty guineas was the fee to the inmates for admission to this preferential spot, followed by eight shillings a week for maintenance, a means by which the governor could extract higher fees than those permitted by Parliament. Drinking parties were held in the yard every night to keep up the spirits of the 'distressed inhabitants' who, despite the exorbitant rates, thought themselves well off in comparison with the wretched occupants of the felons' and common debtors' quarters, who had not even the opportunity of exercise or fresh (after a fashion) air.

Here the cramped, filthy cells were so dark they needed to be lit even in the summertime. Some cells were six inches deep in water, all were infested with rats, and many had no fireplaces, chimneys or even beds. Rations were meagre, consisting of little more than a slop of bread boiled in water, and overcrowding was appalling. Unsurprisingly, the habit of keeping as many as a hundred prisoners in three rooms fourteen by seven feet and seven feet high (an example drawn from the May assizes of 1750), led to frequent outbreaks of typhus, known as 'gaol fever', of which there were three great epidemics in the first half of the century. Newgate life has been described as one of 'debauchery and foul discomfort, the nastiness and squalor of its surroundings, the ever present sickness and infections due to constant overcrowding and the utter absence of all cleanliness or efforts at sanitation',[16] leading to the death of many prisoners before they even came to trial.

With the spectre of Bridewell and Newgate before her, Lavinia felt that if being an actress was perhaps not much better than being a whore, the difference was great enough for her to attempt a career on the stage. Besides, it was safer. She knew that she had talent, and the encouragement she had received from her father's customers, men who knew the town well, suggested that she might have at least a chance of making a living as an actress before succumbing to the inevitability of her mother's plans. Singing came as easily to her as speaking, and she persuaded Mr Fenton to get her lessons from the best masters he could afford. Fortuitously for Mr Rich when he came to cast his Polly, Italian singing was still not widely taught, and certainly beyond the means of a coffee shop-keeper's daughter, so Lavinia learned mainly the English ballad style, which was the perfect preparation for *The Beggar's Opera*. Her simple, true voice was fine enough for one of the customers at Fenton's to arrange a trial upon the stage, and the *Daily Post* of 23 February 1726 duly reported that 'a Gentlewoman who never appear'd on any stage before' was due to take the role of Serina in Otway's *The Orphan*. It was a small part, with just sixteen lines spread over three entrances, and the fact that Lavinia was not mentioned by name suggests that her appearance was by way of a general audition. Nevertheless, it was a start.

Once Lavinia had set her sights upon the theatre, it seemed the ideal opportunity for Mrs Fenton to pursue her own ambitions. While her daughter was going through her lines, Mrs Fenton lost no time in picking up a lover for herself who, when he got a look at Lavinia, offered a generous salve to her pride for switching his affections from mother to daughter. Mrs Fenton thought Lavinia could do better, on the grounds that 'the first market a woman made was always the best, and second-hand goods would fetch but a second-hand price'. Two hundred pounds was the sum she deemed Lavinia's virginity to be worthy of, and she contracted the sale with an old gentleman known as the Fea-thered Gull, who offered the asking price with a set of lodgings thrown in, and a further £200 per annum so long as his purchase remained faithful. If Mr Fenton objected to his wife's schemes (assuming he even knew of them), he did little to stop her. Perhaps he felt that he had no right, having disappointed her so himself, especially as Mrs Fenton was not the type of woman to let him forget it. Lady Mary's sour charge that Lavinia had been bred in the Mint was strictly inaccurate, but Mr Fenton does seem to have been on frequent visiting terms with the Old Bailey. The coffee shop was unable to keep pace with Mrs Fenton's taste for luxury, and the family had fallen on hard times, removing to cheaper lodgings within the walls of the court. Here, a few doors away from

Cowplants, the huge London soap factory, where slimy, stinking tallow was converted with rose and almond oil into balms for ladies' white hands, and a greasy alkaline scum scaled the walls, clothes and skin of the neighbours and their houses, it seemed less likely than ever that any man should wish to assure Lavinia's future as a wife. Mrs Fenton had become ill, and it seemed that gradually the family was sliding down the ruthless scale of London poverty which ended in the horrifying squalor of the St Giles slums. There was no safety net for people like the Fentons, nothing to mitigate the cruel vagaries of fortune, and it was quite plausible that Mrs Fenton saw her daughter's choice as being between relative comfort and security and a wretched, brutalised existence in a freezing rookery, creeping like a starved animal in gin-soaked rags. No mother could want her daughter to become one of the tottering bundles kicked aside by rich men's footmen as their masters strolled to the theatre, and though the Old Bailey clung greasily to its soapy respectability, there were plenty of such examples about.

In the first decade of the eighteenth century, the boom in trade and commerce that was so radically altering both the landscape of London and the lifestyle of the wealthy broadened the morass between rich and poor. Unprecedented wealth accentuated the horrific extremities of the poverty in which a third of the city's population struggled to live. For them, daily life was harsh and cruel, and the threat of joining their ranks was ever-present to those who hung on to the opposing brink of respectability; one historian comments on 'the threat of instability, of liability to sudden ruin that runs through so much eighteenth-century literature'.[17] What little support was offered by the state to the destitute came in the form of the essentially unrevised Elizabethan Poor Law. From 1723, parishes had been permitted to establish workhouses, and refuse relief to those who declined to enter them, but many people were justifiably afraid of entering the poorhouses, which were usually run for profit by their managers. Francis Parent was not seen to be untypical of poorhouse directors when he was prosecuted in 1754 for the abuses he had enacted in Marylebone Workhouse to squeeze profits from the miserable maintenance allowed to the paupers. But the presence of the poor was considered as a fact of life, and reforming urges, though they existed, were few. Those who were vulnerable, whether sick or elderly, unemployed or alone, were expected to make shift as best they could, and this callousness had predictably wretched consequences. As late as 1779, the magistrate Saunders Welch estimated that as many as twenty people died of simple starvation each week in the tenement rookeries of Holborn and St Giles.

One of the main contributors to the appalling conditions of the poor was the 'gin craze'. Between 1720 and 1750, London suffered its worst-ever per capita death rate, as well as a low birth rate. The explanation for this, quite plainly, was gin. By 1734, 5 million gallons of raw spirits were being distilled annually in London, and one in seven houses in the slum district of St Giles was a gin shop. Despite an act of 1729 to arrest the growth of the trade, 8 million gallons of gin a year were consumed by the time the Gin Act was passed in 1743. Unlike established industries such as brewing and baking, distilling was not subject to guild and apprenticeship laws, so anyone with a vat and a still could set up in business, and many did. Dr Johnson observed that 'the great fortunes recently made were ... a convincing proof that the trade of distilling was the most profitable of any now exercised in the kingdom except that of being broker to a prime-minister'.[18] As ever, pleasure (or the ruin it betokened), was politicised.

Gin had originally been associated with the Hanoverian succession, after William III's administration took measures to promote it. 'Mother Gin was of Dutch parentage, but her father, who was a substantial trader in the city of Rotterdam, came to settle in London, where he married an Englishwoman and obtained an act of parliament for his naturalisation.'[19] For the opposition, the depredations of gin represented the destruction of the steady, beer-drinking English character by the corruption of foreign influences (Hogarth's famous prints contrasting the respective effects of gin and beer can therefore be read politically as well as morally). Gin consumption had initially been encouraged in Parliament by the landed interest as a means of keeping corn prices high at a time of abundant harvests, but shortly after Daniel Defoe produced a pamphlet in its favour in 1713, the consequences began to prove themselves in the city's Bills of Mortality. The fact that a landowning Parliament should have attempted to halt the frenzy for gin in 1729 at a time when corn prices remained low reflects just how serious were concerns that gin was literally wrecking the country.

That England appeared to be becoming a nation of drunkards

accorded with a general view of the idleness and fecklessness of the poor, and it was also connected with the perceived rise in crime. Henry Fielding commented in his *Enquiry into the Causes of the Late Increase of Robbers*: 'A new kind of drunkenness, unknown to our ancestors, is lately sprung up amongst us, and which if not put a stop to, will infallibly destroy a great part of the inferior people.' Drink was a cheap means of forgetting for a few hours the misery of everyday life, but of course it also exacerbated that misery. Yet for many people it hardly seemed worth the trouble of dragging themselves out of poverty: the struggle was just too hard. Better to live for whatever pleasures could be obtained today when tomorrow offered no prospects of improvement. 'Is it to be wondered', wrote Bernard de Mandeville,[20] 'that [the people] should be indisposed to attend to anything serious, or that they grow sick of religion which has no comforts for them; that they fly from the church and crowd to the playhouse? It is this unhappy, unsettled state of mind that has introduced a kind of general idleness among the people.'

(Spirits are mentioned frequently in *The Beggar's Opera*, part of the grubby background of Polly Peachum's world. Lucy attempts to poison her rival with 'strong waters', Macheath's whores genteelly excuse their preference for gin on medicinal grounds and Mrs Peachum reserves a delicious 'cordial' for her own consumption.)

If Lavinia herself was terrified by the prospect of poverty, she was still young enough to prefer pleasure to profit, and confounded her mother by eloping, with a Portuguese aristocrat, who was presumably handsomer than the old gull since he certainly wasn't rich. One Friday evening in 1725, a coach was sent to the Old Bailey. Lavinia kept it waiting three hours before she finally stepped into it. Was it fear of her mother that made her hesitate? The consideration that £400 was indeed a fortune in exchange for a few minutes' worth of sour old breath and withered old limbs? Or the knowledge that once the coach rattled away through the city she would have embarked upon a career from which few women escaped with their dignity or, for that matter, their lives? Perhaps the Portuguese gentleman was very handsome indeed, because Lavinia returned on the Monday a ruined woman, and Mrs Fenton, yet again, had to make the best of it.

At first the loss of the Feathered Gull was compensated for by the mysterious Portuguese gentleman's assurances to Mrs Fenton that he would provide for her daughter, but unfortunately his passion for Lavinia was more extensive that his means, and his funds were exhausted inconveniently in advance of his desire, so much so that whether by his own indulgence or the rapacity of the disappointed mother, he bankrupted himself and was sent to prison for debt. It seemed that Lavinia would have to look about for another protector, and according to her more ungenerous biographers, this was precisely what she did.

'It cannot be said by her greatest Enemies, that she was ever a Common Prostitute, as some would insinuate,' ran one such account,[21] suggesting, of course, that this is exactly what she was. When Lavinia became famous, a collection of spoof letters appeared, entitled: *Letters in Prose and Verse to the Celebrated Polly Peachum, From the Most Eminent of Her Admirers and Rivals*, who included the silk mercer again, this time named Philander Flush Cheek, who sighed such nonsense as, 'What have I done, that Heaven should sentence me to die by the Hands of an Executioner who has the appearance of an Angel . . . did you suffer me to go on and discover fresh Beauties in you every day, till the God of Love had fired my Heart beyond all cure that my Grief and Disappointment might sink me to the Grave for my Presumption,' implausibly quoting Dryden for good measure. There was also a barrister who signed himself Sullivan Slaver and a 'Horse Courser' who, in a prurient tale reminiscent of the euphemisms of *Harris's Guide*, wagers fifty guineas he can last a five-minute ride with her, a bet Lavinia supposedly won because he 'foundered between two Hills, and lost Breath in one minute, three seconds and two Moments'. The *Craftsman* of 13 April 1728 implied that Lavinia was indulging in the popular whore's trick of the blackmailing 'memoir'.

> Whereas P-lly P—ch-m hath of Late received innumerable Letters of Love and Gallantry from all Quarters of the Town, this is to give Notice that, the week after Easter she designs to have them printed by subscription, with the Names of the Authors, in two neat Pocket Volumes. The Price to Subscribers is Two Guineas. But if any Gentleman are apprehensive that their Amours should come to the ears of their Wives . . . they may be excused upon the following Terms. For a

Lord, Ten Guineas ... for a Baronet, if he be married, Eight. For a Citizen, Six ... For all gentleman of the Inns of Court, providing they be under Five and Twenty, half a Guinea. Attendance is given, twice a week, behind the Scenes, when Subscriptions are taken in and Hush Money received.

Was it possible that after the willing surrender of her virginity to the Portuguese gentleman, Lavinia had decided to offer it for sale on more liberal terms? Sally Salisbury, the famous prostitute, had after all managed to cut a deal for her hymen a record twenty-six times. (If menstruation didn't assist at a girl's 'deflowering' with 'evidence', a small sponge soaked in animal's blood could be inserted into the vagina to provide the necessary gory proof of spoiled virtue on the sheets and the penis of the client. The method is explained in John Cleland's erotic comedy *Fanny Hill*.) Yet in 1728, the writers whose praise had so quickly made Lavinia a star are determined just as swiftly to cut her down. Like Young, they lazily insisted that as a successful actress she was naturally a more successful whore, so it is difficult to give total credence to their stories. If Lavinia had begun her career as a kept woman, after the incarceration of her lover she sought, and succeeded in finding, a different method of protecting her family from poverty. She had stepped on to the stage as a professional for the first time in 1726. She had also, apparently, remained faithful to her Portuguese admirer, selling the jewellery he had given her to provide for him in prison and allow him to return home, whence he sent her £400 and the comforting assurance that the Portuguese ladies were 'mere Dowdies' compared with his beloved, and returned triumphant to 'Enjoy the Pleasures, which all the World covets'.[21] Lavinia, in turn, lent him £300 in cash to redeem him from yet another arrest. So when the *Craftsman* of 22 June 1728 reported that 'To the great Surprise of the Audience, the Part of Polly Peachum was performed by Miss Warren, who was very much applauded; the first Performer being retired, it is reported, from the stage,' it was assumed by the writers who sought to profit by libelling her that Lavinia and her lover, reunited after their tribulations like a true stage couple, had departed into happy-ever-after. Better than admitting that no one knew the whereabouts of London's most famous actress or why she had, quite simply, vanished.

# 3

# THEATRICAL CRIMINALS

Of all the extraordinary aspects of *The Beggar's Opera*, perhaps the least extraordinary is the mechanism of the plot. Mr Peachum is a 'thief-taker' who makes a living from informing on criminals who, in exchange for his protection, pass him their stolen goods, which he then returns to their owners for a price. Macheath, the highwayman who has married Peachum's daughter Polly, is the principal robber in the gang Peachum controls. Peachum and his wife decide that in the interests of the family they will 'peach' (i.e. inform against) Macheath at the next court sessions, and thus benefit from his death, and accordingly conspire with Lockit, the gaoler of Newgate prison, to have him taken. Macheath has been having an affair with Lockit's daughter Lucy, who says she will try to save him from the gallows if he abandons Polly for her. He agrees, but returns to Polly as soon as he has escaped. He is recaptured, and is set to hang, but on the intervention of the Beggar, as chorus or narrator, is freed once more on the grounds that, since the convention of opera demands a happy ending, 'in this kind of drama, 'tis no matter how absurdly things are brought about'.

Dr Johnson was about to enter Pembroke College, Oxford for his short career as an undergraduate in October of the year of Lavinia Fenton's triumph. He would suggest that *The Beggar's Opera* was written 'in ridicule of the musical Italian drama',[1] and added with polysyllabic pomposity that 'there is in it such a labefactation of all principles, as may be injurious to morality'. Such an unsubtle interpretation owes more to Johnson's ambivalent relationship with the theatre than to any serious attempt to understand the genius of Gay's conception. Boswell, in his *Life of Johnson*, later explained that his mentor was inspired to inveigh against the theatre through jealousy of the superior good looks of the performers and of the success of his protégé, the great actor David Garrick. Along with Garrick's more famous roles, he was also celebrated for his hilarious impressions of Johnson's beloved but rather blowsy wife Elizabeth Porter, but the 'peculiar acrimony' which 'Tetty's' husband will display towards the stage may also have been due to his own singular lack of success as a dramatist. In 1749, when Johnson's drama *Irene* is given a performance at Drury Lane by the kindly Garrick, the author's arrogant refusal to alter a word of his text guarantees a flop, particularly as a result of 'the conclusion, when Mrs Pritchard, the heroine of the piece, was to be strangled upon the stage, and was to speak two lines with the bow string round her neck. The audience cried out "Murder! Murder!", she several times attempted to speak, but in vain. At last she was obliged to go off the stage alive.'[2] Johnson was finally to allow the piece to be altered, so that the unfortunate Mrs Pritchard could die more discreetly in the wings, but still *Irene*, even with the support of the all-powerful Garrick, ran for only nine nights. Johnson, who thought that as an author he ought to look rather dashing, had squashed his bulk into an untypically splendid get-up for the evening, consisting of a substantial scarlet waistcoat set off by a gold lace hat, and though he demurred to the verdict of the public and made little defence of the play, he was never quite to forgive the theatre for his humiliation.

Squirming in his box seat in January 1728, Mr Gay, whose fortunes so far have not run to any majestic accessories for his first night, is well aware of the hostility of audiences to authorial stringency. In fact, he has already satirised it in the character of the pretentious bluestocking Phoebe Clinker in *Three Hours After Marriage*, a farce co-written with his friends Mr Pope and Dr Arbuthnot. Gay's solution to bad notices was rather less dignified than Johnson's was to be: when he heard that the oleaginous actor-manager of Drury Lane and future poet laureate, Colley Cibber, had criticised Mr Pope's involvement in the play, he responded on puny Pope's behalf by punching Cibber on the nose. It was therefore unsurprising, perhaps, that Cibber turned down *The Beggar's Opera* for Drury Lane, with the bloody injury to his dignity resulting in perhaps the greatest error of his career. Cibber attempted to save his damaged face in his memoirs by suggesting that Gay 'gave them [the tasteless public] that Performance as a Satire upon the Depravity of their Judgement (as Ben Jonson, of old, was said to have given his *Bartholomew Fair* . . .), and that by artfully seducing them, to be the Champions of the Immoralities he himself detested, he should be amply revenged on their former Severity and Ignorance'. His rejection of the play, Cibber implies, is thus due to his superior discernment as one who did not share in the 'Ignorance' of the general public, and therefore had no need of Gay's satire. Whether Gay's intention was to mock the Italian opera, as Johnson was to claim, or the public, as Cibber asserted, was of little interest to John Rich, the manager of Lincoln's Inn Fields theatre, to whom Gay presented *The Beggar's Opera* after the 'Old House' had refused it. Rich was badly in need of a hit, and this peculiar combination of English ballads, low-life drama and romance might, he felt, just provide it.

Rich's involvement in the London theatre was part of a massively complex network of familial and political allegiances which spanned the seventeenth century and had their origins, some romantics claimed, in the triumphant era of the great Elizabethan dramatists. (Lavinia Fenton's career just touched on an acting connection which reached back over the closure of the theatres during the Commonwealth. Lavinia was acquainted with the actress Mrs Bracegirdle, who had acted with Mrs Betterton, who had been married to the Mr Betterton who had learned his *Hamlet* from William Davenant, who had his from Mr Taylor, who had his, so legend insisted, from William Shakespeare himself.) After the Restoration of King Charles II in 1660, two theatre companies were established by royal patent: the Duke's men under the management of William Davenant and the King's men under Thomas Killigrew. The Duke's company had begun at the Lincoln's Inn theatre, previously Lisle's Tennis Court, in Portugal Street in the autumn of 1660 – 'the first playhouse, I believe, that ever was in England', Pepys records – then moved to Dorset Garden, leaving the theatre to the King's men after the Theatre Royal burned down in 1672. Ten years later, the King's company collapsed, and the New United Company was formed under Betterton at Drury Lane. In 1687, Davenant's original interest from the Duke's men was bought up by a hard-headed businessman, Christopher Rich, whose methods so offended Betterton that in 1695 he led an actors' rebellion against Drury Lane and founded the Seceded Company, with Lincoln's Inn as its headquarters. Initially, the Seceded Company functioned as perhaps the first actors' collective, on a democratic basis of profit-sharing, but the scheme failed and Betterton resumed sole management in 1700. In 1705, the writer John Vanbrugh, newly issued with a patent from Queen Anne, opened the Queen's theatre in the Haymarket, to which the Seceded Company transferred. In 1708, Rich and Betterton buried their professional differences, and their two companies were reunited briefly at Drury Lane once more, before Rich quarrelled with the Lord Chamberlain, who had jurisdiction over the theatres, and Drury Lane was forced to close in 1709. Eventually, the management of the Old House was taken over by William Collier and Aaron Hill, a former schoolmate of John Gay. Hill's regime was so unsuccessful that in 1710 the actors rioted, and in 1712 control at Drury Lane was passed to Colley Cibber, John Wilks and Barton Booth.

In 1714, Christopher Rich's son John reopened the old theatre at Lincoln's Inn. Since it had been improvised rather hastily from a tennis court during its first occupation by Davenant's company, the Duke's men, the house was too small, and both audiences and neighbours complained about the crowds. The ambitious Rich found the stage area too mean for the spectaculars with which he intended to lure the crowds from Drury Lane, so he completely refurbished the old building, expanding the stage to fifty-six by a hundred feet, larger than Drury Lane's, and undertook a marvellous scheme of decoration involving new scenery, mirrors and paintings. Six chandeliers on iron chains illuminated the house throughout the performances. The *Censor* commented: 'The greatest Pleasure that I received through the whole Play, was to observe those Original Pictures that were the Ornaments of the Gallery, and could not help taking notice that the noseless Sir William Davenant had more fearful Starers from the Pit than any of the rest of his Fraternity.' The link between the theatre and sexual corruption, as exemplified here by Davenant's syphilis-ravaged face, was ever-present.

Mindful of the inheritance to which he owed his new theatre, John Rich, who also enjoyed a highly successful career as an actor, gave an elegiacal prologue in mourning dress at the house's first night, a performance of *The Recruiting Officer*. The form in which Rich, under his stage name of Mr Lun, was to receive most acclaim, and in which he hoped he would trounce his rival actor-managers at Drury Lane, was the pantomime. Introduced from the Italian *commedia dell'arte*, the pantomime involved a set of stock characters and narrative upon which any variety of fantastic, whimsical themes and effects could be imposed. Harlequin is in love with Columbine, but is thwarted in his designs by her father, Pantaloon, his man, Pierrot, and the Squire, a rival for Columbine's love. After a number of convoluted pursuits, dancings, tumblings and trickings, the enchanter Harlequin, who at Lincoln's Inn was inevitably played by Rich himself, prevails. 'Harlequin's only wit consists in his activity,' sniffed Robert Wilkes.[3] In John Rich's hands, the pantomime became an amazing spectacle, employing the latest in costumes, lighting effects, scenery and stage design, while the malleability of its simple plot meant it could serve to illustrate (or corrupt) almost any well-known story or current issue. César de Saussure wrote of Rich's *Harlequin Orpheus*, which cost the unbelievable sum of £40,000 to stage. It featured a set where 'hell' rose to the ceiling to reveal a farmhouse where Harlequin was born from an egg which grew and grew as the audience gaped in astonishment, along with an enormous gold and green serpent so realistic that one of the King's guards drew his sword to it. Machines made trees grow out of rocks, forming a forest where flowers blossomed and fell away to be replaced by fruits. In 1723, the *London Stage* described another pantomime: 'You will see strange alterations, Cloaks flying upon Men's shoulders, Harlequin, Scaramouch, Punch and Pierrot riding upon spirits in the Air, Dancing Wheat Sheaves, flaming Barns, barking Dogs, flying Flasks and Oranges, and fellows, to escape a Scouring, venture their Necks down a chimney.'

Such marvels were not universally seductive. A caricature of 1731, 'The Stage's Glory', sneered at the unsophisticated tastes to which Rich's spectacles appealed:

> What's more in Hercules is Harlequin!
> One slew the Hydra, this can kill the Spleen,
> In him behold the Age's Genius bright
> A Patch-Coat hero to this Town's delight.

And the critics loathed the pantomime – 'that succession of monstrous medlies that have so long infested the stage', harrumphed Cibber – but, as is frequently the case in the theatre, critical disapproval did nothing to dissuade the paying public, and the genre was a roaring success. It is interesting to note that, in the theatre which was to première the low-life *Beggar's Opera*, an earlier 'Patch-Coat Hero' than Macheath should have enjoyed such popularity.

John Gay's first theatrical connection with the London underworld of thieves and thief-takers was established through the pantomime. In 1724 he had published a ballad called 'Newgate's Garland', 'Being a New Ballad, Shewing how Mr Jonathan Wild's Throat was cut, from Ear to Ear, with a Penknife, by Mr Blake, alias Blueskin, the Bold Highwayman, as he stood his trial at the Old Bailey'. The characters involved in this real and unsuccessful assassination attempt were some of London's most famous villains. Jonathan Wild was the self-declared 'Thief-taker General' who for several years was the city's most powerful controller of organised crime. He took advantage of the conditions which made London so plentiful a hunting ground for criminals – a dark, complicated warren of a city whose commercial wealth was expanding while the gap between rich and poor increased, with no police force and an inefficient judiciary which relied on a dubious form of barter to obtain convictions – to turn himself into a one-man industry. Bernard de Mandeville, in his 1725 *Enquiry into the Causes of the Frequent Executions at Tyburn*, admitted that in the absence of a police force the authorities were forced into 'shameful negotiations with thieves' and that therefore 'as soon as anything is missing, suspected to be stolen, the first course we steer is directly to the office of Mr Jonathan Wild'. Wild's system, his 'corporation of thieves', was brilliantly simple, and for a time kept him safely out of reach of the law. From his office in Cock Alley, and later the Old Bailey, he would receive reports from victims of burglary, and would undertake to broker a deal for the return of their stolen goods if no questions were asked. Since the goods were already in his possession, handed in by the gangs of thieves he controlled, he could profit from both thief and victim without committing the felony of actually receiving stolen goods. This protected the thieves by providing a market for materials it would otherwise be dangerous to dispose of, and Wild undertook to safeguard his workers against the gallows so long as they remained obedient to him. He was equally adept, though, at securing convictions as acquittals, and any independent criminal who refused to be part of the system risked being 'peached' by Wild, who would then benefit from the reward or the leverage obtained by informing on him to have one of his own men released. At the height of his success, Wild was rumoured to control large warehouses full of stolen goods, a ship to smuggle them to Holland for sale, a team of artists and craftsmen to alter or reset stolen jewellery and artefacts and numerous well-organised gangs of thieves, divided into districts and specific skills. Wild played the gentleman, keeping a grave clerk and a row of ledgers in his office, placing pompous advertisements in newspapers and sporting a silver cane. He represented himself to the public as a champion of the victim, a ruthless hunter of thieves, but his popularity was ambiguous, as the reaction to the trial of Blueskin and his famous partner, Jack Sheppard, shows.

If Jonathan Wild was London's thief-taker extraordinaire, Sheppard was his burglar equivalent. The intelligent, cheeky product of a charity school, Jack soon abandoned his apprenticeship as a carpenter to pursue a more lucrative line of business, though his skills with his tools were to prove his greatest asset. He began quietly enough, with the theft of two silver spoons from the Rummer, a brothel near Charing Cross, and progressed to relieving one Mr Charles of Mayfair of £7 to £8-worth of silver and four smart suits. He also called on Mr William Phillips in Drury Lane and had £60-worth of goods from Mary Cook's drapery shop in Clare Street. The latter two robberies were committed in collusion with his brother Thomas, who was subsequently captured and sent to Newgate, where he turned evidence against Jack. Jack Sheppard was brought to St Giles's roundhouse, where he embarked on the series of escapes that was to make him a legend by extricating himself from the most secure cell on the top floor of the building using only a razor, a straw mattress and a rope of blankets to force a hole in the roof and clamber down into the churchyard next door.

A few weeks later, Jack stole a watch in Leicester Fields, but while fleeing the scene unluckily ran straight into the arms of a watchman, who had him committed to St Ann's roundhouse. Here he was visited by his lover, a plump prostitute known as Edgeworth Bess, who brought him a spike hidden in a basket. Using this to break the lock, the couple got out of Jack's cell and into the corridor, where they encountered the warder. Both were committed to the new prison in Clerkenwell, where Jack was shackled with weights and a heavy chain. Over the next few days, acquaintances smuggled in sufficient tools for him to attempt another escape, and he duly filed the bars of the window and climbed out into the yard, which faced that of the Clerkenwell Bridewell and was surrounded by a wall twenty-two feet high and topped with iron spikes. Undaunted, Jack used a gimlet to carve footholds in the wooden gates and, with a rope made of sheets and Bess's petticoats, he hauled his portly mistress to safety before nipping over the wall to join her in the quiet anonymity of the dark east London streets.

A more successful robbery followed, the victim being a wealthy tailor named Barton, from whom Jack had £300-worth of goods and cash. Along with his friend 'Blueskin' Blake, he then stole £50-worth of goods from a Mr Kneebone, in whose house he had formerly lodged. Furious, Kneebone called in Jonathan Wild. Wild was already perturbed by Sheppard's activities. Jack had attended one of Wilds 'levées', as Wild pretentiously called what were effectively recruitment meetings for thieves, but later confessed that he had not cared overmuch for the gentleman's acquaintance. Sheppard was a maverick, a showman, and Wild's operations were threatened by his independence. Kneebone's approach gave the Thief-taker General the opportunity to dispose of a nuisance who had dared to oppose his authority. He placed an advertisement in the *Daily Post* of 17 July 1724 offering £20 and a pardon to anyone who would give himself up and 'discover his Accomplices in the Robbery of one Piece of Scarlet Drab cloth with several Pieces and Remnants of colour'd Broad Cloth, two silver spoons, a light Tye Wig and other Things from Mr Wm Kneebone Woolen Draper at the Angel the Corner of Drury Lane in the Strand'. Scarlet scraps, mismatched remnants and the inevitable silver spoons seem poor things for a man to risk his life for, but if Jack was caught, Wild could be confident he would hang.

Forty-eight hours later, Jack found himself in Newgate. Rather pathetically, after the Kneebone robbery he and Blueskin had attempted to set up as highwaymen in the Hampstead area, but in three hold-ups they had amassed only twenty-eight shillings and sixpence between them. Meanwhile, Wild had captured Edgeworth Bess in a brandy shop near Temple Bar and succeeded in forcing her to reveal that Jack was hiding in a tavern kept by Blueskin's mother in Rosemary Lane. Wild worked efficiently. On 13 August, Jack was taken to the Old Bailey to be tried for his life, and returned to prison a condemned man.

His execution was set for 4 September, but a few days before he obtained a file from his cellmate and managed to make a little hole, about nine inches wide, from the condemned hold to the adjoining Newgate Lodge, which the turnkeys used as a bar and sitting room. Edgeworth Bess and her friend Poll Maggot came to the lodge to visit him, in accordance with the condemned prisoner's right to speak to friends from the hold through the partition. As the turnkeys boozed and gossiped, Bess pushed a bundle containing a nightdress and cap through the hole Jack had made. He had prepared himself by sawing away his chains and fetters and now he slipped the disguise over his head, wriggled his sinewy body through the tiny gap and, while Poll made herself scarce, he and Bess, appearing to the turnkey's bleary eyes to be the two girls who had come to talk to Sheppard, strolled casually through the prison entrance and into a waiting coach.

The horses rattled away to Blackfriars, where William Page, a friend who had hired the coach, was waiting. Soon he and Jack were on their way into Northamptonshire, this time disguised as butcher's apprentices, to lie low with some relations of William's. Rustic retirement palled for Jack within a matter of days. It would have been relatively easy for him to disappear permanently into rural obscurity, but some fatalistic urge drew him back to the dangers of London. In his way, Jack was an artist, and a part of him seemed to need the adrenaline rush of the terror upon which his performances were contingent. Wild had been called in again after Jack's escape, and a reward of twenty guineas had been offered by the Keeper of Newgate for his recovery. Within a day of his return to London, rumours of his arrival and sightings began to swell like an epidemic. By now Jack was a hero, and the taverns and coffee houses around Drury Lane were agog for news of his next encounter with the law.

Jack didn't keep his public waiting. On 8 September, he and Page made off with £15-worth of watches from Martin's in Fleet Street. The drama of his exploits now became a comedy, with Sheppard and Page pursued through the town and across Finchley Common by a posse of incompetent Newgate turnkeys. Jack was eventually pulled by his heels from a bundle of farmyard straw and returned in chains to Newgate. The whole of the prison was in a frenzy, and the city without so excited that it ground to a halt. Jack's latest escape and sudden recapture created a sensation amongst all classes, and caused a frenzy of theorizing, betting and speculation. The taverns were crammed with gossips, shops and businesses were neglected, and the cacophony of London's streets was stilled as porters and coachmen left their work to follow the latest news of Sheppard. The stage was set for the most thrilling act of the performance.

The castle, high up a twisting staircase on the third floor, was believed to be the most secure cell in the prison. Here Jack was brought, and chained to the floor. It is a measure of the authorities' incompetence, though, that no one thought to search his visitors, and soon he was once more supplied with tools to help him escape. His bonds were easily dealt with, and after he had been surprised taking a stroll round his cell, he obligingly offered to give a demonstration of his 'magick art' to the prison officials, freeing himself in a matter of minutes before their disbelieving eyes. He was fastened down again, this time with the addition of a huge padlock and a heavy pair of handcuffs disabling his wrists. So severe were his fetters that even Mr Kneebone, after visiting him, pleaded for him to be relieved. But Jack required none of Kneebone's intervention. Incredibly, beginning with a nail extracted from its hiding place in his stocking and held in his teeth, he removed the padlock and handcuffs, broke the chain between his ankles, removed the bricks from the chimney and used the iron bar placed there to prevent escape through the flue to smash a hole in the ceiling above. He then negotiated the spiked partitions of the prison chapel and six stout doors, reinforced with iron, to arrive on the prison roof. It was too long a drop to jump, so he painstakingly retraced his route, grabbed his blankets to make a rope and returned to the open air, climbed down on to the roof of an adjoining house, and slid through the attic window and down two flights of stairs to freedom.

Jack had saved his most spectacular feat until last, but the law had him in the end. He was hanged on 16 November 1724. After he finally swung at Tyburn, the rumour went about that his poor, thin little corpse was concealed at a house in Covent Garden, awaiting sale to surgeons for dissection. Incensed at such treatment of their hero, the spectators who had been so entertained by his death took to the streets and enjoyed an invigorating afternoon's stone-slinging and looting, paying no heed to a local magistrate's rather feeble reading of the Riot Act, until a company of bayonet-wielding dragoons was summoned from the Savoy to disperse them.

The previous month, Jack's old accomplice Blueskin had attacked Jonathan Wild in the prison yard after Wild arrived to give evidence at his trial. Sheppard's friend leaped at Wild and managed to slash his throat to the windpipe before he was dragged away. The Thief-taker General was saved by the convenient presence of two surgeons and the thick fabric of his stock, but Blueskin 'curs'd with many bloody oaths both his Hand and the Knife for not doing it more effectually', declaring that he had intended to cut off Wild's head, and that he would hang with pleasure so long as he could be sure the thief-taker had died before him.

Gay's ballad about the incident was used in a pantomime entitled *Harlequin Sheppard* which was performed eight days after Jack's death (having been hastily written and rehearsed, it not being thought prudent to give time to it while he was alive in case he escaped again and ruined the story). The song's inclusion suggests that Jonathan Wild's power was already declining. His involvement in Sheppard's captures had made him intensely unpopular, and indeed he was himself tried and hanged the next year, though such was the intense hatred of the crowd that pelted him with missiles down from Newgate that he barely made it to the gallows alive.

It was in this song that Gay first made popular use of the layered resonances of the English ballad tradition. It was sung to the tune of 'The Cut Purse' or 'Packington's Pound', a Tudor melody which Ben Jonson had employed in his play *Bartholomew Fair*. In Jonson's version, the song set to the tune is 'Nightingale's Song', which has the refrain:

> Youth, Youth, thou hadst better been starved at Nurse
> Than for to be hang'd for cutting a Purse.

To the audience, the lyrics of the old song would still be present beneath its new words, contained in the memories of a familiar tune which connected them with the popular London free-for-all of Bartholomew Fair itself, where society's rules were inverted for a short, precious time. And it did indeed seem tragic that a young man should die for attempting to relieve himself of want. The richness of such folk tunes made the pantomime vivid for its audiences in a way which the more rarefied wit of gentlemen playwrights could rarely grasp.

So successful were Rich's pantomimes that, much to its disgust, the management of Drury Lane was obliged to compete, presenting a pantomime as an 'afterpiece' to the main play. Mr Booth, sulking in a tavern with his colleagues after appearing in a poorly attended tragedy, argued that 'a thin Audience was a much greater Indignity to the Stage than any they mentioned ... he begged them to consider that there were many more Spectators than Men of Taste and Judgement', and asserted that if it was necessary to use such low devices to draw in customers, the management might at least 'by the Artifice of a Pantomime ... induce a greater number to Partake ... of a good play than could be drawn without it'.[4] There was perhaps no harm in it (not to mention a great deal more money to be made). 'Harlequin is such a hero among the English,' wrote a visitor to London, 'that nothing can be done without him'.[5]

In England, it has been suggested that the court of Charles I represented the apotheosis of the Renaissance ideal of kingship, epitomised in its supreme art form, the masque, whose stately choreography and extravagant settings were termed by Ben Jonson 'the studie of magnificence'. In some form, the pantomime might be said to be a democratisation of this elite tradition of extravagant fantasy, and in pantomime's irreverence, its audacious scrambling of high and low culture, lay a certain rebellious attraction. The lure of the pantomime was the lure of the carnival and Bartholomew Fair, its topsy-turvy charivari reaching into a feeling not so long buried in England, a feeling which connected even the soberest of Augustan theatregoers with the vividness of their medieval past. As high culture ceased to be the exclusive province of the court and entered the realm of commerce, the energy of London's streets, the exuberance of its fairs, the explosive riotousness of its people were encapsulated in the grotesque beauty and violence of the pantomime. In such a strictly hierarchical society, pantomime offered a taste of the old Catholic carnival spirit, and a connection with the even more ancient tradition of the Roman Saturnalia, where scullions could be kings for a day, and the Fool was the Lord of Misrule. Excitingly, spectacle could subvert truth; what appeared to be and what was were increasingly, and compellingly, separated.

# 4

## SEEING IS DECEIVING

Lavinia Fenton would disappear from her incarnation as a famous actress and reappear, some time later, in quite another role altogether. The trajectory of this dramatic reversal in her life places her at the heart of one of the principal debates of the eighteenth century: the construction of the self. The consistency of individual identity was a troublesome problem and actors, the epitome of inconsistency, were representative of the century's struggle to pin down the nature of that identity. Ideally, as expressed in Pope's 1733 poem 'An Essay on Man', every person had a fixed place in the great 'chain of Being', which ascended, in strictly demarcated categories, from animals at the bottom to God Himself at the top.

> Look round our World; behold the chain of Love
> Combing all below, and all above.
> See plastic Nature working to this end,
> The single atoms each to other tend,
> Attract, attracted to, the next in place
> Form'd and impell'd its neighbour to embrace.
> See Matter next, with various life endu'd,
> Press to one centre still, the gen'ral Good.

To recognise one's place in this chain, and to fulfil its obligations, was, Pope suggested, the foundation of a harmonious social order. But Lavinia was an example of someone who succeeded in slipping her social bonds, in shuffling off the coil of destiny, and proving that identity was not so neat or so fixed as Pope's reassuring argument would lead us to believe.

Playing a part was a dubious, potentially immoral evasion of social definition which was the source of the mistrust and condemnation of actors. Yet, as the seventeenth-century philosopher Thomas Hobbes commented, it was also an essential element of all social behaviour: '*Persona*, in Latin, signifies the disguise or outward appearance of a man, counterfeited on the stage, and somehow more particularly that part of which disguiseth the face, as a Mask, or Vizard ... So that a Person is the same as an Actor is, both on the stage and in Common conversation; and to Pesonate is to Act, or Represent himself, or an other.'[1]

Participating in society, then, to some extent necessitated the playing of a part, a fact which Addison acknowledged in the *Spectator*, quoting the Latin '*totus mundus agit histrionem*' (everyone is a player), and thereby 'conjuring up a theatre of the world on whose boards all must perform'. Lord Chesterfield, in his famous letters to his son,[2] insists repeatedly that 'distinguished politeness ... a superior gracefulness' is the qualifying mark of the gentleman, but at what point did good manners, that prized commodity of eighteenth-century social life, slide into insincerity? At what point did 'polite' behaviour become deception? How to know what was innate and what contrived? In Lord Chesterfield's analysis of court behaviour, it is clear that the polish of civilisation is only a veneer placed over savagery: 'Ambition and avarice, the two prevailing passions at courts, found dissimulation more effective than violence; and dissimulation introduced the habit of politeness which distinguishes the courtier from the country gentleman. In the former case the strongest body would prevail, in the latter the strongest mind.' So insincerity was an essential component of social existence, but to what degree was it desirable, and if dissimulation could be learned, where did that leave a faith in some sort of ontological essence of self?

The Earl of Shaftesbury used the metaphor of whoring to examine the apparent contradictions between the polite and the natural self. Writing of social behaviour, he questioned: 'Must not I prostitute myself in the strangest manner, be a Hypocrite in the horridest degree?'[3] The polite self was a tutored construct, created through education, but the century was deeply suspicious of the products of that education at the same time as it embraced them. Dancing masters in particular came in for a good deal of implied moral condemnation, as with Swift's description of a fashionable young man at the theatre: 'There sits a beau like a fool in a frame, that dares not stir his head nor move his body for fear of uncommoding his wig, ruffling his cravat or putting his eyes or mouth out of the order his maître de danse set it in.' Numerous handbooks such as the 1740 *Essay on Polite Behaviour* attempted to instruct their readers on the necessary social performances, but a learned courtesy ran up against the strain of anxiety that politeness was a form of that most dreadful activity: acting.

As the success of Rich's pantomimes proved, eighteenth-century audiences had a tremendous appetite for spectacle. Yet the urge to see was also founded upon the desire to be seen, to engage in judgement of others' displays. Events such as plays, recitals and operas were opportunities not only to watch and listen to a performance, but to become part of it. 'The ostensible reason for a person's presence, seeing the play, attending an auction, listening to a concert, was often subordinate to a more powerful set of social imperatives. The audience were not passive, but incorporated culture as part of their own social performance.'[4] Audiences chattered and gossiped and peered at one another across the stage or assembly room, from the pit to the gallery, over promenades and ballrooms, ogling and quizzing, comparing their visions of one another as well as their impressions of the piece. Even the professional performers like Lavinia were not immune. 'How improper in our theatric ladies is the screening of the eyes and countenance behind a fan, in order to take a sly peep around the boxes,' grumbled Robert Wilkes. This dominance of scrutiny created a concomitant desire to conceal, and hence a period characterised by both its obsession with appearances and the lure of disguises devised a form of entertainment that played with both, and combined the elegance of the court masque and the contrariness of the pantomime to create the masquerade.

Some time after her mysterious disappearance from Lincoln's Inn, Lavinia Fenton sat for George Knapton holding a masquerade vizard, the half-mask often made simply of velvet or ornate with gilding and feathers, that teasingly disguised a woman's face. Her choice of this accessory might be read as a visual challenge. Who am I? it insists.

Where the self and where the disguise? Lavinia was playing with an image which formed the objective correlative to her time's frustrated debate about identity, for the masquerade was one of its most popular and controversial means of playing with the confines of a fixed persona.

Essentially, masquerades were fancy-dress balls with the costumes of the partygoers extended to their faces. To add to their anonymity, masquers even disguised their voices, affecting a high-pitched squeak or low whisper and thereby creating a curiously menacing, jungle-like mutter in hot, crowded rooms where impenetrable Venetian dominos swirled against milkmaids and mermaids, Greek chitons, Roman togas, Turkish warriors, monks, goddesses, sailors, all masked, some in the simple vizard, some in the alarming, colourful distortions of the carnival, pantomime Punchinello. The *Guardian* commented in 1713 on the dubious moral implications of such loose, flowing costumes. The masquerade was an opportunity for social anarchy, dissolving class distinctions of appearance and accent, but also for sexual misbehaviour, permitting spouses to conduct flirtations or adulteries literally in front of one another's deceived eyes. Husbands and wives tried to double-cross each other by changing costume again after arriving at the ball; wives found themselves planning illicit liaisons with their own husbands; gallant gentlemen found that the pretty girl they were attempting to fondle beneath her domino was not a girl at all. Like the theatre, the masquerade was seen as a breeding ground for sin. Hogarth's harlot Moll Hackabout has a witch's costume and a mask displayed in her lodgings, accessories to her trade. In the masquerade scene of Fielding's novel *Amelia* a 'buck' reads aloud a satirical exhortation against adultery, shockingly parodying St Paul's Second Epistle to St Timothy, to the general amusement of the company, while the connection with the morally deplorable new fashion for opera is made apparent by a proposal that the letter should be set as an oratorio by Handel. Amelia, the virtuous heroine, is disgusted when a 'he-domino' attempts to conquer her by appealing to 'avarice and ambition', suggesting that the masquerade was a flourishing marketplace for sexual profiteers. As Bishop Gibson complained, in a sermon to the Societies for the Reformation of Manners in 1724, masquerade disguises gave people 'the freedom of profane discourse, wanton behaviour and lascivious practices without the least fear of being discovered'. In the confusion of the masque, it was impossible to tell whether one was addressing a whore playing a duchess or a duchess playing a whore.

The elusiveness of the self was confounded by dress. In his seventeenth-century manual *The Compleat Gentleman*, Henry Peachum declared confidently that 'nobility being inherent and Naturall, can have (as the Diamond) but the lustre only from itselfe: honours and titles externally conferred are but attendant on desert, and are but as apparel, and the Drapery to a beautifull body'. In the Knapton portrait, Lavinia's mask can be seen as representing her theatrical career; it is as though she is stubbornly emphasising her pride in her success. Since she chooses not to disguise her disguise, she confuses the viewer's perception of her image: an actress playing at being a lady, or a lady playing at being an actress? Since the mask is, like Moll Hackabout's, potentially the badge of another profession, one with which her name was all too frequently associated, she further teased the viewer by sitting for the artist in white satin, playing on the contrast between her virgin's dress and her whore's accessory. If her costume is merely the drapery to her beautiful body, what is the self it contains?

For Hogarth's portrait of her as Polly Peachum, Lavinia Fenton chose the palest blue silk sack, which falls straight back from her shoulders and stretches over the newly introduced oval hoop, so much lighter and more easily manoeuvrable than the starched layers of gummed petticoats known as *criardes* that French actresses had pioneered for the stage, literally increasing their presence by the volume of their clothes. The crucial handkerchief she carried was of delicate lawn, edged with the frothy Brussels lace with which fashionable ladies were replacing the stiff, heavy Venetian work that had been in vogue at the turn of the century. Lavinia had to practise the management of her hoop, which, though for working purposes it could not occupy the eleven-foot circumference of the very latest Parisian look, nevertheless took up an enormous amount of space. At a time when in polite circles a lady's possession of knees was supposed to remain a rumour, the correct manipulation of the hoop, which required tiny, doll-like steps to create the lilting, bell-like swing of the skirt, was an essential sign of good breeding. Clothes were the woman, locating her precisely on the infinitesimally complex scale of social standing upon which 'a society that relied on layers of privilege and servitude'[5] functioned. So minute were such gradations that a woman could transform herself entirely with what she wore, the relationship between perception and thought being so well trained that a lady who adopted her servant's dress could literally become invisible to her social equals. Time and again in the theatre, a plot depends on a lover's inability to distinguish mistress from maid. A woman who dressed beyond her station, who cheated society of the role in which it expected to place her, was therefore dangerous in her ambiguity. For the actress, or the whore, the permitted disguise of the masquerade spilled over disturbingly, transgressively, into everyday existence. It might amuse Lady Burlington, or the Duchess of Bolton, to slip into a milkmaid's smock for an evening of whispered flirtation, since their social Saturnalia ended next morning with everything in its proper place. But for the actress, that slippage, that overspill, meant a disturbing evasion of social control. A silk sack, then, could be an anarchic emblem.

For the uneducated, it was considered that the distinctions of class could be too easily dissolved by clothes. Foreign visitors to England often expressed their surprise at the ease with which the English appeared to treat rank, as though any man with a sword and a decent coat to his back had the right to be considered a gentleman. Yet confusions of status derived from dress were disturbing. 'Eighteenth-century novels are full of references to the social disasters that might ensue if the dress was not appropriate to the ... class of wearer.'[6] Mr Spectator (who often used characteristic 'types' to illustrate his didactic anecdotes) commented of his amiable Tory squire Sir Roger de Coverley that 'he has ever been of the Opinon, that giving his cast Cloaths to be worn by Valets has a very ill Effect on little Minds, and creates a Silly Sense of Equality between the Parties in Persons affected only with outward Things'. For the quality, equality, the sense of distinction carried within the self, as opposed to upon the person, was a troubling issue.

Peering over the limelights as she goes through her part, Lavinia can see them, the ladies in their boxes, as Polly Peachum and Lucy Lockit in their Newgate finery parody the *politesse* of the aristocracy in their quarrel over Macheath:

LUCY: Dear madam, your servant. I hope you will pardon my passion when I was so happy to see you last . . .

POLLY: I have no excuse for my own behaviour, madam, but my misfortunes . . .

But there is another kind of lady in the theatre, as Lavinia knows, as unreal as the two cockney misses genteelly squabbling on the stage. One visitor to London, on a visit to Bridewell prison, the miserable house of correction where Hogarth's poor Moll Hackabout ended her days, saw a beautiful young woman in a magnificent silk gown shivering incongruously in a cell, and a few nights later, he spotted her again at the theatre, 'in one of the principal boxes, dressed like a duchess, and more beautiful than ever . . . every night at the comedy or opera you see women of this class and position occupying the best places'. A short time before, the girl had been starving and beating hemp. Such were the contrasts of a kept woman's life; that terrible, theatrical instability which could see her emerging a duchess from a prison in a matter of days – but always in the knowledge that the transformation could work both ways. Lavinia is at this very moment becoming a star, but just now, as she doesn't know it yet, the soap factory and the Feathered Gull are still a real possibility.

# 5

## ᵁNNATURAL 𝒯ASTES AND 𝒞URIOUS 𝒟IVERSIONS

ℒincoln's Inn desperately needed Lavinia's blue silk dress to be a beauty, Mr Gay's curious play to catch on, Mr Pepusch's music to be sung by every apprentice in town. In comparison with his prosperous rival Cibber at Drury Lane, Mr Rich was doing poorly. That he had accepted *The Beggar's Opera* in the face of Cibber's rejection of the piece was a measure of his need, for Cibber was confident that so outlandish and disconcerting a play would not be a commercial success. After the new King's coronation in October 1727, the two houses had gone head to head, with *Tamurlane* at Lincoln's Inn up against a spectacular production of *Henry VIII* at Drury Lane. The King, Queen and Princess Royal attended the latter, and according to the *British Journal* of 11 November, 'seem'd very well pleased with the Performance'. This patronage was troubling for Rich, whose production of *The Merchant of Venice* made only £86. On 17 November, *Macbeth*, with Mr Quin in the title role, grossed a pathetic £31, and Rich resorted once again to a pantomime, *Harlequin Anna Bullen*, hoping to catch the vogue for royal splendour, but for once even pantomime was a flop. Cibber compounded Rich's discomfort by reviving Vanbrugh's *The Provok'd Husband*, which the critics loathed but audiences loved, so much so that it ran for a record twenty-eight nights, on into January, while Lavinia was rehearsing for Polly. Dr Swift was certain that *The Beggar's Opera* would 'knock down' his own *Gulliver's Travels*, and hoped in turn that Pope's 'Dunciad' would 'knock down the "Beggar's Opera", but not till it hath fully done its Jobb'. Mr Rich, meanwhile, hoped dearly that he had not taken a foolish gamble on his pretty new star.

At present, whether the Portuguese nobleman is loitering opti-
mistically in the wings, or in the imagination of a chilly hack scratching
out an invented 'Life' in a garret near St Paul's Churchyard (for there is
no evidence whatsoever that the amiable if arrest-prone lover was anything but the convenient fiction of a hungry scribbler with a deadline
for his commission and the rent to pay), Lavinia's salary is thirty shillings
a week (five per day with Sundays off). Some actors are 'sharers', paid
in a percentage of the profits, but most are hirelings like herself. Thirty
shillings is hardly enough to keep anyone in silk dresses, and she has to
provide all her costumes herself. Mrs Fenton is sulkily unimpressed at
her daughter's attempts to pursue an honest profession. Still, it is already
an improvement on her initial salary of fifteen shillings. Since 1726, when
her aristocratic protector may or may not have disappeared, Lavinia has
been working hard. It is often assumed that her first role was Monimia,
in Otway's *The Orphan, or The Unhappy Marriage*, which was played
for the benefit performance of a Mr Huddy at Lincoln's Inn Fields in
February 1726, then again at the Haymarket, in the New Theatre, in
April the same year. Other suggestions for roles suitable to Lavinia's
lack of experience that she may have undertaken include the page,
Cordelio. In fact the part was Serina, the trial role she had obtained
through a kind word from one of the coffee-house customers. As she
won further parts Lavinia initially appeared in the cast as 'Miss Beswick',
perhaps to spare her mother's feelings by suggesting that the latter's
'marriage' to the roving lieutenant had been legitimate, but thereafter
she became and remained 'Miss Fenton', under which name she played
Lucilla in *The Man's the Master*, Lucia in *Epsom Wells* and Ginnet in
*The Wits*, throughout July and August.

If Lavinia intended to make a success of her fledgling career, she had
plenty of examples to emulate. Mrs Barry, famously coached for the stage
by the wicked Earl of Rochester, had begun her career in 1673,with her
first hit in Otway's *Alcibiades* coming in 1675, and was the first actress
to be granted a benefit performance in recognition of her talents. Mrs
Betterton, renowned for her Lady Macbeth, Mrs Butler, Mrs Leigh,
Mrs Mountfort and Mrs Oldfield had all proved that women could carve
out a successful, even a respectable career on the stage The great Mrs
Bracegirdle (who the mealy-mouthed Colley Cibber untruthfully
claimed was as famous for her lovers as for her histrionic talent), had

retired from the stage in 1708, but was still living in London at the time of Lavinia's debut. Both Betterton and Barry had developed styles based on emotional intensity and deep understanding of their texts – the Earl of Rochester quoted Horace at his pupil: '*Si vis me flere, dolendum est primum ipsi tibi.*' ('If you want to move me to tears, you must first feel grief yourself.') The sophisticated social comedy of the Restoration period had required that an actress project a carefully controlled amalgam of her own erotic charm and a naturalistic assumption of the intelligence and wit of her character,[1] but by the 1720s a certain grace, restraint and decorum was also expected of female performers. Colley Cibber described his star performer, Mrs Oldfield, as informing the spectator of her emotion 'as much by her eyes as her elocution; for the look is the only proof that the actor rightly conceives what he utters'.[2] (True to rackety theatrical form, however, the sweet and melodious Mrs Oldfield disgusted Dr Swift by playing a virtuous virgin while heavily pregnant. Acting during pregnancy was so common, though, that later in the century the famous Mrs Siddons actually went into labour on the stage.) Despite this increasingly distinguished tradition of a feminine acting style, Lavinia had also to learn the prescribed conventions of her trade.

In 1710, Charles Gilden had published a biography of Thomas Betterton which was essentially an acting manual, with principles adapted from classical orators such as Quintilian and more modern French works of the seventeenth century. Strict instructions were laid down as to the correct movement of body parts which the actor ought to perfect before a mirror. The eyes were to be cast up or down as directed by the passions 'as to deject them on things of disgrace which you are ashamed of, and raise them on things of honour'; the eyebrows had to be 'natural', neither rigid nor always in motion; the mouth controlled, neither biting nor licking the lips; the shoulder more in evidence in comedy than in tragedy, while the hands, as the chief instruments of action, were never to hang down, this being disagreeable to look at and emotionally unconvincing. Similarly, in Pickering's *Reflections on Theatrical Expression*, the legs were precisely attended to: 'In Astonishment and Surprize, arising from Terror, the left Leg is drawn back to some Distance from the other; under the same Affection of the mind, but resulting from an unhop'd for Meeting with a beloved Object, the right Leg is advanced to some distance before the Left. But Anger and Threatening may be strongly supplied with Grand Expressions from these limbs.' A hero or heroine could not do anything so ordinary as walk across the stage, being expected to affect the 'tragic strut', whereby the leading foot stepped out strongly with the other dragging slowly and precisely behind.

In his summary of acting knowledge published posthumously in 1753, Aaron Hill opposed Gilden's mannered style, observing that Quintilian had written for the bar and not for the stage. Actors, he suggested, should look to nature for their inspiration (an idea that Mrs Betterton and Mrs Barry seemed to have grasped some time before). Hill detested what he sarcastically referred to as the graces of the modern stage: 'a puffed, round mouth, an empty vagrant eye, a solemn silliness of strut, a swing-swang slowness in the motion of the arm, and a dry, dull, drawling voice that carries opium in its detestable monotony'.[3] Hill devised a kind of emotional abacus according to which every feeling could be expressed by combining variations on six 'passions': joy, sorrow, fear, scorn, anger and amazement. Jealousy, for example, was shown by combining fear, scorn and anger in the face, while revenge required only the last two. Love was a combination of joy and fear, pity, fear and sorrow. If these equations could be mastered, Hill summarised neatly, then:

> The Actor to the audience can reveal
> He has the will and faculty to feel:
> Moved in himself, all others he controls,
> Commands their thought and agitates their souls.

In addition to worrying about the tragic potential of the left leg and the correct mixture of facial expressions, the diligent actress had also to be concerned about her voice. 'He must be a very ignorant player who knows not there is a musical cadence in speaking and that a man may as well speak out of tune as sing out of time. It was this instrument which distinguished the actor, and audiences divided passionately over their favourites' deliveries. Lavinia's talent for singing suited her to the rather affected diction currently in fashion, in which modulations of the voice were altered, 'raised or sunk, extended or contracted, swelled or soft-ened, rapid or slow, as the Sense and Spirit of the Author, or the several tempers and Emotions of Mind, in different Characters, required'. This emphasis on contrasting tones led to such exaggerations that some actors substituted ridiculous rapids of changing volume for any attempt at sincere expression, a practice known as 'ranting'. 'The taste in general is so depraved that there is little or no applause to be gained in Tragedy but at the expense of the lungs,' sniffed a disgusted Robert Wilkes in 1730. Colley Cibber added a tremendous capacity for ranting to his many other faults. As one journal sneeringly observed of his performance as Richard III: 'He screamed through four acts without dignity or decency … when he was killed … one might plainly perceive that the good people were not better pleased that so execrable a tyrant was destroyed than that so execrable an actor was silent.'[4] Neither Wilkes nor Cibber, however, seemed aware of their own deficiencies of style. Addison was astonished at the vehemence with which Wilkes ranted his way through the ghost scene in *Hamlet*, observing that the Prince of Denmark seemed more enraged than terrified, while Barton Booth, playing the ghost, inquired as to whether Wilkes intended to fight him in the next performance. Cibber commented hypocritically on the same scene that Betterton was much finer, 'solemn, trembling, yet manly'.[5]

Actresses in particular were further exhorted to study ancient sculpture and historical paintings, particularly Diana, Flora and the Three Graces, but it is doubtful that Lavinia had any time for this more gentle aspect of her professional studies, since her talent was already getting the better of her inexperience. When she rejoined the company at Lincoln's Inn for *The Man's the Master*, her name topped the bill, despite her part being only the second lead. Clearly Rich had seen enough potential to poach her from the Haymarket. This greatly irritated Mrs Haughton, a veteran of the company, who had had a bigger role than Lavinia's in *The Orphan* and felt she deserved the billing. Perhaps she eventually had her way, as Lavinia's next part, Ginnet, was merely a maid. Both plays were written by the noseless Sir William Davenant who ogled so fearsomely from the walls of Rich's refurbished Lincoln's Inn. *The Wits* was advertised in the same issue of the *Daily Post* that announced to the public that 'His Grace the Duke of Bolton has set out for the Isle of Wight to take possession of his government of the said Island'. Since everyone knew that the Duke of Bolton was unhappily married to his wife, Lady Anne, perhaps there was some disappointment in the actresses' communal dressing room that one theatrically inclined aristocrat would not be available for the coming season.

In the winter of 1726-7, Lavinia played Mrs Squeamish in *The Country Wife*, a country lass in Rich's harlequin pantomime *The Rape of Proserpine*, Cherry in *The Beaux' Stratagem* and Lucy in *Tunbridge Wells*. Mrs Squeamish was not a leading role, but it was one of Lavinia's most popular parts. Wycherley's *The Country Wife* was one of the great old Restoration comedies whose bawdiness and cynicism were soon to be replaced by the more sentimental, moralistic mood of the eighteenth century. This change was indicative of the growing influence of the middle-class patrons of the theatre. The 'Cits', as they were snobbishly known due to the fact that their wealth came from the city trade, tended to be more sententious and puritanical in their tastes than the swaggering aristocratic rakes who patronised and starred in the plays of the previous century. David Garrick followed this trend when he sanitised *The Country Wife* as *The Country Girl* in the middle of the century, providing the famous actress Dora Jordan with one of her most celebrated roles.

Mrs Squeamish is one of three upper-class women who are lovers of Mr Horner, a cunning seducer who has his doctor put about the rumour that he is impotent in order to gain access to the beds of respectable women under their husbands' noses. The complaint of Mrs Squeamish and her companions is that since 'marriage is rather a sign of interest than of love', they are neglected by their husbands. 'Women of quality, like the richest stuffs, lie untumbled and unasked for.' The sexual hypocrisy of wealthy men, and the similar hypocrisy of their wives, who think there 'is no virtue but in railing at vice, and no sin but giving scandal', is figured with particular reference to the sexual licence of the theatre. 'Foh!', remarks Lady Fidget, ''tis a nasty world.' 'That men of parts, great acquaintance and quality', replies Mrs Squeamish 'should take up with and spend themselves and fortunes in keeping little play-house creatures. Foh!' The women condemn the actresses while secretly envying their freedom to enjoy sexual satisfaction and 'rail at a poor, little, kept player' while yearning for such licence themselves. A further irony for the audience was derived from the fact that it was one such poor little creature who spoke the lines. As her name implies, Mrs Squeamish is a faux prude and a snob, but it was a good comic part, including a scandalous drunken scene, in a play full of risqué *double entendres* and sexual transgression.

Cherry in *The Beaux' Stratagem* was another success, and a curiously prescient preparation for the part of Polly Peachum. Lavinia played an innkeeper's daughter whose father operates a gang of thieves from his tavern. Her father, Boniface, is happy to sell her honour to Archer, one of the two ruined rakes who are the heroes of the play, if it means he has a chance of getting £200, and Cherry who, as a servant, is cheerfully practical about such matters, is equally happy with the bargain, so long as Archer, who is disguised as a footman, is prepared to reveal his true status as a gentleman. Eventually, though, Cherry's feelings get the better of her, and she betrays the gang in order to save the man she loves. Both *The Beaux' Stratagem* and *The Beggar's Opera* are concerned with the increasing commercialisation of contemporary society, and both have disguise as a major theme. As analyses of marital relationships they are pessimistic; husbands are foolish and brutal, wives unfaithful and greedy, and neither adheres entirely to the comic convention of a happy romantic ending.

With Rich, or 'Mr Lun', in the lead role, *Harlequin Proserpine* was also very popular, running intermittently between February and May 1727, but Lavinia preferred the parts of Cherry and Mrs Squeamish, as she was required to do little more in the pantomime than dance and look pretty, and her lack of involvement emphasised what a minor member of the company she really was.

(In April that year, as Lavinia pirouetted in the pantomime, Dr Swift arrived to visit his beloved friends Pope and Gay for their valedictory summer at Twickenham. He was called back to Ireland in the early autumn, to the deathbed of his long-time companion and sometime mistress, Esther Johnson. Kicking his heels for a week in a squalid inn at Holyhead waiting for the weather, he wrote a poem cursing the wind, previously so 'malicious kind', but which now 'With rage impatient makes me wait / A passage to the land I hate'. *The Beggar's Opera* was finished on 22 October, that 'odd, pretty sort of thing' the friends had first discussed over a decade earlier. Swift never saw the play in London, nor London itself, nor the enchanted grotto at Twickenham, ever again.)

Lavinia's status must be considered in the context of the other star performers of the London theatres. Some years before, John Rich had engaged two dogs from Germany, owned by a Herr Swart, who danced the louvre and the minuet. They featured in over twenty packed nights at Lincoln's Inn, and Rich paid them £10 a night for their act. The *Daily Post* proposed that for those who were jaded with theatregoing, an outdoor excursion to see 'two great fishes, allowed to be a great curiosity', twenty feet long and fifteen feet round, might be diverting. As Lavinia goes on stage as Cherry, the Sun tavern in Aldersgate Street features Mr Clench of Barnet, giving his celebrated imitation of the horn, huntsman, pack of hounds, sham doctor, old woman, drunken man, the bells, flute and triple organ, 'all Instruments are performed with his Natural Voice' (Mr Clench's stage name suggests whence that prodigy was emitted). Twenty years earlier, Mr Gay had been inspired by a pair of Hungarian twins, Helena and Judith, joined at the genitals, who were exhibited for public entertainment in Cornhill. When the Scriblerus club of the Smyrna coffee house, whose literary distinction Lavinia had envied when she served behind the counter in Charing Cross, set down their satirical *Memoirs of Martin Scriblerus*, the unfortunate twins would provide the example for the bawdy 'double mistress' episode.

So avid for sensation were London audiences, and so gullible in their admiration for marvels, that even the established theatres were obliged to compete. In 1749, the Duke of Montague would take a night at the Haymarket under an assumed name, claiming that he would play a variety of instruments on a common walking cane, then clamber inside a tavern quart bottle 'without equivocation, and there sing several songs, and suffer any spectator to handle the bottle'. Box seats would be five shillings, the same price that John Rich charged for those wishing to see Lavinia at the height of her fame. The distinguished audience that night at the Haymarket was led by the Duke of Cumberland (aged just seven at the zenith of Lavinia's fame in 1728, and probably just old enough to read to himself the book of charming fables dedicated to him two years before by the aspiring poet John Gay in yet another of his rather pathetic attempts to secure a royal pension). When the hoax was discovered, the audience enjoyed a lovely riot instead, which was just as much fun, especially for the Duke of Cumberland, who had grown up to become the famous Butcher of Culloden, and who was apparently happy to take out his indignation on the long-suffering harpsichord in the absence of any Scotsmen to murder.

While Lavinia has been preparing for her role as Polly in the 1728 season, she has also had to cram the other parts she will play in the repertoire, Nanny in *The Fortune Hunters*, Alinda in *The Pilgrim*, Ophelia in *Hamlet*, Leanthe in *Love and a Bottle* (which does not end in a riot), Betty in *A Bold Stroke for a Wife*, Marcella in *Don Quixote* and Jaculine in *The Royal Merchant*. On top of this she will appear as a singer and dancer in the entr'acte. Life is exhausting, as even though Lavinia generally keeps a whore's hours, rising late and not bothering to dress before she leaves for the theatre in the late afternoon, there are other rehearsals to attend before the performance in the freezing auditorium, barely lit until the audience begins to arrive, to save money; there are costumes to be mended, lugged to the dressing room in a large straw basket and placed in readiness next to her allocated looking glass and single candle, dance steps to practise. It is a far more prosaic existence than she had imagined, gazing from the other side of the footlights. Swift's recollection of attending a theatre rehearsal makes it sound unglamorous and banal: 'I was this morning at 10 o'clock at the rehearsal of Mr Addison's play called Cato ... We stood about on the stage, and it was foolish enough to see the actors prompted every moment, and the poet directing them, and the drab [the maligned Mrs Oldfield] ... out in the midst of a passionate part and calling out "What's next?" '[6]

Alinda was Lavinia's first 'breeches part', a cross-dressing stock role very popular with audiences because it gave the men a chance to see a woman's legs, but irritating to actresses, as it meant more expenditure on stockings and garters. At least comedies were performed in 'modern dress', which entailed less expense, although they were harder work for the actress, since audiences often enjoyed a lavish costume so much that a performer with enough tragic plumes in her hair could carry off a triumph without having to do very much at all. Steele's prologue to Vanbrugh's 1705 play *The Mistake* commented:

> In Lace and Feather Tragedy's express'd
> And Heroes die unpity'd if ill dress'd.

Consequently, the *Spectator* was discerning enough to observe that 'the ordinary Method of making an Heroe, is to clap a huge Plume of Feathers upon his Head',[7] but most audiences cared less for technique than for spectacle, so much so that playwrights like Aphra Behn wrote in the costumes especially. Compared with Widow Ranter's feathered gown, or the robes that Betterton wore for *Love and Honour* (kindly lent by Charles II after his coronation), Lavinia's silk sack for Polly is, she feels, rather a disappointment.

Of course the real earners in the theatre, whose lavish lifestyles all the other actresses envied and admired, were the great opera singers, the most celebrated of whom in Lavinia's time were Signora Cuzzoni and Signora Faustina, and the castrato Senesino. In 1723 Gay had written to Dr Swift: 'As for the reigning amusement of the Town, it is entirely music; real fiddles, bass-viols and hautboys, not poetic harps, lyres and reeds. There is nobody allowed to say "I sing" but an eunuch or an Italian woman. Everybody now is grown as great a judge of music, as they were in your time of poetry and folks that could not distinguish one tune from another, now daily dispute about the different styles of Handel, Bononcini, and Attilio . . . Senesino is daily voted the greatest man who ever lived.'

It is noteworthy that one of the most emblematic figures of the eighteenth century should be the castrato. If constructions of the self were concerned with the conflict between art and nature, then the castrato, whose lost, enchanted voice was at once the most refined expression of civilisation and the consequence of a vicious barbarism, played out in his person the contradictions between the instinctive and the aesthetic which so engaged his time. 'Imagine a voice', runs one description, 'that combines the sweetness of the flute and the animated suavity of the human larynx, a voice which leaps and leaps, lightly and spontaneously, like a lark that flies through the air and is intoxicated with its own flight; and when it seems the voice has reached the loftiest peaks of altitude it starts off again, leaping and leaping, still with equal highness and equal spontaneity, without the slightest sign of forcing or the faintest indication of artifice or effort; in a word, a voice that gives the immediate idea of sentiment transmuted into sound, and of the soul into the infinite wings of that sentiment.'[8]

Francesco Bernardi, known as Senesino, may have been hailed as the greatest man who ever lived, but this accolade rested rather cruelly on the fact that he wasn't entirely a man. Between 1600 and 1750, an estimated 70 per cent of operatic performers were men who had had their testicles surgically removed. Since 1599, this practice had been sanctioned by the Catholic Church under Pope Clement VIII, on the pretext of St Paul's instruction that women ought to remain silent in church, and that therefore God's music must be sung exclusively by males. St Paul had not offered an opinion on whether the voices of choristers ought to be improved by a barbaric operation, but the voices of the castrati were so intoxicating that their angelic sound was considered sufficient justification for the cruelty by which they were created.

The procedure, properly called orchidectomy, was usually performed on boys who had shown promise as singers when they reached the age of about eight. (The butchers of Norcia, an Umbrian town famous for its prosciutti and salami, were supposedly the most efficient in performing the operation.) After the child had been drugged with opium and lowered into a bath of milk, the groin was slit with a knife, the spermatic cord detached and the testicles removed. The physical effects as the child matured were curious: castrati tended to be tall, with disproportionately long limbs, an infantile penis, no Adam's apple and an inclination to plumpness, with odd fatty deposits on their lips and eyelids. Since the larynx had failed to develop as usual in teenage boys, the vocal cords stayed close to the resonating chambers in the torso, creating a voice which retained a childish purity combined with the register of a woman singer and the power of a man. Not every boy who was thus mutilated, however, would attain the extraordinary purity and sweetness of the ideal castrato voice. Sadly, the operation in no way guaranteed its purpose, and many castrati, sold to unscrupulous surgeons by impoverished families, limped through their lives in obscurity without ever knowing the adulation that a few of their fortunate peers commanded.

For Europe was infatuated with castrati. In Smollett's *Humphrey Clinker*, one character remarks that when she hears this strange 'thing from Italy' sing, she can believe herself in paradise. Singers such as Senesino and Carlo Broschi, known as Farinelli, were able to push their voices to limits that seemed otherworldly; so perturbingly beautiful were they that they did indeed sound superhuman, angelic, divine. Their voices could swoop and soar between octaves with impossible ease, and the castrati developed showpieces such as the *virtuosita spiccata*, in which they sang separately every note in a trill, or the *messa di voce*, which was an agonisingly drawn-out crescendo, beginning quietly, rising sometimes for a full minute to a climax and then very slowly falling away. Farinelli, who famously liked to duel with a trumpet, matching the instrument note for note until the player was exhausted, was particularly famous for his ability to hold a note until the audience were so tense they forgot to breathe. To utilise their extraordinary abilities, composers created the 'Opera Seria' form specifically for the castrato voice, but the singers were often anxious to show off their finest tricks, insisting that certain showpieces, known as 'portmanteau arias', be included in every score. Not content with that, the castrato could also use his voice to manipulate the score on stage, adding impromptu embellishments to show off his range, much to the confusion of the orchestra.

It is hardly surprising that theatre managers and composers grew exasperated with their stars, even as they coveted their profitable talents. From 1720 onwards, the quarrels between Handel and Senesino were almost as famous as their music. Handel had hoped that Senesino would star in the opera he created for the Royal Academy's opening season in 1720, an adaptation of Lalli's *L'Amor Tirannico* called *Radamisto*, but contractual complications meant that the castrato was not free to sing the role at the Haymarket until December that year. Meanwhile, London had already gone wild for Senesino in Bonnoncini's *Astarte* the previous September, much to the irritation of Handel, who wanted his music to introduce this incredible new sound to the public. By the time Senesino came to sing for Handel, he was a far greater star than the composer, and Handel's jealousy of what he considered to be less a human being than a walking musical instrument led to shouting matches which the public lapped up as eagerly as they did the operas. Nevertheless, Handel went on to create eighteen roles specifically for Senesino, as well as rewriting pieces such as *Radamisto* for his voice.

The capricious, hysterical behaviour of the famous castrati was well known, and often attributed to a kind of malformation of the spirit matching that of their butchered genitalia. 'Fat, volatile and conceited' was the blunt summation of one critic.[9] Yet although they were almost worshipped by their public, they were also exposed to cruel ridicule, and made to feel that were it not for the gift of their voices they would be seen as monsters who deserved no place in society. Fans happily bought medallions featuring their idols' faces which they wore round their necks in tribute, but seemed unaware of the pain they could cause by their shouts of encouragement: *'Eviva il coltello!'* ('Long live the knife!'). The castrati were also looked upon with suspicion by 'real' men as they were, curiously enough, reputed to be wonderful lovers, able to continue intercourse far longer than the average man, and of course without the risk of pregnancy for their partner. Farinelli was particularly well known for his conquests, and the famous incident in which a woman in the audience during his London season of 1734 cried out, 'One God, one Farinelli!' before fainting into the pit (a scene satirised by Hogarth in *The Rake's Progress*) was spiced up by the suggestion that the lady was not referring exclusively to the singer's vocal powers. By the nineteenth century, however, the stricter moral climate had no place for the distastefully ambiguous status of the castrato, and when in 1825 one such singer, Giovanni Battista Velluto, attempted to make a comeback, the city which had swooned and screamed for Senesino a century before now condemned him, with newspapers exhorting theatre managers to ban women from the audience rather than expose them to such a hideous travesty of nature.

Female opera stars were almost as fascinating to the public. Cuzzoni had been in vogue since 1723, when the *London Journal* reported that she had earned as much as 50 guineas a ticket for her benefit performance in *Ottone*. Predictably enough, she was reputed to set almost as high a price on her body as on her voice. 'She is already jumped into a handsome chariot, and an equipage accordingly,' the *Journal* also slyly remarked. 'The gentry seem to have so high a taste for her fine parts, that she is likely to be a great gainer by them.' But in 1726 a new singer, Faustina Bordoni, had appeared from Venice, with her salary set at the same enormous £2,500 a season as Cuzzoni's, and immediately the press set about fanning the flames of a rivalry. The costumes of the respective singers became ever more extravagant and they demanded increasingly spectacular special effects, such as cages of live songbirds being released to trill about their heads as their voices reached a climax.

Throughout the spring and summer of 1727, duelling 'claques' prevented the voice of their favourite's rival being heard. 'I suppose you have heard', reported Lord Hervey, 'that both Cuzzoni and Faustina were so hissed and catcalled last Tuesday that the opera was not finished that night: nor have the directors dared to venture the representation of another since.'[10] High society was divided, with hostesses ceasing to invite the advocates of their favourite's rivals. The Countess of Pembroke was all for Cuzzoni, while the Countess of Burlington and Lady Delawarr admitted no one to their drawing rooms who did not champion Faustina.

Hervey deplored the fact that audiences were prepared to pay so much for the pleasure of hissing the singers off the stage, and suggested that the rivalry between the two divas was feigned to increase their price. Both were constantly throwing tantrums and threatening to leave, but '1,500 guineas are mediators whose interposition they'll never be able to resist'. Public interest in the ladies' lovers was almost as great as in their professions, and aside from the death of King George I in June 1727, the battle of the sopranos was the biggest news story of the year. A few days before the King's demise, the *Journal* reported of an encounter in the Haymarket that 'the contention at first was only carried on by hissing on one side, and clapping on the other; but proceeded at length to cat-calls, and other great indecencies: And notwithstanding Princess Caroline was present, no regards were of force to restrain the rudeness of the opponents.'

One pamphlet summed up the concerns of the nation during that hot spring, as the court waited tensely for the outcome of the succession and the merchants of the exchange gloomily unrolled their black stuffs for an unprofitable season of court mourning. 'The Devil to Pay at St James's: Or, A Full and True Account of the Most Horrible and Bloody Battle Between Madame Faustina and Madame Cuzzoni' announced: 'It is not now (as formerly), i.e. are you High Church or Low, Whig or Tory; are you for Court or Country, King George or the Pretender: but are you for Faustina or Cuzzoni, Handel or Bocconcini. There's the question.' Apparently, the only issue worth debating in polite society was which soprano was superior, and the very real anxiety about 'blood and slaughter' in the event of the son of the deposed James II, the 'Old Pretender', making an attempt upon the Crown when the King died was facetiously transposed into a concern that the English, who had seemed a little softened by the gentle airs of Italian music, should allow their 'native ferocity' out and produce such violence on the stage.

# 6

# *O*PERA, *W*ALPOLE AND THE *M*AKING OF THE *S*TAR

*I*t was impossible for an actress like Lavinia not to be aware that the theatre was a forum for the expression of political as well as dramatic allegiances. Just as she had learned how the party factions of London swarmed and formed around the various coffee houses according to the shifting loyalties of the day, so she appreciated that theatre audiences represented a concentration of public opinion which was influential beyond the range of the limelights. The creation of 'stars' like Faustina and Cuzzoni, and indeed Lavinia herself, was evidence of a change in political emphasis which was increasingly concerned, under the Prime Minister Sir Robert Walpole, with consumption. Generally, 'the period [was] characterised by transition from aristocratic to mercantilist culture'. This new obsession with celebrity reflected 'an unprecedented propensity to consume, unprecedented in the depths to which it penetrated the lower reaches of society'.[1] If commercialisation had given birth to the possibility of the star, a new form of money-spawned 'aristocrat', it also called into question the practices of a government which was seen by many as obsessed with gain at the expense of the people. One of the themes of *The Beggar's Opera* is a condemnation of this mercantilist tendency, which encouraged consumerism for profit and then hypocritically deplored its effects on the morality of the country.

Lavinia's celebrity was thus both a product and an emblem of the same conflict between interest and probity that was reflected in the press by the debate surrounding opera. The philosopher David Hume observed in his essay 'Of Refinement in the Arts' that 'the spirit of the age affects all the arts',[2] but the extent to which the state of those arts was celebrated or deplored was very much a matter of partisan affiliation. 'Court or Country . . . Handel or Bocconcini' were therefore opposed pairings indicative of a very real political and cultural divide. The opera separated audiences, certainly, but as a metaphor for factions of allegiance it had more significance than whichever diva the town preferred on a given day.

Opera in the Italian manner had its English debut in 1705, with *Arsinöe*, introduced by John Rich's father Christopher, who had been provoked into staging it by the news that Vanbrugh was to open an opera house in the Haymarket. The composer, Thomas Clayton, claimed that its aim was 'to introduce the Italian manner of music on the English stage, which has not been before attempted',[3] although the libretto, by Peter Motteux, was in English. Immediately, opera provoked professional hostility among actors and managers, for it reduced their audiences – so much so that in 1707 a sympathetic charity was formed 'for the better support of the comedians in the Haymarket, and to endorse them to keep up the diversion of plays under a separate influence from opera'.[4] Nevertheless, *Arsinöe* was followed by *Camilla* in 1706, and *Thomyris* at Drury Lane in 1707, the first opera to use an Italian castrato. Nicolini starred in the first bilingual opera, *Pyrrhus and Demetrius* in 1708–9, while in October 1709 the first entirely Italian performance, *Idaspe*, was sung, with translations provided for the audience to follow the plot. The craze continued with *Almahide* and Handel's *Rinaldo* at the Haymarket in 1711.

John Gay met Handel in connection with the latter performance, introduced in February 1711 by Aaron Hill after Hill left Drury Lane to take over the Haymarket. *Rinaldo* was reprised under Hill's management with, as the *Spectator* noted, a 'very short allowance of thunder and lightning', though the theatre was 'exceeding generous' with the rather cheaper fire and smoke. Always alert to opportunities for poking their own brand of supereducated fun, Gay and Pope were quick to capitalise on the more absurd features of the latest theatrical craze to vex an old enemy, the critic John Dennis. In his *Reflections on Pope's 'Essay on Criticism'* that year, Dennis had roundly abused little Pope by comparing him to a venomous hunch-backed toad. In revenge, the friends devised a satire on Dennis in which, after the fashion of the opera's grandiose characters, Dennis is named 'Don Rinaldo Furioso, the Critic of Woful Countenance' and depicted astride a wooden hobby-horse, a favourite Scriblerian motif. Dennis's literary pretensions are mocked in the comparison with the posturings of opera heros, and with the *Spectator*'s criticism of the inadequacies of Hill's staging: like the Haymarket production, poor Don Rinaldo has very little in the way of verbal thunder and lightning.

One commentator on English culture, Louis de Muralt, gave a measured, moderate view of the new theatrical fashion: 'The music seems to me but indifferent, the machines near as good as those at Paris, the decorations are fine, but above all that made of satin is extraordinarily magnificent. They don't dance as well as the French, but on the other hand they dance less frequently and perhaps more to the purpose. The same thing may be said of their singing, they sing only the airs and recite the rest. There's something uncommon and agreeable in these airs, and in my opinion more suitable to the taste of melancholy people than others.'

To native eyes, though, it seemed that as the rage for opera developed, it represented a new low point in the nation's cultural decline, corrupting the good solid taste of the English with its baroque excess. This accusation soon took the form of alliance with other partisan quarrels. Music, it seemed, was seducing the nation. 'Operas and masquerades, and all the politer elegancies of a wanton age, are much less to be regarded for their expense (great as it is) than for the tendency which they have to deprave our manners. Music has something so peculiar in it, that it exerts a willing tyranny over the soul into whatever shape the melody directs,' warned the *Craftsman*. The soul might willingly succumb to the dictatorial demands of Cuzzoni's arias, but for many of the audience who watched Lavinia's debut as Polly, there were other tyrannies abroad. For the Tory party, the death of the last of the Stuarts, Queen Anne, in August 1714 had proved fatally divisive. Unlike the Whigs, who were almost unanimous in their support of the new Hanoverian King, George I, who arrived at Greenwich in September, Tories were uncertain in their loyalties. Some were acknowledged Jacobites, supporters of the Old Pretender, James Francis Edward, titled 'Chevalier de St George', son of the deposed James II, who was regarded by some as heir to the throne of England by divine right. Other Tories, while anti-Hanoverian, distrusted James's Catholicism and his French allegiance, and wished to restore the King but preserve the Church of England, whereas still others supported George as legitimate monarch but hoped he could be brought to favour their policies. Henry St John, Viscount Bolingbroke, Secretary of State to Queen Anne, attempted to form an alliance between Tories and the few dissident Whigs, but he was defeated by Robert Walpole, who led his own band of Whig reformers into government and into the start of his own brilliant political career.

Quick to recognise that he could consolidate his new position by playing on fears of a Jacobite uprising, Walpole was swift in categorising his Tory opponents as sympathisers of the Chevalier's. The Tory press responded by comparing his activities with those of Jonathan Wild, an acknowledged criminal protecting himself with the image of a public defender. (The comparison was also drawn morally, with Walpole supposedly 'debauching the political morals'[5] of his acolytes just as Wild had lured young men into crime.) The Tory party line was rather more complicated, as indicated by the popular epigram:

> God bless the King! I mean the Faith's Defender
> God bless – no harm in blessing! The Pretender
> Who that Pretender is and who that King,
> God bless us all! Is quite another thing.

The atmosphere of suspicion and disgrace left many Tories feeling they had very little choice but to join the rebellious side. 'No matter how little sympathy most of the party had with ideological Jacobitism, they were steadily under pressure to rally to the Stuart cause as the only alternative to an exclusionary policy that the Whigs seemed intent on maintaining indefinitely.'[6] From the moment that Bolingbroke, so influenced by this logic that he believed himself (with some justification) in fear of his life, set off for France disguised in a black bob wig, a laced hat and ordinary clothes' to throw in his lot with James Stuart, the Jacobite cause begins to take on the fabulously implausible plot twists of an opera.

Though they had a poor reputation for political acuity, romance has always been firmly on the side of the Stuarts. Never terribly good at hanging on to their thrones, they were majestic in the leaving of them. In 1715, and again in 1745, it is hard not to feel sympathetic towards those dark, rather effetely handsome princes and their draggled band of gentlemen, trudging through the mists of the north that the King might come into his own once more; hard not to recall the final moment of heroism of their ancestor Charles I who, having lost his people through imperious stubbornness, was determined at least not to be seen to shiver on the block. The fact that the 1715 rebellion was largely undermined through the duplicity of a woman is also appropriate to that other famous Stuart weakness: susceptibility to a pretty face. On arriving in Paris that year, Bolingbroke had taken up with an old flame, a former nun named Alexandrine de Tencin. Having broken her vows to God, she was not overly scrupulous about temporal promises, and she neglected to mention to Bolingbroke that she was also sleeping with one Abbé Dubois, an intelligencer in the pay of the English ambassador the Earl of Stair. Thus the Whig government had ample time to prepare themselves against invasion by incarcerating all those Jacobite sympathisers in the south of England who had not fled, and forcing James, who had originally intended to sail for Plymouth, to change his plans and make for Scotland. The Stuarts' penultimate standard was gallantly raised by the Earl of Mar at Braemar on 6 September. Rather bathetically, the orb immediately fell off the top into the mud, which was felt to be a very bad omen by the Highlanders gathered to fight for the Pretender. Two months later, their superstition was justified when the rest of the standard fell to pieces in the Jacobite defeat at Preston and, following a further battle in Scotland, at which James, betraying another typically unfortunate Stuart characteristic, turned up late, it was seen no more for thirty years.

The '15 was a cause of great personal inconvenience to Lady Mary Wortley Montagu. Since practically every country gentleman in England had ridden south on the Queen's death to be in with a chance of advancement under the new regime, she was forced in her husband's absence to move into neighbouring Castle Howard, which she claimed was no better than a nunnery. To compound this irritation, her sister Frances had been married the previous year to the Earl of Mar ('a good Whig marr'd by taking a Scotch Jacobite for a husband', as the obvious pun had it), and for a time was left destitute in London with her young daughter while her husband escaped to France with the Pretender. That year, Lady Mary had been frequenting the studio of the painter Charles Jervas, which Pope made his London lodging, and mixing with Pope, who had recently published 'The Rape of the Lock', and his young friend Gay, already well known for his Scriblerian collaborations and his *Shepherd's Week*. Lady Mar's distresses were an embarrassing interruption to her sister's literary ambitions.

The failure of the '15 caused, however, considerable excitement in Newgate prison, whose officers called for liquor 'after an extravagant manner' and drank to 'their good luck, which was the ruin and loss of lives and fortunes in many good families'.[8] Mr Pitt, the governor at the time, was reckoned to have cleared between £3,000 and £4,000 in additional press yard fees as a consequence of all the Jacobite gentlemen he was obliged to house. Even in the face of charges of treason, class struggles broke out among the defeated rebels, with a Mr Forster claiming himself to be 'slighted and ill used' in being imprisoned in Newgate and not in the Tower, as he was a member of Parliament. He consoled himself by becoming the shuttlecock champion of the press yard. Meanwhile, Walpole had suspended Habeas Corpus and established a military encampment in Hyde Park.)

Even by 1728, the libertarian economic practices of the Whig junta had not extended to political liberty, and Gay and his friends had been touched by the oppressiveness of the new age. The Earl of Oxford, friend and patron to the Scriblerians, had spent two years in the tower, as had Swift's friend William Wyndham. Dr Arbuthnot had lost his job as official physician to the court. Swift's letters had been opened by spies operating under the authority of his former friend Joseph Addison with the aim of implicating him in a Jacobite plot. The association between the Scriblerians and Bolingbroke intensified the suspicion with which these literary subversives were regarded after the latter's flight to France, and Swift was counselled: 'If you have not already hid all your papers in some private place in the hands of a trusty friend I fear they will fall into the hands of your enemies.'[9] Everywhere, Tory sympathisers had been hounded from their posts. Pope had complimented Bolingbroke in the preface to his *Iliad*, as had Gay in *Shepherd's Week*. Their mutual friend Charles Jervas advised Pope that since he had made room for the errant viscount in one book, he ought to leave some space for Walpole in the next, so as to keep the balance even. Ever prudent when it came to politics, in his letters to Gay after Queen Anne's death Pope shows some rather forced indications of Whiggish views, as though the poet knew his correspondence might be scrutinised, and in his 'Farewell to London', he is careful to enumerate his Whig friends.

Pope wrote tensely to Swift: 'This is not a time for any man to talk to the purpose. Truth is a kind of contraband commodity which I would not venture to export.' When *Gulliver's Travels* appeared in 1726, England was satirised as Tribnia, where 'the bulk of the people consisted wholly of discoverers, witnesses, informers, accusers, prosecutors, evidences, swearers: together with their several subservient and subaltern instruments; all under the colours, the conduct, and pay of ministers and their deputies'.[10] For many readers, this analogy might not even have seemed hyperbolic.

England in 1728, then, was considered by many little better than a police state, and the debate about liberty, individual and political, was transferred into the less dramatically dangerous arena of the theatre. Yet the network of allegiances surrounding the opera was internally complex, even contradictory. At first, before the Jacobite rebellion in 1715, opera had been jingoistically condemned as an example of the corrupt foreign influences that were polluting the nation, just as the French Catholic sympathies of the Pretender threatened to overthrow the State.

> Begone, our nation's pleasure and reproach!
> Britain no more with idle truths debauch;
> Back to thine own unmanly Venice sail,
> Where luxury and loose desires prevail.

Thus Sir Richard Steele rather breathlessly captured the argument. Opera's link with Latinate corruptions prevailed throughout the century, with Lord Chesterfield considering the contemporary dominance of music as Italy's principal art to be emblematic of the country's decline as late as the 1740s. If sovereignty could be associated, artistically and thus politically, with masculinity, the opera might appear to threaten the virility of the nation. As Swift playfully suggested, the craze for opera represented 'that unnatural taste for Italian music amongst us which is so unsuitable to our Northern climate and the genius of the people, whereby we are overrun with Italian effeminacy and Italian nonsense. An old gentleman said to me that many years ago when the practice of an unnatural vice grew frequent in London and many were prosecuted for it, he was sure it would be a forerunner of Italian operas and singers, and that we should want nothing but stabbing or poisoning to make us perfect Italians.'[11] 'Effeminate', 'unmanly'; the adjectives suggest that the seductions of the opera are emasculating the nation, producing a body politic as unwholesome and ineffective as that other warped Italian import, the castrato.

The disgruntled Tories, with their suspected, covert allegiance to the King Over the Water, might therefore be cast as champions of this threatening alien form, and indeed, Lord Burlington, the principal mover behind the establishment of the Royal Academy in 1719, was closely associated with the Scriblerian circle, who were Tory and anti-Hanoverian, though he himself was a 'progressive' Whig. However, subscribers to the Academy, which was to be run along the lines of the newly fashionable joint stock companies, included not only Burlington but George I himself. Thus opera could also be seen as representing a different kind of foreign corruption, that of the German-speaking monarchs who had displaced the Stuart dynasty. Support for the opera could be interpreted as support for the new, mercantilist philosophy of the Whig administration, and yet again, more confusingly, the chief subscribers to the Academy were drawn largely from the landed interest at court, numbering seven dukes, a marquis, twelve earls and four viscounts.

The aim of the Royal Academy was to encourage the presentation of operas at the Haymarket, to be subsidised by payments of at least £200-worth of stock per member. (Burlington gave £1,000, and the King committed to the same amount). To supplement the income from the performances, the Swiss impresario 'Count' Heidegger, hired by the Academy to manage the opera, gave spectacular masquerade balls, capitalising on the trend for those scandalously fashionable private parties. As many as 700 guests would attend at a time, their squeakings and philanderings lit by a 'monstrous extravagant' glow of wax candles. If anything, of course, masquerades were seen as even more subversive than opera, since, like the playhouses, they allowed promiscuous dissolution of the social hierarchy, and yet the supposed upholders of that hierarchy were hypocritically making a profit from them, a charge which was being levelled, without the rarefied context of the masquerade, at the administration in general.

The debate surrounding the opera is captured in Hogarth's daring and controversial print *The Bad Taste of the Town*, issued in 1723. As ever, Hogarth's timing was perceptively topical. The Haymarket theatre is shown on the left of the picture, with Heidegger leering from the window. His finger points to the sign, based on Vanderbank's print of Handel's *Flavio* of 1723, starring Cuzzoni and Senesino. At Cuzzoni's painted feet languishes a nobleman (specifically Charles Mordaunt, third Earl of Peterborough), brandishing £8,000, while the customers for the masquerade, disguised as clowns, bishops and milkmaids, are led towards the doors by a devil brandishing a £1,000 note.

In the middle is the elegant Palladian façade of Burlington House, the magnificent new Piccadilly residence of Richard Boyle, third Earl of Burlington, its gates adorned with figures of Michelangelo and Raphael. Burlington House astonished Londoners, who had never seen such a building – a north Italian palazzo transposed to one of the town's busiest thoroughfares. Lord Burlington visited Italy several times, and the new design for the house was greatly influenced by his travels, and by two publications which held tremendous importance for the architecture of the eighteenth century in England, Campbell's *Vitruvius Britannicus* (1715) and Leoni's edition of Palladio's *Quattro Libri* (1717). For those among the elite who considered an understanding of Palladio essential to any claim to be a gentleman, Burlington House was the symbol of a refined classical spirit which was the ideal of a cultivated aristocracy. For others, the very decoration could be seen as pretentiously deferential to the obsession with the superiority of European over British art, and the mansion was derided by traditionalists as the epitome of poor taste. Since nothing in Augustan London was free from contorted partisan connections, it is curious to note that Palladian architecture was seen as a Whig innovation and conventionally loathed by nostalgic Tories, though its greatest artistic champion, Pope, was also the greatest of the Tory writers.

Burlington House is firmly closed to the public crowding towards Rich's Lincoln's Inn theatre, to the right of the picture, wrestling for a place to see the pantomime *Dr Faustus*. (The choice of pantomime, one of Rich's most popular, has self-evident implications about the selling of souls for worldly pleasure.) In the foreground, a woman pushes a wooden barrow full of scrapbooks, her sales cry: 'Waste paper for Shops.' Inside are the works of Congreve, Shakespeare, Dryden and

Jonson (Addison is also included, but this might be a sly double-bluff on Hogarth's part, as Addison himself had tried to cash in on the opera craze in 1707 with his English version of *Rosamund*, which had flopped after a miserable three nights). Hogarth makes two obvious points: that the current cultural fashions of London are inferior to the classics of the English canon, and that the supposedly 'highbrow' tastes of those flocking to the Haymarket cannot really be distinguished from the low-class sensationalism exemplified by the pantomime at Lincoln's Inn. Gay's *Beggar's Opera* will enact this latter point by uniting high culture with low-life characters in the same piece.

Yet like much of Hogarth's work, *The Bad Taste of the Town* is a subtle visual essay rather than a didactic illustration. Just as in Gay's play, Hogarth connects the spheres of court and finance through the symbolism of the opera. Heidegger, the master of revels, can be seen to represent Walpole: the devil leading the masqueraders waves his thousand pounds, George I's Academy donation, implying that Walpole stands in the same relation to the King, an impresario of illusion, as Heidegger to the Academy. Walpole's capacity for theatrical deceit was reflected in one of his recent nicknames, 'Skreen Master General', a reference to his conduct in the affair of the South Sea Bubble.

The South Sea Bill had been presented in the Commons in April 1720 as a means of assisting the national debt. The South Sea Company would take over the debt in exchange for 5 per cent interest and a monopoly on trade to the Pacific islands and the West Indies. As parcels of stock were handed out to significant men to ease the passage of the bill, gambling fever struck London, and the city went wild for South Sea stock. Two million pounds were raised, but this capital was dispersed in bribes, and by the time the bill was passed there was nothing left, even though the stocks had tripled in value. When, in August, crowds gathered outside South Sea House demanding to sell for cash, thousands of people were ruined. Even Pope was scathed. The building of his villa at Twickenham, where Gay would so happily work on *The Beggar's Opera* in 1727, had to be interrupted, as Gay explained in a letter to Swift. 'He has engag'd to translate the "Odyssey" in three years, I believe rather out of the prospect of gain than inclination, for I am persuaded that he bore his part in the loss of the Southsea.' If Pope's magnificent *Odyssey* and Guy's hospital, built with the huge fortune acquired by Thomas Guy before the bubble burst, were two good things to have come out of the crash, many people blamed Walpole for the trail of bankruptcies and suicides that followed in its wake. Ministers were accused of secretly manipulating the market to enable the court to make a killing, and then blocking questions in the Commons when MPs tried to find out the truth. Walpole shielded many involved in the scandal, and discontent was so high that the MP for Guildford, Arthur Onslow, remarked that if the Pretender could have arrived at that moment, 'he might have rode to St James's with very few hands held up against him'. The absurd amounts of cash waved by the operagoers in Hogarth's print, then, illustrate this crazed atmosphere of greed, corruption and luxury that is bankrupting the old institutions of England for Walpole's profit. Operas and masquerades symbolise the intrusion of this dishonest commerce into the solid structures of the city, which is tottering and growing simultaneously, metamorphosing like a theatre set into the strange landscape of a corrupt new order. As Mr Pope's elegant zeugma has it, 'And now a bubble bursts / And now a world.'[12]

The costumes of the masqueraders have another, more sinister implication. Walpole's Jacobite witch hunt was continuing at the time of operas and masquerades and, in 1723, what became known as the 'Black Act' was forced almost without dissent through Parliament. This statute was the most vicious and unjust law ever to be passed in England, if not in Europe. Aimed ostensibly at a group of supposedly Jacobite poachers who blackened their faces as camouflage, the bill made many existing criminal offences capital, and created a set of new crimes which were punishable by death, many of them concerned with injuries to property in even minor degrees, when committed by any person with his face blackened or otherwise disguised. Anyone so concealing himself could be arrested as a criminal, and many men, women and children were hanged for offences so negligible that they would be laughable were their punishment not so barbaric. In 1748 a ten-year-old boy was hanged, in 1777 a fourteen-year-old kitchenmaid who had been bullied by her employer into hiding some counterfeit shillings. The wealthy crowds jostling for a ticket at the Haymarket were, of course, exempt from the deadly suspicions their costumes might now legitimately arouse. Thus Hogarth emphasises that the new administration cares more for the property of the rich than for the lives of the poor.

In 1727, when the rivalry between Faustina and Cuzzoni was at its height, and the theatre managers prepared themselves for the slow season following on the official period of court mourning, there was some doubt as to whether Walpole would retain his position of pre-eminence. The coronation of 1727 was particularly significant in that George II's succession was the first time a Prince of Wales had ascended his father's throne since Charles I in 1625, that is, for over a century, and it therefore represented, to pro- and anti-Hanoverians alike, a sense of dynastic continuity unknown since the Civil War and the Glorious Revolution. Despite a general confidence that 'There would be no Twenty Eight to follow 1727 as there had been a Fifteen to follow 1714,'[13] there was some speculation as to whether the Pretender would make another attempt upon the Crown. The coronation passed off smoothly, attended by all the peers of the realm, including the Duke of Bolton, with his Duchess, costumed like the other women of her high rank in a long red robe, lined in white satin and bordered with green silk, beneath an ermine-trimmed cloak with silver tassels.

Though the coronation was a powerful display of solidarity among the ruling class, many remained uncertain as to whether the first minister would maintain his hold over the new King. According to Lord Hervey, George II had always referred to Walpole as 'a great rogue', and many considered, incorrectly, that his reign was over. Yet Walpole, who had become particularly close to Queen Caroline when she and her husband, at their rival 'court' at Leicester House, had represented a rallying point for Whig opposition in 1716–20, adroitly granted a new civil list of £800,000 to the King, and raised the Queen's jointure to £100,000. So Walpole continued in office, despite the hopes of the Tories, and his privileging of commercial interests, as depicted previously in Hogarth's print and, possibly, in *The Beggar's Opera*, suggested that the new order was here to stay. The loathing of Walpole this inspired was not confined to the opposition; even Sir John Perceval, a staunch Whig, described 'the prostitution of the character of a first minister in assisting and strenuously supporting the defence of dunghill worms, let their cause be ever so unjust, against men of honour, birth and fortune'.[14]

The 1720s and 30s saw a boom in wealth under Walpole's guidance, that process of commercialisation which made Lavinia Fenton a star. The constant denunciations of the 'luxury' of the age, however, suggest that there was an uneasiness felt even towards relative peace and prosperity, as though the battles of political principle that had torn English society apart in the preceding century had been replaced by squabbles in the counting house. The results of this prosperity were everywhere visible, at least in the lifestyles of the wealthy – 'exotic trees for the park, strange birds and creatures to divert visitors, exquisite porcelain from Delft, Meissen and Sèvres, perfumes, fruits, wines, elegant tables and chairs, vases from China, statues from Italy, paintings, tapestries – all the worldly goods that made a Robert Adam mansion so different from the plain, simple and empty rooms of the early Jacobean houses'[15] – but it was also evidenced in fashionable language. It cannot be accidental that the 'town' declared itself in hyperbolic adjectives: 'monstrously', 'immensely' and 'extravagantly' were the *mots du jour*. Similarly, it has been suggested that an important feature of *The Beggar's Opera* is the 'commodification' of the characters' language. In one sense, the object of Gay's satire might be seen to be the bourgeoisie, rather than the conventional aristocracy; it is Peachum, who puts profit before anything, who is the real villain of the piece. 'These characters have no other vocabulary for their emotions than that of the balance sheet,' as one critic notes.[16] In the *Opera*, the commercial practices of trade and court are equated, and if Gay was not prepared to suggest, à la Walpole, that trade was the only basis for honour, he investigated the idea that 'honour' was no more or less a commodity to be traded upon than any other. 'Honour', even for Polly, is not an abstract principle, but a concept derived from the language of the marketplace.

The consequences of this invasion of culture by commerce are criminalised, linguistically and geographically, in Pope's 'Dunciad'. Of all the Scriblerian productions, this poem is the trickiest, a dense web of symbols and allusions which contains the complexity of the relationship between politics and the arts with a deceptively elegant conciseness. Like much of Pope's poetry, it is concerned with miscegenation; images of abortions and monsters run throughout, and the goddess Dulness, the 'Daughter of Chaos and Eternal Night', is created in an anthropomorphised Grub Street, the Cave of Poverty and Poetry, from whence nightmarish 'Miscellanies' spring. This blurring of literary distinctions, 'How Tragedy and Comedy embrace; / How Farce and Epic get a jumbled race', suggests the pollution of morality brought about by commercial corruption. Thus Poetic Justice is no longer an unprejudiced arbiter of the truth, but in thrall to money. 'Where in nice balance truth with gold she weighs, / And solid pudding against empty praise.' The starveling hacks of Grub Street are prepared to produce abysmal literature to serve the interests of the nation's rulers, brought together in the figure of Walpole.

The action of 'The Dunciad' is 'the removal of the imperial seat of Dulness from the City to the polite World; as that of the "Aeneid" is the removal of the Empire of Troy to Latium'. Dulness, 'Hymning Tyburn's elegiac lines', takes possession of 'Britannia' in a progress across London which follows the convict's route east to west to the gallows. East London is the home of criminals, of Peachum and Macheath, as well as of the Grub Street writers who plunder literature for financial gain, but it is also the citadel of bourgeois commerce. The west, by contrast, is the locus of fashion, wit and power, so Dulness's journey enacts the corruption of London's morals by the incursion of commerce and crime into the culture of polite society.

Just as Gay's *Beggar's Opera* links the worlds of crime, court and commerce, so Dulness, in her admiration for Walpole, illustrates the connection between the new monarchy and the debasement of the nation's politics and literature: 'Hold! – to the Minister I more incline/ To serve his cause, O Queen, is serving thine'. (To serve Walpole was to serve Queen Caroline, hence to serve Walpole was to serve Dulness.) The goddess is identified with the 'Good Old Cause', as is Walpole's Whig party. The 'Cause' was the exclusion of James II and his descendants from the English throne, which was in some measure supported by those dissenters whom Anglicans and Catholics accused of the murder of Charles I, and whose own descendants were now important figures in the new commercial order. The new class of magnates, Pope suggests, are the patrons of the Grub Street writers whose putrid productions are threatening to overwhelm the city.

> Dulness! Whose good old cause I yet defend,
> With whom my Muse began, with whom shall end! . . .
> For thee I dim these eyes and stuff this head,
> With all such reading as was never read;
> For thee supplying, in the worst of days,

Notes to dull books, and Prologues to dull plays;
For thee explain a thing 'till all men doubt it,
And write about it, Goddess, and about it.

The dubious taste of the town was figured with masquerades, as well as bad literature, and Pope, like Hogarth, implies a connection between the masquerading craze and Walpole's regime. Dulness is anointing her acolyte (the poet Lewis Theobald in the 1728 version) with opium, suggestive of sleep and a stultifying of the faculties, and as she does so, a bird settles on his head. 'And lo! Her bird (a monster of a fowl/ Something betwixt a Heidegger and owl) / Perched on his crown.' The owl is classically associated with Athena, and thus with the wisdom that a true hero, a real Aeneas, ought to possess. But since it looks like Heidegger, who was so famously ill-favoured that he was known as 'Count Ugly', the bird's symbolism is inverted, and it comes to represent the vulgar immorality of the masquerade. Since Heidegger was appointed George II's master of revels that year, the link between masquerades, Walpole and the King (Dunce the Second) is made, just as in Hogarth's print.

Pope did not forget Lavinia. In a later edition, one of 'The Dunciad's' deliberately bewildering library of footnotes alludes to *The Beggar's Opera*, mentioning that it has been acted throughout England and Wales, and lastly in Menorca. 'The person who acted Polly,' Pope adds, 'till then obscure, became at once the great favourite of the town; her pictures were engraved and sold in great numbers, her life written, books of letters and verses to her published and pamphlets made even of her sayings and jests.'

It was not only among the public that Lavinia became a favourite. Her undoubted talent had already projected her far beyond the limited sphere of ambition that might be expected for the stepdaughter of a struggling coffee house keeper, bringing her into direct contact with the elevated aristocratic world that Gay had so successfully satirised on the stage. More particularly, Polly Peachum would famously draw the attention of one of the most powerful men within that tiny clique, the Duke of Bolton. When Lavinia suddenly disappeared from the stage, it was to enter an obscurity of a very different nature from that of her early career as an unknown actress. Her absence from the theatre established a presence which was to become, in its own way, even more scandalous than the disturbingly double role she had enacted. Who Lavinia Fenton was, the location of that 'self' so praised and disputed by her century, was about to undergo another radical mutation.

This reference of Pope's to Lavinia's 'obscurity' was, then, simultaneously correct and misguided. As the star of *The Beggar's Opera*, Lavinia had become famous not only in her own right, but as a representative figure in the cultural debate about the direction of the nation's politics. The status of her own 'honour' formed part of a discourse about changing attitudes to wealth and probity. Given the repressive stance of the government, discussion of the evolving role of opera and literature was one of the few means by which dissent against these new mores could be expressed. What was dangerous to write as a political treatise could be aired in poetry, or on the stage. In the theatre, Polly pleads for Macheath's life, poor Mrs Pritchard staggers off to gales of laughter, Signora Faustina dies in her lover's arms six times a week at 50 guineas per death, but at Tyburn, where Dulness arrives triumphant, where the same crowds pause expectantly in that tiny moment, so plenteous in its smallness, the taut caesura between two worlds before the rope snaps tight; at Tyburn, death is real and savage and cold.

# 7

## POLLY PEACHUM'S LOVER

Coat of Arms: sable, three swords in pile, points downwards, proper, pommels and hilts or. Crest: a falcon, wings displayed, or, belled of the same and ducally collard gules. Supporters, two hinds purpure, semée of estoiles and ducally gorged, or. Motto: Aimez Loyauté.

Unlike the Fentons, whose family tree stretched back a mere generation or so, the Paulet family had solid centuries of ancestors behind them. The first of the family had arrived in England in the entourage of Geoffrey Plantagenet, the Earl of Anjou, third son of Henry III, and been given an estate at Paulet, in Somerset, whence derived the family name, though spellings of it varied between different branches. By the sixteenth century, there was a William Leigh-Paulet with land at Leigh in Devonshire, and it was through him that the family began their ascent from genteel rural obscurity to significant political influence. William Paulet's character was distinguished by a kind of malleable tenacity; when asked late in life how he had maintained his position through the turbulent reigns of three Tudor monarchs – reigns that had seen many of his peers go to the block at the royal displeasure, as martyrs or criminals – he replied: 'By imitating the willow rather than the oak.' William was lucky as well as flexible, miraculously surviving the plague to play host to Henry VIII on a rare westward progress, a visit which cost him the incredible sum of £2,000 per day, but which rewarded him with a title, Lord St John of Basing. Under Henry's son Edward VI, William was appointed Lord High Treasurer of England, a position he retained for thirty years, and created Earl of Wiltshire and subsequently Marquis of Winchester in 1551. The family motto, Aimez Loyauté (Love Loyalty), suggests that William's unusually long tenure in office was due to his ability to serve his monarchs faithfully but, as imitators of the willow, the Paulets' loyalty seems principally to have been directed to their own interests. The family had, like nearly all English people, been Catholics before the Henrician reformation of the Church, but William Paulet's appointment as treasurer was made under the Protestant Edward. Edward's older half-sister, Mary, was ferociously Catholic, so William was able to make a show of returning to his original faith, but how he explained a third conversion, back to Protestantism, just in time for the ascension of Elizabeth I, is a testament to his diplomatic skills. William's lack of religious partisanship saved him the trouble of having to die for his faith, and enabled him to build his enormous house at Basing in Hampshire, in which he died aged ninety-seven, extremely pleased with himself and leaving an impressive 103 descendants.

Having neither simple faith nor Norman blood, William thought he might as well dispense with the kind heart, too, and concentrate on coronets. The first Marquis may have taken pride in his durability, but some commentators were less than admiring. Writing in the early nineteenth century, the radical thinker William Cobbett expressed his disgust at William Paulet's willow-like qualities:

> A man most famous in the world for sycophancy, time serving and all those qualities which usually distinguished the favourites of such kings as the Wife-Killer [Henry VIII]. This Paulet changed from the Popish to Henry VIII's religion, and was a great actor in finishing the Papists. When Edward VI came to the throne this Paulet was a great actor in punishing those who adhered to Henry VIII's religion. When Queen Mary came to the throne this Paulet turned back to Papist, and was one of the great actors in sending papists to be burned at Smithfield. When old Bess came to the throne this Paulet turned protestant again, and was, until the day of his death, one of the great actors in ... putting to death those who still had the virtue and courage to adhere to the religion in which they and he had been born and bred.[1]

By the middle of the following century, William's great-grandson John, the fourth Marquis, had returned to the faith of his French ancestors and the Paulets were once again devout Catholics. Either they had sensed which way the religious wind was blowing with the ascension of the Stuart monarchs, or they had been skilfully secret recusants under Elizabeth all along. Whatever the case, their Roman allegiance was sufficient for them to take the pro-Stuart, proto-Catholic side in the English Civil War. Basing House became a Royalist garrison, from which John Paulet withstood a siege that lasted two years. Eventually, he and 400 others were captured by Cromwell's men, who were apparently so enraged by the family motto inscribed on the windows of the house that they burned it to the ground in 1645. They were prudent enough, however, to carry away over £200,000-worth of loot from Basing before putting it to the torch. Impoverished but undaunted, the Marquis and his sons were thrown into the tower, where they sought to raise the £7,500 fine demanded by the Parliamentarians for their release. A mortgage was raised on the ancient deer park of Hackwood on the Basing estate, and the Paulet men were able to buy their freedom.

As Cromwell's men were besieging Basing, the seat of another Catholic family, the Scropes, was also under attack. Bolton Castle, a solid medieval keep on a high bank overlooking Wensleydale in Yorkshire's North Riding, was the home of Mary, one of four illegitimate children of Lord Scrope. Scrope was vastly wealthy, despite the depredations of the Civil War, and when he died he took the unconventional step of leaving this wealth to his 'natural' children, a son and three daughters, by his mistress Martha James, along with a thoughtful allocation of funds for lawyers to prevent his legitimate relations from depriving them of it. Quite how Charles Paulet met the heiress Mary Scrope is unknown, but perhaps their religion, the persecution they had suffered and their first-hand experience of defending their homes against the finest army England had ever seen made them feel they were made for each other. Or perhaps Charles had the lucky Paulet eye for the main chance. The couple married less than six months after Charles's release from prison, in 1653.

With the return of Charles II in 1660, Mary and Charles had no difficulty, as staunch Royalists, in releasing the funds to build a fine new home, Bolton Hall, in the valley below Bolton Castle. The house, imposing but rather dour, was completed in 1678. By the time of the Glorious Revolution two years later, however, Charles had forgotten his family's Stuart loyalty, and as the deposed James Stuart sailed dismally for France, the fifth Marquis of Winchester was busy facilitating the coronation of the staunchly Protestant William of Orange, who replaced James as William III. Charles had never got on with James II, and had in fact earlier supported the rebellion of Charles II's illegitimate son the Duke of Monmouth. Perhaps he hoped that his famous eccentricity would absolve him from royal blame if the Stuarts turned up trumps in the end.

Charles's contemporaries were intrigued by the contradictions of his character. Bishop Burnet wrote that 'he was a very knowing and a very crafty politic man; and he was an artful flatterer, when that was necessary to compass his end, in which generally he was successful; he was a man of profuse expense and a most ravenous avarice to support that; and though he was much hated, yet he carried matters before him with such authority and success, that he was in all respects, the great riddle of the age'.[2]

Charles may or may not have been traumatised by the violence of his youth, but as he grew older he certainly became very peculiar indeed, his 'infinite whim' making him a figure of fear and curiosity in the north country. Later in life, he refused to speak, supposedly out of fear of demons, since it was rumoured that he had sold his soul to the Devil in order that his family, unlike so many other Stuart sympathisers, might rise unscathed from the ashes of the interregnum. He hunted his hounds across the moors at midnight, their baying and the thrum of the hunting horns terrifying the cottagers, and for his private pleasures he built a little banqueting tower one and a half miles along the avenue from Bolton Hall. Hexagonal, two storeys high and topped with a cupola like a marchpane ornament on a cake, the tower's large, rectangular windows gave a perfect circular view of the surrounding countryside. Perhaps this was to allow the Marquis to look out for the Devil coming to claim him, but the reports of the bacchanalian orgies that took place in the tower might have shocked Satan himself had he troubled to call. Charles hated his guests to leave the table, bullying them to remain until he had drunk himself insensible, perhaps because he was afraid of being alone. Even in death he was still on the watch for Lucifer, insisting on being buried upright in his stone coffin in Wensley Church. Local rumour suggested that the contract for the Marquis's soul was eventually honoured, as his skeleton supposedly hung out of the coffin as evidence of his last attempt to evade his bargain. The church was presented with silver plate (now in Ripon Cathedral), inscribed as being donated by

Mary Scrope, Marchioness of Winchester, and Charles's wife was buried alongside him. Her heart, however, was disposed of elsewhere, a gesture which clarified her private opinions of her husband's antics.

Maybe Charles did have the luck of the Devil, because despite this operatic behaviour, William III thanked him for his turncoat support by creating him first Duke of Bolton in 1689. Never one for gratitude, Charles grumbled that the new King and his court were as dissolute as the Stuarts. Since he was rumoured never to speak, William never got wind of this latest Paulet disloyalty and created Charles's eldest son Lord Lieutenant of Ireland. The second Duke, born to Charles and Mary in 1657, married three times. His first wife, Margaret Coventry, didn't last long, dying in 1682 as a bride of three years at the age of twenty-five. The Duke then married Frances Ramsden, the daughter of William Ramsden of Byron, York, the same year, and managed to beget a son, another Charles. Frances died not long afterwards, and in 1697 Henrietta Crofts, the illegitimate daughter of the Duke of Monmouth (who could therefore claim Charles II as a grandfather, although the blanket of legitimacy had been turned so many times as to have no sides left), became Duchess of Bolton. Despite his wife's royal connections, the second Duke was unable to improve upon his father's court repu-tation. Bishop Burnet, who had found his father such a conundrum, dismissed him with the remark that he 'does not make any figure at Court',[3] to which Dr Swift appended in spiteful italics: 'Nor anywhere else. A great Booby.'

Charles Paulet, who was to become the third Duke of Bolton, was born in Chawton in Hampshire on 3 September 1685. As the heir to a marquisate and, after the age of four, to a dukedom, he was a member of a unique and tiny elite, one of only 1,003 people who would hold a peerage in the whole of the eighteenth century. Though this number is negligible, it nevertheless represented most of the political power and still considerable economic influence in England. The number of peers available for an active public life was, however, diminished by the exclu-sion of those who were lunatics, such as the third and fourth Earls Ferrers, and those disadvantaged by the gender equivalent of madness, the forty-nine women who were peeresses in their own right. They wielded very little political power, though a great deal of social influence. Sixty Catholic peers were also disbarred from public office. They and their families formed an aristocratic microcosm of their own, isolated and incestuous, but little Charles, despite his family's topsy-turvy religious history, was not educated to be one of them. He was to take his place among the minuscule governing class which was his birthright.

As a Paulet, Charles could take pride in the established (if not by aristocratic standards ancient) lineage of his family. The nobility of the eighteenth century complained, as they always had, that vulgar upstarts were soiling the bloodline of the ruling classes and pushing their way into high-ranking positions. This lament had been going on since the Norman Conquest, but did nothing to prevent Robert Walpole's son Horace, who really was a parvenu since his family had only been ennobled in 1723, from railing as vigorously at the shocking state of the aristocracy as Charles's ancestors had done when Edward II's lover, Piers Gaveston, was ennobled in 1307. Charles may not have been able to boast that his family had come over with the Conqueror, but they had not been far behind, and thus from childhood he was conscious of an apparently invulnerable social superiority, which the Paulet resistance to political change over the previous two centuries served only to reinforce.

This was just as well, since the Paulets were not noted either for their looks or for their intellectual accomplishments. Charles was painted, in full ducal regalia, by Sir Godfrey Kneller in 1723, presumably very shortly after his succession to the title in 1722, since Kneller died the next year. The Duke's father's portrait had been painted by one of Kneller's followers, and there is a strong resemblance between the two men which contrasts with the physiognomy of the first Duke. Portraits of Charles's wicked grandfather show him as much harder-looking than his namesake, somehow more clearly delineated, with a pronounced hooked nose which has straightened in his grandson, and sharp, beady eyes, on the lookout for the Devil, which two generations later have become heavy-lidded, larger, lazier. Charles and his father share those eyes, the same high domed forehead, rather jowly cheeks and softly dimpled chin. They appear rather indolent men, solidly confident in their ermine, and there is a sense that their strength, if roused, would show itself as clumsy and bear-like, though no less certain than the vulpine wiriness of their ancestor. Even allowing for changing fashions in the depiction of faces as the more delicate Van Dyck influence of the seventeenth century gives way to the spoon-faced countenance of the early eighteenth, Charles appears pompous rather than clever, not unpleasant-looking, but with very little charm.

As a younger man, he was perhaps in possession of sufficient good looks to attract women, since his headmaster at school had to write to the second Duke in 1699 complaining that the fourteen-year-old Lord Winchester (Charles's courtesy title) was too busy chasing girls to pay attention to his Latin. The rather stubborn self-confidence which shows in his portrait at thirty-seven was evident in the teenager, as the Reverend Robert, master of Uvedale's school in Enfield complained: 'He declines all business, and refuses to be governed, absenting himself from school, and by no persuasion will be prevailed on to follow his studies, but takes what liberty he thinks fit on all occasions.'[4]

Charles was infatuated with Lord Falkland's daughter, who lived in the neighbourhood of the school, and the boy so neglected his lessons in pursuit of her that the exasperated Reverend informed the Duke that he refused to be responsible for his son for even one more hour. It is surprising that young Charles was not neglecting his classics at Eton or Westminster, by far the most popular and prestigious schools for the sons of the nobility at the time, and certainly a more appropriate choice for a family of the Paulets' wealth and position. The fact that in the early eighteenth century attendance at a public school had not yet become the standard pattern of education for the rich, as it was in the following century, is one explanation. Either that, or the second Duke simply thought his son too stupid to make the fees worthwhile.

Reading and writing were not Paulet strengths. Lord William, brother to the second Duke, was challenged to a duel by a man who claimed William had slandered him in a scurrilous pamphlet. He demanded a written denial, but poor Lord William got no further than 'This is to scratify that the buk ...' before his laughing adversary declared that he could not possibly have been its author. Another Paulet accidentally presented a lady friend with 100 monkeys from the East Indies, his spelling of the word 'two' as 'too' on the commission being mistaken for a figure. The second Duke himself was described by Lady Cowper in her diary as generally to be seen with his tongue lolling out of his mouth, a posture which is rarely indicative of intellectual profundity. When Charles grew up, Lord Hervey was as scathing about his intelligence as Lord William's adversary had been about his spelling, declaring with reference to Charles's support of a land tax: 'The Duke of Bolton ... would have been more extraordinary than all the rest, if it had not been for that great and common solution for the many otherwise unaccountable riddles in people's conduct, which was his being a great fool, but this explains a multitude of differences in judging multitudes of people as well as the Duke of Bolton, for when one can without hesitation pronounce a man absolutely a fool, to wonder at any of his actions afterwards or seek a reason for them is only putting oneself in his class, and I am no more surprised to see an understood fool act against his interest than I am to see a blind man go out of his way.'[5]

Lord Hervey was notoriously waspish, but then Charles does seem to have been something of a dunce at school. After leaving Uvedale's when his master washed his hands of him, Charles did not even take the conventional route of the nobleman: a pleasant few years of drinking, gaming and idling at one of the two universities. It was quite usual to matriculate at either Oxford or Cambridge at a young age – the Duke of Beaufort began at University College, Oxford aged thirteen in 1720, and the future Earl of Shaftesbury at New College in 1724, and given that no qualifications for a degree were required of peers save their presence, it should have been easy for the newly expelled Charles to graduate. As the *Terrae-Filius* disparagingly acknowledged in 1726, it sounds as though university would have suited him: 'A nobleman may bring any-thing from College but learning, but there is generally effectual care taken that His Grace shall not want temptations to entice him from studying too hard. A Gentleman Commoner, if he be a man of Fortune, is soon told that it is not expected from one of his form to mind exercises.'

Charles may have been disappointed not to have gone on to uni-versity, but at least he was now free to pursue the things he really loved – drinking, women, racing and the theatre. Drunkenness was considered the least of such vices. Walpole himself had learned to drink at his father's table, encouraged by the friendly advice that a son ought to drink two cups to his father's one, lest he risk seeing his elder's intoxication. Charles's own father had been described as 'a most lewd, vicious man, a great dissembler and a very hard drinker'.[6] In gentlemen's houses all over England, the ladies retired after dinner to leave the men to the serious business of consuming a bottle of port apiece, pissing in the chamber pot placed under the table for their convenience, and eventually rolling on to the floor to join it. In contrast with the French, who preferred the mixed conversation of the salon to the strictly masculine convivialities of the table, the English took the view that a man who couldn't hold his bottle (or three) was hardly a man at all. The playwright Sheridan and the politician Pitt the Younger were both respected as six-bottle men, with no apparent detriment to their other talents. (It should be noted that bottles were much smaller in the eighteenth century, but then, so were people). Walpole's opponent Viscount Bolingbroke was well known for drinking all night, wrapping a wet handkerchief around his eyes to stave off his intoxication and proceeding immediately to business. Dr Johnson, recalling his own youth, observed that all the respectable people in Lichfield got drunk every night and no one thought the worse of them for it. Alcohol was not seen as an impediment to working. In 1725 Benjamin Franklin gave a wide-eyed account of a typical workman's drinking: 'My companion at the press drank every day a pint before breakfast, a pint at breakfast, a pint between breakfast and dinner, a pint in the afternoon about six o'clock and another pint when he had done his day's work.'[7] Strong beer was believed to give strength to labourers, but unless shouldering a gun on the moor could be considered labour, Charles drank excessively, as did most young men of his class, simply because he liked to.

Spirits, aside from brandy, were not a gentleman's drink, and the rich were protected from the terrible consequences of gin as they affected the poor in London's slums. Gambling was a more exclusive way for a gentleman to ruin himself. The Paulets were a racing family and, following the fashion for the sport introduced by Charles II, had constructed tracks at Bolton Hall and at Hackwood in Hampshire. A silver gilt trophy survives from a race at Hackwood in 1684, estimated to be worth £250,000, demonstrating that Charles's family took their hobby seriously.

Cards were the greatest temptation to the aristocratic gambler, and though Charles never reached the excessive notoriety of the century's most dashing gamester, Charles James Fox, who once lost £140,000 at Brooks's in a single night, he played high all his life. In town, the most fashionable house where a young man could lose a fortune he had not yet inherited was the old club, at White's in St James's, established under Queen Anne and swiftly joined by Boodles and Crockford's in the same street, and Almack's in nearby Pall Mall. These clubs were sophisticated, elegant and well organised. Of the latter (which moved round the corner to become Brooks's in 1778), Horace Walpole wrote: 'a thousand meadows and cornfields are staked at every throw, and as many villages lost as in the earthquakes that overwhelmed Herculanaeum and Pompeii.'[8] Games included hazard, faro and basset, and even the King and Queen were known to play high. Charles's father, the second Duke, had written repeatedly to his own father to complain of the meagreness of his allowance and request advances for London extravagance, and Charles followed this example, running up hefty gambling debts. In this, as in everything else, he was unexceptional, since men of fashion were notoriously prepared to bet on virtually anything, and when more elegant gambling palled, there were stakes to be made on rougher chances such as prize fighting, cock-fighting, bear- and bull-baiting at Marylebone and Hockley-in-the-Hole and even bare-armed wrestling between women stripped to their shifts, which remained popular throughout the century, producing champions like Bruising Peg who, according to a newspaper account of a 1768 battle at Spa Fields, 'beat her antagonist in a terrible manner'.

Despite all these temptations to profligacy, and the fact that he had not been a shining light at school, Charles managed to occupy several important positions from a young age. At twenty, he became an MP for the first time, affiliated to the Whig party, for the seat of Lymington, which he held until 1708. He continued his parliamentary career by representing Hampshire for two years, and followed this with the important post of Lord of the Bedchamber to the Prince of Wales in 1715. Charles combined his political and court duties with a colonelship in the smart regiment of the Horse Guards, which eventually promoted him to lieutenant-general.

Charles's life may have seemed enviably free of responsibility, but there was one obligation his class required of him, which was the begetting of future members of it, most particularly sons. If until this point his life had been too unchallenging for any of his achievements to really count as successes, it was in respect of his marriage that he first experienced the bitterness of failure. Admittedly, it was never going to be easy for him to do his duty. Lady Anne Vaughan was selected from the range of eligible young ladies by his father, as was conventional, for her fortune and her breeding, both of which were impeccable. She was the daughter of Lord John Vaughan, Earl of Carbery in Ireland, Baron Molingart in England and Baron Emlyn in Wales, and even more importantly, was his sole heiress. Lord Berkeley reported in February 1713: 'There is such running after my Lord Carbery's rich daughter as you never saw. My Lord Lumley makes the greatest bustle ... My Lord Winchester and Lord Hertford are also in pursuit.'[9] According to her friend Lady Mary Wortley Montagu, Lady Anne was as well educated as she was well bred and wealthy, having spent most of her life in quiet study with a governess on one or another of her father's estates. As she had several suitors to choose from, she must have been attracted to Charles, as a month after Lord Berkeley mentioned the attention she drew, he was able to inform his correspondent: 'My Lord Winchester is to be the happy man that marries my Lady Anne Vaughan.'

'Happy' was a diplomatic adjective. Anne, too, was painted by Kneller, as Duchess of Bolton, in 1722. Her portrait is much simpler than that of her husband, even severe. Her heavy-browed, plain face seems impassive, as though sitting for her picture is another of the social duties in which she has been so well trained, but not one which can arouse her to an expression of interest, much less animation. She seems thoroughly bored. Kneller did his best, but even allowing for the considerable licence given to artists when painting the aristocracy, whose physical charms were deemed as much a function of rank as of nature, there is no doubt that Anne is extremely disagreeable-looking. Horace Walpole was cruelly to the point. 'Unluckily, she was a monster.'[10] By 1713, Charles had had nearly fifteen years in which to indulge his taste for pretty women, and though, given his background, he was likely to have been perfectly prepared to marry without love or even much attraction, he baulked at his ugly bride, and violently opposed the match. The Duke had to force it upon him, threatening him with disinheritance if he refused to obey, and, at the age of twenty-eight, Charles pronounced his vows through gritted teeth.

However, there is some possibility that the young Marquis and Marchioness of Winchester were never quite legally married. As well as the actual ceremony, marriage required consummation to be binding, and Charles's contemporaries were quick to gossip that this event had never taken place. 'Winchester, being forced by his father to marry her for her great fortune, was believed never to have consummated,' reported Walpole gleefully.[11] Lady Mary Wortley Montagu, though loyally silent on the subject of her friend Anne's looks, also hinted at the state of her unfulfilled relationship. Given the importance of consummation in validating a marriage, such speculation was very common. Walpole apologised in a letter for his lack of spicy wedding-night anecdotes after Lord Fitzwilliam's marriage in 1744, while of Lord Beauchamp's, George Selwyn reported that His Lordship was 'seen about so early in the morning that it does not look as though much business was doing'. While the custom of public bedding on the wedding night, though still prevailing for royalty, was gradually dying out, a country marriage meant that it was still likely Charles and Anne would have been put to bed by their families, with much smirking, and quiet, sheltered Anne may have found this public assault on her virginity too distasteful to contemplate. More likely, given his propensity for the bottle, Charles may have swallowed, in the new phrase, more 'Dutch courage' than was wise, though in a spirit of desperation rather than celebration. Whether or not Charles ever managed to overcome his physical distaste for his wife, they had no children, which suggests that either Anne was infertile, or that the rumours were true.

Until Charles succeeded to his title in 1722, he and Anne behaved like many young couples of their class and managed to see very little of one another. Anne was presented at court in her new rank of marchioness with her husband in attendance, and at first they maintained a polite façade on the rare occasions they appeared together in public, though for much of the time they barely lived in the same house. Charles pursued his military and political activities in London, while his wife preferred the country. This was by no means odd behaviour in an era when most wives expected to spend relatively little time with their husbands, who moved, through much of the daytime at least, in the masculine environments of club or coffee house, but there were unpleasant rumours that Lady Anne was made wretched by Charles's drunkenness and infidelities. Although Charles found her sexually disappointing, she was not a stupid woman, and her manner was apparently quite pleasing, but perhaps he was not discerning enough, or simply not interested enough, to attempt to form even a friendly relationship with her, particularly as it became clear they were not to have children. Lady Anne was hurt perhaps not so much by the idea of his drinking and whoring, which were seen as perfectly reasonable activities in a married man, but by the fact that Charles took pleasure in flaunting his debauches in front of her, as though he was so bitter and frustrated with the failure of their marriage that he wanted to confront her with this humiliating evidence of its inadequacy. On one occasion, Charles and a few cronies brought a group of whores back to the couple's London home in the middle of the night. When the Marchioness, alarmed by the racket, sent her maid to investigate downstairs, her husband, barely bothering to raise his eyes from the body of the woman with whom he had been disturbed *in flagrante delicto*, was said to have cursed both maid and mistress roundly, and told the servant to convey the message that Anne should find somewhere else to sleep if she meant thus to interfere with his business.

These cruelties were particularly hard to take since Anne's Welsh connections had helped her husband to two more prestigious posts. He became MP for Camarthen in 1715, two years after their marriage, and was appointed Lord Lieutenant of counties Carmarthen and Glamorgan the same year. The latter was a lucrative sinecure, and had perhaps been offered to Charles as an inducement to accept his ugly bride.

As soon as he succeeded to his dukedom in 1722, Charles ungratefully set about putting as much distance as possible between himself and his wife. Effectively, they had been separated in private since 1714 – Lady Mary Wortley Montagu had reported in November of that year that 'My Lord made her an early confession of his aversion' – but now they began to maintain separate households as well, and in January 1724, the Duke of Bolton brought a petition to the House of Lords requesting that his wife might be allowed a bill to raise money independently on her own lands. Anne's property had been, since their marriage, legitimately and entirely his, and it seems that this step was a way of dividing their financial affairs without recourse to a divorce. Even for a man with such wealth and power, a divorce, which would seem the obvious solution for a couple so wretchedly ill suited, was not an easy thing to contemplate. Before 1740, only three peers had obtained one – Lord Roos in 1670, Lord Macclesfield in 1698 and the Duke of Norfolk in 1700 – and in total, only ten British peers were to divorce in the entire eighteenth century. It would not have been impossible for Charles to cast Anne aside by a private Act of Parliament, as the Duke of Beaufort was subsequently to do to his wife, but the expense and humiliating publicity of such a step was daunting. Either Anne would have to be proved adulterous (and given her unfortunate appearance, this might have required some very hard evidence indeed), or Charles himself would have to endure public exposure as a cruel husband which, by the standards of the time, he really was not. The final option was the ground of non-consummation, but perhaps Charles could not bear to be branded impotent especially as this was patently untrue. Nevertheless, since the primary duty of an aristocratic wife was to breed, Charles may have felt legitimately annoyed, since he was not impotent, that he had made such a bad bargain.

The Duke of Beaufort had no such scruples. Attempting to divorce his wife for adultery, he disproved her counter-charge that due to his impotence the marriage had never been consummated by organising a private demonstration of his erectile capacities at the house of one Dr Medes. Two doctors, three surgeons and the Dean of Arches were invited to witness, from behind a screen, that the Duke was man enough for the job, and Horace Walpole reported delightedly that 'Colley Cibber says "His Grace's — is in everybody's mouth."'[13] Charles was not alone in his frustration at his wife's apparent barrenness, since one-fifth of eighteenth-century aristocratic marriages were similarly unblessed, but infertility, though traditionally viewed as the responsibility of the woman, could not be absolutely proved. As Caleb Fleming noted in *The Oeconomy of the Sexes* in 1751, 'Every man who taketh a wife, may, and ought, to know, that fruitfulness is not at her pleasure or in her power; and therefore the capacity of intercourse is all he is to expect from her, relative to propagation; which being found, consummates the contract.' Nor was Charles alone in his unwillingness to perform his conjugal duties. The Duke of Bedford, who was a virgin on marriage due to his inclinations lying elsewhere, declared that he would prefer 'to let his estate go to his brother rather than go through the fitting drudgery of getting an heir to it'.[14]

The Duchess of Bolton was depressed by her failure to fulfil the role for which she had been raised, and her frequent visits to spas such as Tunbridge were made in the hope of a cure (which suggests that at some point she and her husband must have at least attempted to sleep together). Newspapers were full of remedies for infertility, and spa waters were recommended to strengthen the womb. Desperate women were more than ready to make the journey; Lady Carteret, for example, of whom Horace Walpole commented: 'My lady is going to Tunbridge, which don't look so flaming vigorous on my lord's part, but there is a hurry for a son.' Anne may well have agreed with the writer of the *Treatise on Warm bath Water*, who claimed that he 'pitied the poor innocent new married women, who have heat and stewed themselves in hot baths . . . thinking that the deficiency lay on their side . . . when alas the fault was in the vile and wicked whoremasterly husband, broke and bankrupt in his bed tackle'. Easier for Anne's pride, perhaps, to believe that her husband was too exhausted by whoring to come to her bed rather than too repulsed by her person.

It was a relief, then, for both Anne and Charles when Anne's bill, which passed through the Lords for the first few months of 1724, was granted in April, eventually permitting the estranged Duchess of Bolton a degree of dignity and independence. She was permitted to settle £1,000 per year from her estates as she wished, and Charles was left free to pursue his whores as he wished. Of course, he could not marry again, and beget the all-important heir, but Anne's health was poor, and he callously hoped that she would die, so that he could take a younger, fertile and more attractive bride.

Did Bolton even bother to say goodbye to his wife when he left to take up the governorship of the Isle of Wight in 1726? He was gone for two years, and it is hard to believe that Anne missed him. In 1728, though, Charles returned. It was then that, perhaps for the first time in his life, he fell in love.

# 8

# PLAYING THE GENTLEMAN

One troublesome aspect of performing as an actress in 1728 is the difficulty of getting through one's part without tripping over members of the audience who insist on joining in the performance. Since the 'apron' of the stage, from which the prologue and epilogue are traditionally spoken, projects into the auditorium, beyond the two-piece curtain which hangs from a rod across the proscenium, it is quite easy for enthusiastic patrons to clamber on to the stage and to make their way through one of the entrance doors, of which there are four, two pairs on either side of the curtain, and find themselves in the thick of the action. Thus the *Spectator* reports of one young man who broke the boundaries of spectating and spectacle:

> This was a very lusty Fellow ... who getting into one of the Side-Boxes on the Stage before the Curtain drew, was disposed to shew the whole Audience his Activity by leaping over the spike; he pass'd from there to one of the entr'ing doors, where he took Snuff with a tolerable grace, display'd his fine Cloaths, made two or three feint Passes at the Curtain with his Cane, then fac'd about and appear'd at t'other Door: Here he affected to survey the whole House, bow'd and smil'd at Random, and then shew'd his Teeth ... After this he retir'd behind the Curtain, and oblig'd us with several Views of his Person from every Opening. During the time of Acting he appear'd frequently in the Prince's Apartment, made one at the Hunting Match, and was very forward in the Rebellion.

Spitting was also a problem.

95

As *The Beggar's Opera* continues its triumphant season, Lavinia Fenton shares her stage with two lovers, one theatrical, one real, both aristocrats of a different kind. 'And are you as fond as ever, my dear?' asks Polly meekly, lowering her eyes.

'Suspect my honour, my courage, suspect anything but my love,' replies Macheath gallantly. 'May my pistols misfire and my mare slip her shoulder while I am pursued, if I ever forsake thee!' His reply hints at both his profession and his pretensions, since while his language is that of a hero of a thrilling drawing-room romance, his references are to robbery. 'Captain' was a common courtesy title in Newgate where, as Fielding observed, one might find '. . . many worse Men in the World than those. Gentlemen may be driven to Distress, and when they are, I know no more Genteeler way than the Road. It hath been many a brave Man's Case . . . and men of as much Honour too as any in the World.'[1] Captain Macheath has a gentleman's tastes and a gentleman's vices; he gambles away his earnings, and is betrayed, like his real-life predecessor James Hind, the original 'gentleman of the road', by his whore.

Highwaymen, at least as they were portrayed in the sensational pamphlets Lavinia and her friends had read so avidly at school, were romantic figures. The dying speech of Claude Duval, hanged in 1670, was addressed to those fair ladies of England who had treated him so well, and was still popular reading in the 1720s. Duval, like many highwaymen, had begun his career as a footman, picking up the gentry's taste and possibly an old lace coat as well as the useful skills of an outrider. Villain he may have been, but Duval had style, and after all, as Charles Johnson remarked, 'Duval was a pickpocket, and what is a court favourite but a picker of the people's pockets?'[2] Imitating the swaggering, swearing, rambunctious aristocrats of the Restoration, Duval became as celebrated a lover as he was a thief, on one occasion forcing a lady victim to dance with him to his own accompaniment on the flageolet before 'charging' her husband for the dance. When Duval eventually took his last ride to Tyburn, 'so much had his gallantries and handsome figure rendered him the favourite of the fair sex, that many a bright eye was dimmed at his funeral, and his lifeless corpse was bedewed with the tears of beauty'.[3] One of the emblematic figures of the eighteenth century, the highwayman, in his swaggering boots, bestrode the chasm between criminal and gentleman with captivating insouciance. As Mrs Peachum puts it: 'The youth in his cart hath the air of a lord, and we cry, "There dies an Adonis!" '

In his last days of freedom, Jack Sheppard had assumed just such a gallant air, a victim, perhaps, of his own legend, which required him to go out in style. Ten days after his astonishing last escape from Newgate he robbed the Rawlins brothers of Drury Lane of two tortoiseshell snuffboxes, a gold watch and diamond ring, two wigs, a ruffled shirt and a suit of black cloth in the latest fashion. He topped off his glamorous new appearance with a silver-handled sword, and strolled about the streets like a member of the quality. He picked up two pretty girls and treated them to meals and wine, and even drove with them in a hired coach right up to the lodge of Newgate prison. Such bravado, though it cost him his life, seems an almost necessary gesture, an appropriate finale to Jack's personal drama. He laughed at the law as he evaded its physical restraints, then he dressed up as a gentleman and strutted through the fashionable brandy shops to tease it yet again. He escaped authority and then made a pantomime of it, and his mockery contained a threat.

Paul Lewis, a former lieutenant in the Royal Navy, was nicknamed 'Captain' after Macheath when his career on the road landed him in Newgate. Like another highwayman, John Rann, known as Sixteen-String Jack, he gave a dinner party on the night before his hanging, where he sat at the head of the table, sang obscene ballads and swore at the parson.

Swift's 1727 poem 'Clever Tom Clinch' sums up the arrogant attitude to death which contributed to the highwayman's legend.

> As clever Tom Clinch while the rabble was bawling,
> Rode stately through Holborn to die in his calling,
> He stopt at the George for a bottle of sack,
> And promised to pay for it when he came back,
> His waistcoat and stockings and breeches were white,
> His cap had a new cherry ribbon to tie't,
> The maids to the doors and the balconies ran,
> And said 'lack-a-day, he's a proper young man'
> But, as from the windows the ladies he spied,
> Like a beau in the box, he bow'd low on each side.

The highwayman is a self-invented character, a radical chameleon who challenges the minutiae of the social hierarchy, making his fake bow to the ladies in their fake boxes on the way to the theatre of Tyburn. The gentleman criminal, with his fine clothes and polite airs, demonstrated how flimsy that hierarchy really was, how much it depended on collusion and delusion. Sheppard and his cohorts were disturbingly rebellious, inverting the mores of the society that punished them in the gravest moment of the punishment's enaction. On his way to die, the highwayman is a star.

In Hogarth's *Harlot's Progress* series, the artist plays with the connection between highwaymen and whores just as Gay had done in *The Beggar's Opera*. The whore Moll Hackabout takes her name from one Kate Hackabout, who was arrested in the brothel where she worked in June 1730, two months after her brother Francis, a highwayman, was hanged. In the paintings, Moll is the lover of another highwayman, James Dalton, whose hatbox is displayed above her bed in the third plate of the sequence. Dalton's escapades had made him popular with the public; he claimed to have travelled in the cart to Tyburn in his own highwayman father's lap to see him hanged, to have become the pirate captain of the ship intended to transport him to the colonies and even to have attempted to rob the Queen (fortunately for Her Majesty, he picked the wrong coach).

Such compelling audacity fascinated Gay's audiences when personified by the character of Macheath, and indeed the imitative romancings of subsequent gentlemen of the road such as Plunkett and the famous Dick Turpin might be said to owe as much to Gay's creation as to real-life prototypes like Duval or Dalton. (William Harrison Ainsworth, who created Turpin's dashing legend in the nineteenth century, certainly thought so, since the real Turpin was essentially a horse-stealer, albeit famously handsome.) Plunkett numbered several 'respectable' women among his mistresses, and lived in prison in some style upon their contributions while awaiting his execution. Just as Goethe's Werther was later to provide a model for young men who fancied that melancholia and fancy shirts amounted to poetic genius, so Macheath's swashbuckling gallantries were an inspiration to a generation of well-educated boys who wanted to play at rebellion. The Duke of Richmond was not above disguising himself as a highwayman for fun, and Dr

Johnson's biographer James Boswell associated himself with the character, having played him at a country house party in Scotland, and did his best to go to the bad in the grand style by frequenting the illegal theatres of Edinburgh, to his father's despair. London proved a more satisfactory source of dissipations and, having escaped Scotland for good, Boswell, when not in sycophantic pursuit of his shambling idol, drank and whored his way round the capital with Macheath never far from his mind. Of an evening with two whores (a Polly and a Lucy) at the Shakespeare's Head tavern in Russell Street, Covent Garden, he recollected: 'I surveyed my seraglio and found them both good subjects for amorous play. I toyed with them and drank about and sung "Youth's the Season", and fancied myself Captain Macheath.'[4] The earnest doctor himself was not immune to Macheath's casual air of power over women, though as ever when he attempted to be theatrical he ended up looking faintly ludicrous. Boswell recalls Johnson disputing with two ladies, Mrs Williams and Mrs Hall, and crying out, '"Nay, when you both speak at once it is intolerable" . . . then he brightened into a gay humour and addressed them in the words of one of the songs in "The Beggar's Opera"; "But two at a time, there's no mortal can bear". "But what, Sir" [said Boswell] "are you going to turn Captain Macheath?"'[5] The contrast between handsome Macheath and lovely Polly and saucy Lucy, and portly Johnson and his elderly, peevish ladies was deliciously absurd.

In making Macheath such an attractive character, Gay was also making a darker comment on the misery of those lives in comparison to which the highwayman's end seemed preferable. The wealthy might amuse themselves by playing at bandits, but for many, the myth was an escape from a wretched reality. In a description of the criminal classes of London, the German traveller Lichtenburg commented: 'They grow up without learning to read or write, and never hear the words "religion" or "belief", and not even the word "God" excepting in the phrase "God damn it". They gain their livelihood by all kinds of work in the brick-kilns, helping the drivers of hackney coaches and so forth, until the old Adam in them is aroused; then they take to stealing and are generally hanged between the ages of eighteen to twenty six. A short life and a merry one is their motto, which they do not hesitate to proclaim in court.'[6]

Similarly, Swift's satirical *Directions to Servants* observes: 'To grow old in the office of footman is the height of all indignities: therefore ... I directly advise you to go upon the road which is the only post of honour left you.' Beneath the comic instructions on how to behave when going to be hanged – only confess to your comrades in return for a pardon, get a speech written by a good Newgate author, be sure to have a fine Holland shirt and look pious in the cart in order to 'make a figure at your exit' – is the bleak reality that for many of London's poor, the attraction of the road was the only opportunity to enjoy some sort of wretched significance.

This potentially pernicious influence of *The Beggar's Opera* in promoting the glamour of the highwayman was summed up by Charles Dickens in the nineteenth century. 'Johnson's question, whether any man will turn thief because Macheath is reprieved, seems to me besides the matter. I ask myself whether any man will be deterred from turning thief because of Macheath's being sentenced to death ... and remembering the Captain's roaring life, great appearance, vast success and strong advantages, I feel nobody having a bent that way will take any warning from him.'[7]

Macheath was Gay's creation, but his glamorous image owed much to the part as created by Lavinia Fenton's co-star Tom Walker. The role had originally been offered to James Quin who, in an error of professional judgement he was to regret, expressed distaste for it and persuaded the writer to offer it to his younger colleague. Ironically, Quin himself was an example of the connections between the stage and Newgate. As an actor, he had first made his name as understudy in the part of Falstaff at Lincoln's Inn, but soon moved on to leading roles. During a performance of *Cato* with Quin in the title lead, another actor, Williams, had to announce that 'Caesar sends health to Cato'. Unfortunately, he mispronounced the name as 'Keeto', to which the recumbent Quin laconically replied, 'Would that Caesar had sent a better messenger,' which set the house roaring. Afterwards in the green room, Williams complained that Quin had made him so ridiculous that it could be the end of his career, and insisted upon satisfaction, a demand that Quin greeted with mocking laughter. Williams left the theatre and lurked in Covent Garden, and when Quin passed on his way home, Williams attacked him with his sword. Quin drew, they fought and Williams was killed on the spot. Quin immediately gave himself up, was committed, tried for manslaughter and branded on the hand, a punishment which did not prevent him from continuing as a successful actor.

'Mr Quin's murderous quarrel', as it was known, may have suited him to the part of Macheath, but instead the role made Walker a star. Walker perhaps began his theatre career as early as 1716, there being mention of him as having played Lorenzo in *The Merchant of Venice* that year. Apparently, he had little formal training and limited musical experience, but he was enterprising enough to create a show of his own, as the *Weekly Journal* for 15 September 1722 reports. 'We hear that the Dramatick Entertainment of Valentine and Orson, which Mr Walker has prepared for the Diversion of the Town during the time of Southwark Fair, meets with universal Applause.' If Lavinia had benefited not only from the combative intellectual climate of the coffee shop but also from observing the debtors who lolled around her family's lodgings in the Old Bailey, and from the whores who trulled their way to Covent Garden across the Charing Cross Road, then Tom Walker had also prepared for his part among the pickpockets and shysters of the great London fairs. As a result he was able to create a Macheath to make apprentices stamp and ladies swoon. It helped, of course, that he was young and handsome, and just as the use of the vernacular in *The Beggar's Opera* was seen as a counterblow of English character to the injurious Italianate posturings of Cuzzoni and Senesino, so Walker's Macheath was viewed by the enthusiastic as exemplifying a sturdy English virility as opposed to the eunuch castrati who had captivated women of fashion a few seasons before.

> If Wit can please, or Gallantry engage
> Macheath may boast he justly charms the age . . .
> The Fair in Troops attend his sprightly Call
> No longer doat upon an Eunuch's squall,
> Well pleased they blush, and own behind a Fan,
> His voice, his looks, his actions speak a Man.[8]

Walker's recent familiarity to London audiences was effectively used by Gay in another of the parodies contained in *The Beggar's Opera*, which is not concerned with opera but with poking fun at heroic tragedy, a previous target of Gay's in *The What D'Ye Call It*. In the final act of Otway's *Venice Preserv'd*, Pierre exits to his doom to the sound of a tolling bell, a scene directly recalled by Macheath's departure for the scaffold in Act III of the *Opera*. Since Walker had played the part of Pierre a few weeks previously, theatre-literate audiences would quickly grasp that Macheath's dramatic exit was sending up the pomposity of Otway's play.

Just as Lavinia is accused of augmenting her theatrical earnings with a little extra-curricular whoring, so Tom Walker is slyly charged with taking advantage of women's desire for the 'sprightly' Captain Macheath to turn a profit. Inevitably, too, it is suggested that their onstage romance is more than acting, and there is even speculation in the press that they will marry, but Lavinia, whether or not she is seduced, like all the other women in London, by Tom Walker's wide eyes and soft brown hair, is keeping her head.

It is doubtful she has time to give much thought to Tom Walker, since Polly is by no means the only part she has worked on during the run of *The Beggar's Opera*. In March, she has performed as Alinda in Beaumont and Fletcher's *Pilgrim* for Mr Quin's benefit, as Ophelia once more, as Leanthe in Farquhar's *Love in a Bottle* for Tom Walker's benefit, and as Marcella in D'Urfey's *Don Quixote*. With Mrs Fenton in the background urging her on, Lavinia seems possessed by the need to work, to reap as many gains as possible from her moment in the sun. She learns a 'skating dance' in the latest mode and performs it with the dancer Nivelon. On 29 April she plays Cherry in *The Beaux' Stratagem* once again for her own benefit, and earns £95 19s 6d. Whether it is she or her mother who has an eye for the main chance, Lavinia pushes her expectations too far at her first benefit performance as Polly, when she asserts that the 'Pittites' ought to pay the same for the privilege of seeing Polly Peachum as the grandees in the box seats. Uniquely during the run of the *Opera*, a majority of tickets are returned, but Mr Rich generously takes the meagre proceeds as his own and arranges a second benefit for his star on 4 May. This performance is marred only by the noise of Lavinia's supporters, who drown out her voice with as much clapping as Cuzzoni or Faustina might command, and the volubility of their enthusiasm is reflected in the takings, and Lavinia earns £155 0s 4d.

Does Mr Rich, as is of course rumoured, really have more than a professional interest in Polly, or is he merely taking care of his profits by assuring that she remains contented in her role? After all, Rich himself will make a staggering £9,000, at the best estimate, from the *Opera*. The hacks are claiming that there is a certain understanding between Lavinia and 'nimble Harlequin', though if she is sleeping with Rich, Tom Walker, the mysterious Portuguese gentleman and half the *beau monde* besides, it is remarkable that she should have the time to do Polly at all, let alone have a care for her theatrical profits.

Even if it is partly true that 'Polly becoming the most celebrated Toast in Town, she gain'd new Admirers every Time she appear'd on the Stage, and Persons of the highest Rank and Quality made Love to her; insomuch, that by the Presents she received, she lives in Ease and Plenty, keeps her Servants and appears abroad in as much magnificence as a Lady,'[9] there is really no evidence at all that Lavinia Fenton has ever turned whore. True, the Fentons have departed from the shadows of the Old Bailey to more salubrious quarters in St James's, and Lavinia does indeed receive gifts from admirers, even from fashionable ladies who are prepared to overlook her dubious status as an actress in order to have the season's most popular performer grace their musical soirées with a ballad, but her acceptance of what are after all conventional tokens of appreciation does not in itself argue for her offering her body in exchange. Her exigency over her benefit strongly implies that despite the rumours as to the fortune she earns on her back, she and her parents are currently relying on her wages as an actress, and even with benefit funds and presents, it is hard to maintain a state of 'magnificence' on thirty shillings a week.

Frankly, the quality of most of the literary *demi-monde* who haunt the theatres falls a good way short of magnificence, too. Dr Swift has declared of the young men who pose and gossip in the taverns and coffee houses of Drury Lane: 'They writ and rallied, and rhymed and sung, and said, and said nothing, they drank and fought and whored and slept and swore and took snuff, they went to new plays on the first night, haunted the chocolate houses; they talked of the drawing room and never came there; whispered a Duchess and spoke never a word; exposed the scrawls of their laundress for a billet-doux of quality, came ever just from court and were never seen in it ... got a list of peers by heart in one company and with great familiarity recited them in another.'[10] Lavinia has spent enough time at the counter of the coffee house not to be deceived by such pretensions, and now she is safely beyond the aspirations of the young men on the make, if not their tongues.

Not all the pamphlets, though, support the view that Lavinia is a whore. When the press tire of knocking Polly down, there is just as much fun to be had in defending her, particularly in the context of the ongoing feuds between opera fans.

> Some Prudes indeed, with envious Spight
> Would blast her Reputation
> And tell us that to Ribands bright
> She yields, upon occasion.
> But these are all invented Lies
> And Vile Outlandish Scandal
> Which from Italian Clubs arise
> And Partizans of Handel.[11]

This rhyme expresses the confusion about the tangled satirical objects of *The Beggar's Opera*. It suggests that those who seek to besmirch Lavinia's reputation do so on musical rather than political grounds, but it yokes together 'Italian Clubs' (the progressive 'Palladians' like Pope and Burlington) with supporters of Handel, who were linked to George II, whom the Palladians despised, thus rendering a musical defence a matter of party faction. The quarrels at court between pro- and anti-Handelists had reached such a pitch by 1728 that Lord Hervey quoted the Princess Royal as saying that 'she expected in a little while to see half the House of Lords playing in the orchestra in their robes and coronets'.

Again and again, Lavinia Fenton was the focus, through her portrayal of Polly Peachum, of the political debates enacted vicariously on the London stage. Sometimes, however, even the dramatic sublimation of the play was insufficient to contain the passions of partisan audiences, and the theatre duly became the location for all too realistic rioting. This aggressive behaviour was just one indication of the general violence of Lavinia's world. The popularity of public executions at Tyburn continued until 1783, when they were removed to the relative privacy of Newgate, much to the disappointment of Londoners. (In Swift's *Directions to Servants*, the temptation to sneak off to watch a hanging is one of the principal below-stairs distractions.) Even hanging was not the most gruesome entertainment on offer. The last woman to be burned alive for 'petty treason' (the malicious killing of a victim to whom the criminal owed a loyalty, such as servant to master or wife to husband), perished as late as 1788. In Lavinia's lifetime, two other women, Catherine Hayes and Anne Hutchinson, were burned for the crime, and a third, Anne Sowerley of York, was similarly executed in 1767. Until 1772, the heads of the thirty-eight Jacobite rebels who had been dragged on hurdles to Kennington Common, where they were hung, drawn and quartered, mouldered in full view on Temple Bar. The bodies of gentlemen of the road swung rotting in chains from gibbets at the roadside. For some, even such grisly reminders of the power of the law were not sufficient. *Hanging Not Punishment Enough*, a tract of 1701, suggested that criminals be broken on the wheel before being flogged, strung up in chains and publicly starved to death.

The success of *The Beggar's Opera* among the poorer sections of its audience resulted from the fact that characters like Macheath enacted upon the stage the 'true crime' stories churned out by Grub Street for the entertainment of the lower classes. Yet their knowledge of his probable end was also a recognition of the savage power that lay behind the polished manners of the rich, the brutal obduracy that could be concealed beneath fine linen and a gracious air. Crime could be seen as a form of rebellion against a social order which would hang a man for stealing a shilling. Since the passing of the Black Act, the presentation of criminals as heroes represented an inclination towards defiance against such ruthlessness, as the Beggar's final lines after Macheath's comic reprieve make cruelly clear. 'Through the whole piece you may observe such a similitude of manners in high and low life that it is difficult to determine whether (in the fashionable vices) the fine gentlemen imitate the gentlemen of the road, or the gentlemen of the road the fine gentlemen. Had the play remained, as I at first intended, it would have carried a most excellent moral. 'Twould have shown that the lower sort of people have their vices in a degree as well as the rich: and that they are punished for them.'

Glamorous Tom Walker played a thief who plays a gentleman, but real gentlemen, too, were schooled in the ways of violence. Macheath's consciously absurd evasion of the law hints at a darker irony, that indeed 'fine gentlemen' could flout it with impunity. Polly Peachum stays true to her highwayman, but Lavinia, when she took her lover, chose a member of that class which sanctioned the vicious destruction of those who dared to ape their betters.

# 9

## 𝒯HE 𝒫OLITICS OF 𝒮ATIRE

𝒯he success of *The Beggar's Opera* was in part due to its burlesque on the conventions of the opera, which so fascinated audiences
even as they reacted xenophobically to its perceived corruption of good
old English taste. Polly Peachum and Lucy Lockit were recognised as
parodies of Faustina and Cuzzoni, and the town's enjoyment of Gay's
ridicule attests as much to its attraction to these stars as to its contempt.
London was both compelled and repelled by the intoxicating music and
capricious stars of the opera in the same way as it was both absorbed and
disgusted by the latest scandals at court. The histrionics surrounding the
opera were as appropriate to its melodramatic self-importance as the
highly dramatic form of its expression, and *The Beggar's Opera* is thus
doubly allusory, suggesting the thieves' society is as much a parallel
world to the opera, with its 'vain pretending superstars affecting the air
of gods and heroes whilst inciting their supporters to bursts of partisan
spite',[1] as the court itself.

Yet if the humorous targets of the play might be said to include Italian
opera, it is not sufficient to assume that Gay merely attempted to ridicule
the form, as Dr Johnson subsequently suggested. In adapting the sixty-
nine popular tunes he chose for the piece, Gay and his orchestrator,
Pepusch, the musical director at Lincoln's Inn, used many of the conventional structures of formal operatic performance, such as the variations between arias, choruses and duets. Though Gay had rewritten
the lyrics to suit the progression of his narrative, they had been initially
selected for their well-known and often bawdy words, so that the comic
effect obtained from the tension between the charm of the lyrics and the
corruption of the dramatic circumstances in which they were delivered

was heightened by association, in the audience's mind, with the former, more saucy versions of the songs. Gay simultaneously relied on his audience's experiences as amateurs of the Italian opera to deepen their appreciation of his burlesque.

For Gay himself was a fan, if not a partisan, of the form, along with Dr Arbuthnot and their mutual friend and patron Lord Burlington. Burlington managed to remain neutral in the great Handel-or-Bocconcini dispute, but by the time of *The Beggar's Opera* London's theatrical world was split into two bitterly opposed parties. Lord Burlington had met Handel on his return from his first tour of Italy in 1715, and invited him to move into a suite of apartments at Burlington House. At the time, George I was displeased with his former favourite composer, who had remained in London instead of returning to Hanover as the King wished. Burlington intervened in the quarrel, and Handel was restored to favour. When Burlington returned from his second visit to Italy, he was accompanied by Buononcini (as his name was properly spelled), who immediately became Handel's rival. Despite the two musicians' mutual loathing, Burlington's relationship with the latter remained cordial well into the 1750s, but in 1727, when George II, who was an uncompromising Handel-phile, ascended the throne, his opponents (who included his own son Prince Frederick) became vehement in their support for Buononcini. The King and Queen took this so seriously, according to Lord Hervey, that an 'anti-Handelian' was viewed as an anti-courtier. Gay made reference to both composers in the *Opera*.

Gay's principal patrons, the Duke and Duchess of Queensberry, were important supporters of Bocconcini, though not humourless enough to object to Gay parodying him. Indeed, the Duchess of Queensberry was present at one of the early rehearsals of *The Beggar's Opera* and employed her own knowledge of the opera in persuading Gay to use Pepusch's talent after an unsuccessful trial in which the songs were delivered without music. In addition, given the fact that Gay also collaborated with Handel on several occasions, not least for the *Opera* itself (he used Handel's music for ''Twas When the Seas' and 'Let Us Take the Road'), it seems absurd to assume that interpretations of the play as anti-opera were derived from the aims of the author himself.

Not that this prevented champions of the 'old English' style in which Lavinia Fenton had been trained from suggesting that Gay aimed to

Miss Fenton; engraving from painting by John Ellys. Lavinia's contemporaries disagreed
about her looks, but the critics found her captivating.

The greatest poet of the Augustan age. Alexander Pope with his dog Bounce (*c.* 1718), attributed to Jonathan Richardson. Pope's description of the first night of *The Beggar's Opera* shows vividly how Lavinia turned a near disaster into a triumph.

Alexander Pope's villa at Twickenham, from the river. Here John Gay began work on his *Beggar's Opera*, during a summer idyll which united him with Swift and Pope, together for the last time.

John Rich with his cats. Rich was the most ambitious impresario of his day. As 'Mr Lun' he acted alongside Lavinia in pantomime, and it was rumoured that they were lovers.

OPPOSITE PAGE John Gay (1685-1732), author of *The Beggar's Opera*. Portrayed by his friends as childishly innocent, Gay nevertheless shrewdly profited from the success of his master-piece, though his worldly ambitions were never satisfied (painted by Jonathan Richardson).

*The Beggar's Opera*, scene III, Act XI, painted by William Hogarth (1729). Hogarth painted several versions of this famous picture. Here, by following the line of Lavinia's gaze, her relationship with the Duke (seated right) is clearly shown, although the picture was produced after their elopement.

A variation of one of Polly Peachum's most famous scenes, pleading for the life of her highwayman lover Macheath (also by William Hogarth).

LEFT Old Theatre Royal, Haymarket. RIGHT Ticket for a benefit performance in Covent Garden, engraved by Joseph Sympson 'for the benefit of Mr Walker'. Handsome Tom Walker played Macheath, and, of course, the two co-stars were rumoured to be in love. BELOW *Strolling Actresses Dressing in a Barn* by William Hogarth. The wonderful rackety vivacity of this picture gives a sense of backstage atmosphere. Lincoln's Inn may have been a grand London theatre, but actresses still had to mend their own costumes and provide their own comforts.

LEFT A scene from *The Beggar's Opera* engraved by Thomas Cook (1744–1818). Gay's play was undoubtedly the most successful of the eighteenth century, achieving record runs and box office profits. RIGHT Robert Walpole, 'the English Colossus'. Walpole was the most dominant political figure of the first half of the eighteenth century. His abilities were as extraordinary as his corruption was legend. BELOW *The Idle 'Prentice at Tyburn*, plate XI of *Industry and Idleness*, published in 1833 by Hogarth. For many Londoners, a 'Tyburn holiday' was a great treat, and hangings had a circus atmosphere.

Charles Paulet or Powlett, 3rd Duke of Bolton (1685-1754), painted in his ducal robes by Godfrey Kneller. Bolton was a member of a tiny and immensely powerful elite, and though he had never made much of a figure before succeeding to the title, as a Duke he was protected from his own foolishness all his life by flattery.

Lavinia, with a mask, painted by Allan Ramsay (c. 1739). Above all, Lavinia's was an age of masks. Masquerade balls were a delight and a scandal, and Lavinia's choice of accessory here is audaciously symbolic.

Anne, Duchess of Bolton, also by
Kneller. Bolton was reluctant to marry
Lady Anne Vaughan, whom Horace
Walpole called 'a monster'. The
marriage was never happy, and the
Duke and Duchess led separate lives.

Lavinia Fenton, attributed to John Ellys.
Lavinia had been taught to sing in the
English, rather than the Italian style, and
though she could never compete with
great stars like Faustina and Cuzzoni, her
voice was perfect for *The Beggar's Opera*.

Little Will, the well-known waiter at the Turk's Head coffee house, 142 The Strand, London, where Johnson and Boswell were regulars. Coffee houses played an essential role in politics and the arts in eighteenth century London, bringing discussion into public places.

Button's Coffee House (c. 1730) showing a gathering of the Kit-Kat Club – Pope in the middle. Different coffee houses had different affiliations, but Fenton's in Charing Cross never acquired a distinctive reputation.

Jonathan Swift (1667–1745), painted by Charles Jervas. Swift and Gay discussed the 'odd, pretty' idea of a 'Newgate pastoral' for years, but Swift never saw the play in London. He was a touchingly keen collector of *Beggar's Opera* memorabilia.

'Life is a jest, and all things show it.' Monument to John Gay by John Michael Rysbrack in Westminster Abbey triforium, after it was removed from its original position in the 1930s. Gay's funeral was a splendid occasion, and 'Polly Peachum' was rumoured to have attended.

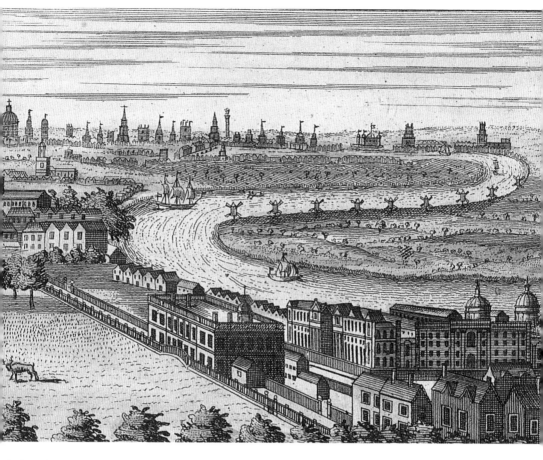

A view of Greenwich from Flamstead Hill (*c.* 1750). Lavinia spent much of her life at Greenwich, peacefully removed from her London origins. Her house at Westcombe was much praised for the beauty of its location.

Lavinia, Duchess of Bolton (c.1740), looking matronly, painted by Hogarth. Horace Walpole said of her shortly before her death, 'after a life of merit, she relapsed into her Pollyhood'.

Lavinia's last resting-place – St Alphege's Church, Greenwich – but no plaque marks the exact spot today. Lavinia chose to be buried here, in a new church which has something of the appearance of a theatre. Her coffin was placed in an underground vault.

rout the foreigners from their eminence, and from using Lavinia when it suited them as a symbol of fresh English beauty and virtue to rival the exaggerated posturings and easy morals of her foreign colleagues. The *Craftsman* of April 1728 proclaimed:

> Of all the belles that tread the stage,
> There's none like pretty Polly,
> And all the music of the age,
> Except her voice, is folly.
> Compared with her, how flat appears,
> Cuzzoni or Faustina?
> And when she sings, I shut my ears
> To warbling Senesino.

Similarly, an early review of *The Beggar's Opera* in the *Daily Journal* of 1 February 1728 noted that 'On Monday was represented for the First Time ... Mr Gay's new ENGLISH Opera, written in a manner wholly new, and very entertaining, there being introduced INSTEAD of ITALIAN AIRS, above 60 of the most celebrated OLD ENGLISH and SCOTCH tunes. There was present then, as well as last night, a prodigious Concourse of Nobility and Gentry, and NO Theatrical Performance for these many years has met with so much Applause.'

If some elements of Gay's satire were indeed directed at the Italian opera, Lavinia was also playing a part in the most politically controversial play of the times. *The Beggar's Opera* had, almost from the opening night, acquired a reputation as a satire on Walpole's administration, though the extent to which Gay intended this response is uncertain. Certainly he had reason, both politically and personally, to dislike the new Whig government. After the death of George I in 1727, during the charmed summer when Gay, Pope and Swift had worked together at Twickenham, the latter and his fellow influential political writers were determined to make an attack on Walpole's power; 'a firm settled resolution to assault the present administration and break it if possible', as Swift wrote to Sheridan.[2] Swift and his cohorts, it must be emphasised, were not marginalised malcontents but significant figures, particularly Swift himself who, after the publication of *The Drapier's Letters* (an attack on the privatisation of Irish coinage which had taken place in the early 1720s), was seen as an eminent asset to the opposition. Swift had even dined with Walpole in 1725 with the aim of alerting the Prime Minister to the true state of affairs in Ireland, an object in which he self-confessedly failed. Yet Gay's own attitude was initially more ambiguous.

Although his literary career in 1727 was moderately successful, and his literary friendships extremely impressive, Gay's financial situation was precarious. While Swift may have been determined to 'break' the administration, neither he nor Gay apparently saw much contradiction between this intention and Gay's own desire to improve his position by obtaining a comfortable court sinecure. To this end, Gay set about scheming with his friend Mrs Howard, who most conveniently happened to be the new King's mistress. As Gay's Tory friends became increasingly alarmed by the measures Walpole was taking to suppress opposition in the guise of protecting the country from the Jacobites, they certainly deplored and privately rather despised the fact that Gay might be content to fritter away his time and talent in the drawing rooms of a King they distrusted, though not to the extent that this caused a breach.

With the accession of George II it seemed to Gay that his long-cherished hopes of court preferment might finally come to fruition, and he was rather unappealingly determined to make the best use he could of a government that was harassing some of his most respected fellow writers.

The popularity of Gay's *Fables* had, he felt, done much to improve his position at court. The moral of these pretty animal stories emphasises the importance of resisting flattery and avoiding cruelty, neither of which maxims seem to have had a lasting effect on the little Duke of Cumberland, to whom they were dedicated (though the lines 'the bones that whiten all the land' in Fable I and 'the butcher trained' in IX may have had some influence on the adult victor of Culloden), but they might be said to apply to their author, who famously characterised himself as the hare.

> A Hare, who in a civil way,
> Comply'd with everything, like Gay
> Was known by all the bestial train,

Who haunt the wood, or graze the plain:
Her care was, never to offend,
And evr'y creature was her friend.


Perhaps because of this naïve self-image, it was not only disappointing but bitterly humiliating for Gay when he discovered that the post he had so assiduously courted was to be that of attendant to a two-year-old child, the Princess Louisa. As gentleman usher to the little princess, he would receive £150 a year. It seemed almost a calculated insult, and one indicative of the attitude towards literature of 'Dunce the Second'. Gay wrote glumly to Pope: 'My melancholy increases, and every hour threatens me with some return of my distemper . . . O! that I had never known what a court was! Dear Pope, what a barren soil (to me so) have I been striving to produce something out of . . . I find myself in such a strange confusion and depression of spirits that I have not strength even to make my will.'[3] This reaction might seem melodramatic, even after such a blow, but Gay's health had never been strong and he was subject to bouts of melancholy. It seems significant that it was in this letter that he gave his dear friend the instructions for what would be his notoriously irreverent epitaph.

Gay's friends attempted to console him. Pope observed that only fashionable fools would sneer, or perceive the appointment as a failure; his real friends would like him the better. 'You will enjoy that, and your own integrity, and the satisfactory consciousness of having not merited such graces from them as they bestow only on the mean, flattering, interested and undeserving.'[4] That Gay had been quite prepared to become such a servile flatterer, had the position been more prestigious and remunerative, was kindly glossed over. In his 1731 poem 'To Mr Gay', Swift made a similar point:


Say, had the court no better place to choose
For thee, than make a dry nurse of thy muse?
How cheaply had thy liberty been sold,
To squire a royal girl of two years old!
In leading strings her infant steps to guide,
And with her go-cart amble side by side.

111

Gay decided that since he wasn't in a position to sell his liberty dear, he might as well have his integrity (especially as no one else seemed terribly interested in buying that, either), and refused the position, explaining to Queen Caroline that he felt he was too old to do the job well. It is possible that this was the beginning of a real animus against Walpole, since Swift had convinced his friend that it was the fat fraudster who had crushed Gay's hopes by maligning him to the Queen in revenge for a libel against himself of which he believed Gay to be the author. Since Gay was the author, it does not seem altogether unreasonable for Walpole to have reacted in this way, but given the viciously satirical relationship that obtained between writers and government, it seemed unsporting to single out Gay in particular for disapproval. (Walpole might well have enjoyed an exceptional degree of personal power, but he was equally subject to extremes of personal abuse which were astonishingly crude. Both he and the King were frequently caricatured with their buttocks exposed, farting and shitting. Casting him as a thief was a relatively mild insult: the 'Norfolk dumpling' was also compared respectively to Nero, the homosexual favourites of King James I, Henry VIII and Cardinal Wolsey, French bishops, Chinese tyrants, Bunyan's Mr Badman, the Devil himself, a child murderer, dancing master, bootlicker, serpent and the perverter of the Magna Carta.) Nevertheless, it seemed to Gay that orthodox aspirations of worldly advancement must now be abandoned. 'So now,' he wrote, 'all my expectations are vanished; and I have no prospect but depending entirely on myself and my own conduct.'

While it might therefore seem that John Gay had a motive for a piece of literary spite, *The Beggar's Opera* was not designed to be a specific satire on Walpole. If Swift's suggestions about Walpole's role in the usher fiasco are true, Gay may have felt that he had no further need to censor himself, since he had nothing more to hope for from the restraint of his wit. It is pleasing to see his worldly disappointment as an artistic liberation, but as ever with a member of the Scriblerian circle, neat explanations are dubious. The idea for the 'Newgate pastoral' had been present in his imagination for some eleven years, and his decision to chase it into performance may have been as much commercial as poetic. Mrs Howard wrote to him: 'Your head is your best friend; it would clothe, lodge and wash you; but you neglect it, and follow that false friend, your heart, which is such a foolish tender thing that it makes others depise your head that have not half so good a one on their own shoulders.'[5] In fact, though it pleased Gay's friends to characterise him as a child when it came to practical or financial matters, he was far more shrewd than they gave him credit for, and the lack of direct anti-Walpole satire in *The Beggar's Opera* may be an indication that he was not, as yet, prepared to sail too close to the wind. Gay did caricature Walpole quite precisely, as Sir Headstrong Bustle in his posthumously published play *The Rehearsal at Goatham*, but Bob Booty, the character in the *Opera* who is often assumed to represent Walpole, has a very minor role indeed, and his name might owe as much to its pleasing alliteration than to any abbreviation of 'Robert'. Gay may have intended his connection between court and criminal corruption to be general rather than specific, as he wrote to Mrs Howard as early as 1723, before his hopes of preference died, 'I cannot indeed wonder that the talents requisite for a great statesman are so scarce in the world, since so many of those who possess them are every month cut off in the prime of their age at the Old Bailey.'

The Scriblerians were as passionately concerned with what they perceived to be the decline of language as with its manifestation in the corruption of modern mores, and *The Beggar's Opera* also engages in an aesthetic debate that was essential to the Scriblerian ethos, though far less obvious to audiences. Pope and Swift particularly were outstanding classical scholars, concerned with the manner in which the poetry they revered could be manipulated through a modern idiom while retaining its 'purity'. In 1709, the publisher Tonson brought out a *Miscellany* that featured the work of Ambrose Philips, a poet whose personal interpretation of the pastoral form relied, unlike Pope's (admittedly contentiously outdated) idealised Arcadianism, on a rather twee presentation of rustic sentimentality. Philips' poems had been much praised, and Pope, ever standing on his four-foot-something of dignity, felt himself slighted. He responded with a piece in the *Guardian* full of sarcastic compliments to Philips, but seriously posing the question, as his biographer phrases it, 'How far can unmitigated reality or nature be made compatible with the significant forms sought by art?'[6] Gay proposed a comic answer to this question in his *Shepherd's Week*, published in 1714, observing in the 'Proeme': 'The Language of my

Shepherds; which is, soothly to say, such as is neither spoken by the country maiden nor the courtly Dame … it having too much of the Country to be fit for the Court, too much of the Court to be fit for the Country, too much Language of old Times to be fit for the Present, too much of the Present to have been fit for the Old, and too much of both to be fit for any Time to come.'

Thus *The Beggar's Opera* is also concerned with the 'authentic' manipulation of language. The pastoral ideal is subverted by the Newgate setting, but the realism of the language is also an investigation of the possibilities of modern idiom played off against a satire of a classical genre.

Since the Civil War and the forced abdication of James II, Tory poets like Gay and Pope had been at a loss as to how to translate their faith in the heroic tradition into modern works. The nobility of classical ideals, or at least of the ideals their scholarship was determined to draw from the classics, was as symbolically defunct as the divine right of kings. The use of the mock-epic or mock-pastoral therefore represents a certain worldly cynicism, the denial of the potential for heroism in modern times. *The Beggar's Opera* makes (anti)-heroes of thieves and whores, whose parodying of the manner of the aristocracy also reflects the new power of the commercial classes, since the thieves, like the aristocrats in real life, depend for their livelihood on the power of the 'bourgeois', as represented in the play by Peachum and in politics by the Whig administration. Thus the play must be seen as a general commentary on changing times rather than a pointed political allegory, and indeed, it could not have supported its popular longevity were its action entirely dependent upon a knowledge of the details of Walpole's personal power.

Nevertheless, *The Beggar's Opera* soon became a rallying point for the ideas of the anti-Walpole opposition. The *Craftsman* was quick to qualify the piece as 'the most venomous allegorical libel against the government that hath appeared for many years past'. The scene featuring the song 'When You Censure the Age', where Polly's father and Lockit, the Newgate gaoler, settle their accounts, was viewed by Charles Macklin[7] in his memoirs, as a direct reference to Walpole. Macklin quotes the story of William Cooke, who claims the scene was intended as a caricature since it had, in the presence of the minister himself, 'such an effect on the audience that, as if by instinct, the greater part of them threw their eyes on the stage box where the minister was sitting, and loudly encored it. Sir Robert saw this stroke instantly, and saw it with ... discretion, for no sooner was the song finished than he encored it a second time himself, and by this means brought the audience into so much good humour with him that they gave him a general huzza from all parts of the house.' (Walpole's typically quick face-saving response might have had its origins in the reception of Addison's *Cato*, whose rehearsal had so disappointed Dr Swift fifteen years previously. Inspired by Plato's treatise on immortality, Addison's pompous heroic tragedy has Cato the philosopher committing suicide as a symbolic martyr to freedom in opposition to the tyranny represented by Caesar. In 1713, the Whigs, who at the time were in opposition, were keen to interpret the piece as a reference to the Treaty of Utrecht, which they saw as a betrayal of the nation and of democracy, twelve peers having been specially created to force the bill through. The Tories were too clever to openly disapprove of a play which made their own corruption obvious and instead made a point of cheering every speech in favour of liberty as though this were a peculiarly Tory virtue.) Macklin assumed that the audience's association of Walpole with the accounts scene was due to his very public quarrel with his brother-in-law and fellow politician Lord Townshend. During the scene, Peachum and Lockit address one another as 'brother' ten times, and when they argue they seize one another by the throat, which subsequent critics read as a reference to a real-life incident between Walpole and Townshend. Yet this celebrated dispute did not actually take place until 1729. The origin of the Cooke story as quoted by Macklin seems to have been a letter written by Swift, who refers to 'the two great ministers in a box together and all the world staring at them', one of whom said to the other, apropos the scene, 'That was levelled at me.' Yet, like so many of the stories associated with *The Beggar's Opera*, there is no sound reason to suppose that this ever happened.

Walpole may have seethed in private, but his well-timed applause was his only official reaction to the *Opera*. It was left to the moralists to denounce the play, and they did so in great numbers and with great gusto. Gay's old enemy John Dennis called it a 'low and licentious piece, designed for the encouragement of gentlemen of the highway and their female associates in Drury Lane'.[8] Dr Thomas Herring, the King's chaplain and later Archbishop of Canterbury, took the trouble of giving a sermon in Lincoln's Inn chapel which denounced the piece as an endorsement of crime, much to the delight of its author. 'I have had the honour,' wrote Gay to Swift, 'to have had a sermon preached against my works by a court chaplain, which I look upon as no small addition to my fame.' Swift himself was inclined to a cautious political reading of the *Opera*, writing in the *Intelligencer* of May 1728 that 'without enquiring whether it [the play] affects the present age, it may possibly be useful in times to come. I mean, where the author takes the occasion of comparing the common robbers of the public, and their several stratagems of betraying, undermining and hanging each other, to the several arts of politicians in times of corruption.'

It was not until December, long after Lavinia Fenton had left the theatre, that the *Craftsman* drew a direct analogy between Macheath and the Prime Minister.

> If Macheath you should name in the midst of his gang
> They'll say 'tis an hint you would somebody hang,
> For Macheath is a word of such evil report,
> Application cries out 'That's a Bob for the c(our)t.'

The precise degree of anti-Walpole references, the nuances of Gay's attack on his society's corruption, may have been fascinating to the court wits and their opponents, but most of the spectators at Lincoln's Inn attended purely for the pleasure of the comedy, the music and, of course, Lavinia. However complex subsequent interpretations of *The Beggar's Opera* became, its popularity depended upon enjoyment rather than analysis, and Lavinia's fame was far more a consequence of her personal charm than of her status as a representative of a lost political joke.

# 10

# AN EXCUSABLE PROSTITUTION

Those who had Walpole's money in their pockets were obliged to clap for shame, and those who had not applauded from envy. Either way, it was true that anyone who was anyone in town felt it imperative to be seen at a performance of *The Beggar's Opera*. John Rich frequently had to make apologies to aristocratic patrons, including the Countess of Oxford, who were unable to get a seat. The Duke of Bolton, according to legend, had no such difficulty, since it was reported that he assiduously presented himself at all sixty-two of Lavinia Fenton's appearances as Polly. Like so much else connected with Lavinia, though, this was an exaggeration, and it is likely that even for a duke, a ticket was hard to come by. On 22 February 1728, the royal family attended a command performance, occupying twenty-eight box seats with an extra one for a yeoman of the guard in the pit; the Duke, however, did not attend until 8 April. Clearly captivated, he returned on the next two nights, and again on 13 April, but when he reappeared once more a month later it was in the surprising company of his estranged Duchess.

If the Portuguese gentleman ever had existed, it was as well for Lavinia at this juncture that he remained rather flimsy. Unlike her faithful counterpart Polly, ready to give all for love, Lavinia had a very profitable proposal to think over. His Grace the Duke of Bolton's offer to his Polly was rather more generous than that of the Feathered Gull with whom Lavinia's mother had proposed she begin her career. Twice as generous, to be precise. Four hundred a year to be settled on her at His Grace's pleasure, and £200 remaining in the case of His Grace ever being displeased: as much for incurring his displeasure as the old gull had offered in total for delight.

### ACCOUNTS AND AFFECTIONS

Whatever the town's opinion as to the state of one's morals, the offer from the Duke of Bolton seems worthy of serious consideration. What is to be gained by it, and what lost? At night, after the play, you scratch out your accounts by candlelight (admittedly wax candlelight these days), attempting to balance future security with present success. You have set your price high, but not too high, after all. Either the Duke disbelieves the town, which claims he could have you for much less, or he is so determined to have you for his own that he will pay anything for the privilege of meeting your dressmaker's bills. Perhaps £600 and £400 for displeasure would have been possible, but £200 is what you shall have as a minimum in the event of your failing to please indefinitely. It is less than you have earned this season, but who knows how long this success will last? One year? Two? You know that you are not strong enough; that in the end, the town will be proved right after all, and that though you may not be a greater whore, indeed, you will certainly be an older and cheaper one.

Four hundred for pleasure, then, but what are His Grace's tastes? What does he know of you, and how, from this presumed knowledge, will he proceed? A quiet supper in a temporary lodging, few candles so as to soften the cheap hastiness of the arrangements, silver dishes brought to dazzle you from the London house, and the door to the adjacent bedchamber propped suggestively ajar? Or something more theatrical, designed to appeal to the artistic temperament? Will Bolton creak to his ducal knees and recite a few rehearsed bits of sonnet (sweet that, to imagine him getting his lines), a willing fool for love? Or maybe a brusque approach, *à l'anglais*, shift up, breeches unfastened, view halloo and straight to the chase? Does boldness make him hotter, or coyness, a feigned Pollyish reluctance? Does His jaded Lordship require correction to illuminate his amorous fire, or are his likings even more recherché? Or perhaps not that, not that at all. There are a hundred, a thousand willing girls in Covent Garden to accommodate his tastes, however oddly inclined. He wishes, you think, to own, to possess, to have for his own the magic that stills the house, night after night, from gallery to pit, to keep whatever holds the people there, and you try to find it in you: your voice perhaps, the angle of your jaw as you twist your neck in supplication, the bronze of your hair by limelight, the pulse of your bosom as you plead. What is it in you that he wants so badly? Which Lavinia does he need, and how are you to know how to give her to him?

You have ascertained, from the scrawl of his letters, that the Duke is not a cultivated man. Not quick and easy like Mr Gay, whose pantomime-Hodge looks, all rotund belly and snub nose, belie his sharp wit, or brittle, waspish Mr Pope, so correct in his pitiful laboured attempts at flirtation, so alien both of them when they skip into other tongues and laugh together in a language you will never understand. The Duke is more simple. He wants, and he is not used to wanting. He is a man used to getting.

At the pinnacle of her fame, Lavinia Fenton was so besieged by admirers as she left Lincoln's Inn each night that a group of young men formed a bodyguard to see her safely home. This might have seemed a romantically excessive bit of gallantry, but as the famous story of Captain Hill and Mrs Bracegirdle shows, Lavinia may have had good reason to be grateful for such solicitousness.

Whatever the town may have said about her – and her morals were as maligned as Lavinia's were to be – Anne Bracegirdle had been not only a successful actress but a remarkably chaste one. So chaste, in fact, that the attentions of a young officer, Captain Hill, who wished to make her his mistress, were refused with a firmness that drove the boy to distraction. In 1692, Mrs Bracegirdle had been returning from a supper party with friends and family when she was set upon by a band of soldiers, who attempted to manhandle her into a waiting coach. The scheme had been dreamed up by Hill and his equally young friend Lord Mohun, who had engaged a coachman to drive the kidnapped actress to Barnet, where Hill hoped that a week of forced country retirement would suffice to convince the lady of his charms. Her prospective seducer used soldiers from his own company to set upon the beautiful Bracegirdle and her companions, isolate the lady and deliver her into his hands. Despite the fact that the two boys had made a great performance of their plan, appearing at the theatre that afternoon and giving a cloak-and-dagger display of changing their coats, and despite the fact that their assistants, with the unusual exception of the coachman,

William Dixon, were drunk, it appeared for a moment that the abduction would succeed. As Mrs Bracegirdle left her friends' house in Drury Lane, the soldiers pushed her host and brother aside and shoved the lady, who was screaming for help, towards the carriage. Hill and Lord Mohun, liberally adorned with pistols, were waiting inside. Luckily, the actress's mother, who was also present, had had a lifetime's experience of backstage admirers, and the vigorous old lady elbowed the soldiers out of the way, threw her arms about her daughter's waist and clung on grimly, determined that Hill should not escape with Anne. Old Mrs Bracegirdle set up such a racket that Hill ordered the coach away and the two women were able to escape to their lodgings. Hill and Mohun, incensed by the failure of the scheme, did not, however, return home, but instead made their way to the house of the actor William Mountford, whom Hill was certain was his successful rival and the barrier to Anne's affections. At about midnight, poor innocent Mr Mountford was stabbed through the heart with Hill's sword and died the following day.

It is unlikely that His Grace will press his suit quite as violently as Captain Hill, but Lavinia uses her unofficial protectors to keep her admirer at a distance, for a while at least. She needs time to reflect, and she has no intention of allowing too easy a winning to make her a light prize. It will do him no harm to wait a little. Luckily for Mr Hogarth, who stands to make a fair profit from the theatrical sensation of the season, she makes Bolton wait long enough for the pugilistic little portraitist to sketch him.

The scene in which the Duke's enchantment with Lavinia begins is the same one that has so captivated the restive audience at the *Opera's* first night. John Rich chooses to commemorate this essential point in his theatre's fortunes by commissioning Hogarth's first version of his *Beggar's Opera* painting in 1728 and a second the following year. Lavinia is on her knees, handkerchief fluttering, her hand clutching pathetically at the coat of Mr Hippisley, playing Peachum, while Mr Hall, as Lockit, Mrs Egleton, as Lucy, and Tom Walker look on. In total, Hogarth makes five versions of this crucial scene, and Lavinia's relationship with the Duke is reflected in the development of his pictures. In three of them (one of which will be said to have been bought rather disloyally by Horace Walpole for his home at Strawberry Hill), Lavinia's eyes are directed at her stage lover, Macheath, and the Newgate set on which she kneels is small and uncarpeted. Only the actors are portraits, the first-night audience being represented by more or less good-natured caricatures. Yet in the remaining two, painted in a looser 'Venetian' style, the space is more expansive, the floor covered and the audience themselves have become recognisable individuals, while Lavinia's eyes yearn upwards towards Bolton himself, who is seated downstage to the right. In the box with the Duke are Major Paunceford and Sir Robert Fagg, Mr Rich, talking to Mr Cook the auctioneer, and Mr Gay. Stage left is a satyr, sculptures of which were a distinctive part of the décor at Lincoln's Inn, but which is an appropriate feature to highlight in the context of the other characters in the picture.

The dull, slightly hazy background of Hogarth's Newgate is undoubtedly more finely rendered than the moveable scenery John Rich had had painted for the real *Opera*, but true to the unique, shadowy, flickering light by which the Duke first sees his Polly. The apron of the stage is lit by 'floats', troughs full of candles from whose guttering, yellowish light Lavinia, in her pale silk sack, gleams ethereally, Hogarth's high relief on her delicate, smooth complexion contrasting with the roughness of her surroundings in an ironic suggestion of vulnerable purity. Lavinia's pose may vary slightly between the paintings, but she is always their focal point, a centre of brightness that seems curiously still, despite the urgency of the moment. In the painting, Hogarth elaborates on Gay's satire with a mocking gesture which reflects those of *The Beggar's Opera* but is also entirely personal. At first glance, the arrangement of the figures seems classical, their postures unusually conventional for Hogarth's style. This 'pastoral' composition is immediately disturbed by the unlikely juxtaposition of the subjects with their environment. Just as Gay creates a correlation between the values of the 'quality' and of the Newgate lowlife in the similarity of the language they employ, as when Polly and Lucy quarrel over Macheath in the vernacular of the tea-party rather than that of the gutter, so Hogarth plays with the visual similarity of a thief got up as a gentleman, while the real gentlemen, the aristocrats who so inconveniently infest the stage, are practically indistinguishable by their appearance from the thieves. When Polly looks out to the Duke in version V, Hogarth himself must have seen, even if Bolton did not, that his image was a realisation of Gay's essential point about the relationship between thieves and gentlemen, illustrating one of the central themes of *The Beggar's Opera* by 'placing the criminals next to the equally culpable aristocrats who are watching them and urging them on'.[1] The spectators who swarm over the stage in the earlier versions are less kindly rendered than the members of the audience: 'their faces are distorted into caricatures of exploiters and degenerates', to the point where the painting manifests visually what the play implies – that there is little to choose between a gentleman of the road and one of the court.

So there is the Duke on the stage for ever, in Hogarth's hand, gazing at Miss Fenton. Does Lavinia find her hopeful lover an attractive man? Horace Walpole describes him as 'an old beau, fair complexioned, in a white wig, gallanting the ladies about in public'.[2] Lady Stuart will be rather kinder, calling him a 'handsome, agreeable libertine',[3] but at forty-three, the Duke is surely past his prime. Specious Portuguese aristocrats aside, though, Lavinia has never made much of physical beauty. She has resisted the charms of handsome Tom Walker, after all, whatever the town might say.

As to his character, there is even less to inspire here than in his looks. Though he has never kept a regular mistress, the Duke of Bolton's whoring is as well known as his drinking, and though there is nothing in that to set him apart from other members of his class, he does not, it seems, command the same respect in public as his fellow peers, however much they gamble and drink and whore in private. The 'Royal Register' is precise about his lack of accomplishments: 'No man was ever more indebted to rank and title than this nobleman, for no man stood more in need of the consequence which is derived from them. Weak and whimsical, but persuaded, like many good mistaken people of the same kind, that he possessed the opposite qualities, he naturally became no infrequent subject of mirth, raillery and cajolement.' In other words, people flattered him, sponged off him and laughed at him. However, snobbery won out when he inherited the title on his father's death: 'The moment which brought his dignity along with it, silenced the laughter and changed the arch look of ridicule into the submissive gravity of respect. The ducal coronet, by its magic power, exalted frivolity and weakness into stability and good sense, and the crowd who used to indulge their humour at the expense of Lord P. think themselves favoured by the society and court the protection of the Duke of B.' He may be as great a booby as his father before him, but rank can supply any number of deficiencies. The best that is said of him is that he is amiable and good-natured, gentle like Mr Fenton, perhaps, and fond of his comforts.

Was it Lavinia's hesitation that prompted the Duke to take the uncharacteristic step of attending a performance of the *Beggar's Opera* with his wife in April? If so, it seemed not to have had the effect of a threat, for Lavinia took almost three months to decide. Supposedly, she had once hidden herself away for hours in her parents' lodgings in the Old Bailey, uncertain as to whether to step into the coach sent by the Portuguese nobleman and change her life for ever, but now her decision, once taken, is brisk and practical. No more cheap lodgings for her. A duke is a duke, after all, thinks Lavinia Fenton, and makes up her mind.

The Duke of Bolton was not Lavinia's only aristocratic admirer. Among 'several Noblemen who have distinguish'd themselves both in the Field and the Court' who declared themselves to be Polly's 'humble servants' was one whose title was 'no less than an Earl'.[4] Bolton, however, offered a settlement in writing, and whether it was this assurance of security or whether his attractions, however limited, surpassed those of the earl, Lavinia wrote to him accepting his proposal on 18 June 1728. The very next evening, she took her last bow as Polly Peachum, and walked off quietly, through the applause, into her new life.

Surprisingly, there had been no gossip about the relationship between the Duke and the town's most famous actress, no sly pamphlets or insinuations in the newspapers. It was only after the connection became public that Hogarth included the portrait of Bolton in his *Beggar's Opera* series, which suggests that even among the tight circle surrounding the production, nobody knew of Lavinia's intentions. (One subsequent 'life'[5] did mention Bolton as a man tired of marriage who gave Lavinia £60 for a night with her, which would indicate that even when the story did get out, the details were confused.) A few weeks after Lavinia's departure, in early July, Gay wrote rather laconically to Swift that 'the d— of — I hear hath run away with Polly Peachum'. He was, however, aware of the precise terms of the settlement, which leads one to believe that the topic had been much discussed. As the season was ending, and most of the 'quality' departing for their country estates, it was relatively easy to keep the matter quiet. Lavinia now had lodgings in Old Bond Street, where Bolton visited her, and shortly after her sixty-second performance, the old satyr of the pit and his Newgate nymph retired to the country.

It was quite possible, when Lavinia eventually did elope with a lover, that she was still a virgin. If she had been too careful to fall into the hands of any of the Drury Lane mediocrities, and the libels on her virtue were no more than libels, then there is no proof that she had any other relationship with a man before the Duke. If so, was the experience of lovemaking for the first time traumatic? A later poem describes a young woman's first taste of vice thus:

> From that dire moment Hell and Honour rise:
> Peace from her violated mansion flies.
> Hourly with Sighs the troubled Bosom heaves;
> Which Hope, Life's latest Consolation leaves.
> Succeeds, in chearful Innocence's Room,
> An everlasting, a remorseless Gloom.[6]

Even if Lavinia had pragmatically avoided sex, and thus the risk of venereal disease and pregnancy, she was far too sensible for such nonsense. She had other mansions in mind. It was hinted later, though, that the Duke, having first acquired Lavinia out of a passion motivated by vanity, was led to keep her by a surprising discovery of the state of her virtue. If this was the case, he must have been delighted with his famous bargain.

# 11

# $\mathcal{V}$ALLEYS OF $\mathcal{P}$LEASURE

Before that old fraud Wordsworth got his hands on her, Nature was not a member of polite society. The end of the eighteenth century would see a boom in sentimental journeys, with ladies and gentlemen who had previously viewed majestic landscapes as uncomfortable and inconvenient barriers between country house parties suddenly rattling all over them in their coaches, anxious to demonstrate the poetry of their souls by swooning over the nearest lake or mountain to hand. What one disgruntled visitor to Chatsworth described as a 'waste and howling wilderness'[1] will become the last word in fashionable back-drops. 'Capability' Brown had pioneered a passion for naturalising the geography of country estates, even if the perfectly natural inhabitants of them had to have their cottages knocked down so as not to interfere with the squire's contemplation of his chestnut trees. Hodge the farm-hand was tidied away beyond the wall of the estate, and characters like Jane Austen's vacuous Mr Rushworth could study Nature's sublimity unimpeded. Vanbrugh swamped the village of Hilderskelfe to improve the grounds of Castle Howard, Viscount Cobham shifted an incon-venient village and, in Norfolk, Thomas Coke removed the settlement adjacent to his great house at Holkham, though he remarked rather mournfully afterwards: 'It is a melancholy thing to stand alone in one's own country. I look around, not a house to be seen but for my own. I am Giant, of Giant's Castle, and have ate up all my neighbours.'[2] Fashion was ruthless, though; wild grandeur was the mode, and Nature was no longer geometrically partitioned, sliced into the formal parterres and ordered gardens made fashionable by Louis XIV's gardener Le Notre in the seventeenth century. She had ceased to be a troublesome intruder upon civilisation, to be disciplined where she could not be ignored, and had become an exciting stranger whose uninhibited beauty might be allowed to encroach upon the very walls of the drawing room.

Since Lavinia Fenton is unaware that her attitude to landscape will be desperately unfashionable in fifty years' time, she feels no need to pretend to herself that Yorkshire is anything other than very wet, very cold and really rather unpleasant. Her experience of blasted heaths has thus far been limited to Mr Quin's *Lear*, and there is something curiously oppressive, she thinks, about such a very great deal of sky. Like most native Londoners, Lavinia has hardly ever left the confines of the city. A Sunday outing to Hampstead, the wells at Islington or Marylebone, or a trip down the river to the cool heights of Greenwich, are the boundaries of most of her townsmen's universe.

Banked in behind the green lump of Wensleydale, Bolton Hall sits in a hollow with the village over its left shoulder, and the remains of Bolton Castle, the original seat of the Scrope family, looming gothically over its right. In the East Meadow, the grooms walk the horses gingerly through the claggy mud of the Duke's racecourse, wary that a stubborn slurp of bog might sprain a precious thoroughbred leg. From the drawing-room window, the corner of her vision glancing over the damp grey-green stone of the staircase to the door, Lavinia can see across the straight lawn and its low wall, the plain, flat fields dipping over the ha-ha to the bridge over the River Ure, and then along up the avenue, a mile and a half, to the fat little tower built by the second Duke for his nocturnal wickednesses. Beyond that, the woods, and the heaping of the land up to the freezing plateau of the moor.

Lavinia has seen a map of her lover's northern estate, made by Will Godson in 1724, a huge wonderful thing that it takes two men to unroll, bright with jewel-like ink and populated like a Chinese tea service with tiny, busy figures ploughing and herding, perfect down to the minuscule hoes in their hands. Every great tree is marked, and the well and the ditches, there are sheep and horses in the fields and implausible fruit abounds in the neat orchard. Mr Godson's map makes the landscape alive, as purposeful and occupied as Charing Cross, but Lavinia wonders how she fits into it. Would she feature like a porcelain doll in this miniature world, a stiff figure in her London fashions, stumping up and down the avenue to the tower at Capple Bank that the future will name, perhaps gratifyingly but certainly erroneously, Polly Peachum's Folly? The name comes about, the village unkindly suggests, because His Grace is tired to death of the warblings of his London opera singer and banishes her and her scales to the tower so that he can have some peace. Unkind because no one in Yorkshire has heard Lavinia sing, or knows or believes that her voice was good enough for the most fashionable crowds in London; unkind because even were she to burst into an Italian aria as she plods up and down the avenue to Capple Bank, in imitation of Signora Cuzzoni, nobody would understand what she sings any more than if she were speaking Chinese, or even plain English.

The north of England is, to Lavinia, another country. In 1761, George Colman writes: 'It is scarce half a century ago, since the inhabitants of the distant counties were regarded as a species, almost as different as those of the metropolis, as the natives of the Cape of Good Hope. Their manners, as well as dialect, were entirely provincial; and their dress no more resembling the habit of the Town than the Turkish or Chinese.'[3] It is difficult, in fact, for anyone in Yorkshire to understand a word Lavinia says. Her tight southern vowels are too quick, too clipped, for the slow, thick rhythms of speech in this place, so that every time she opens her mouth, to speak to a servant or to say good morning, incomprehension and stifled mockery remind her of just how far she is from home. She makes Charles laugh, in the evenings, by mimicking the heavy local accent, so broad it might as well be a foreign tongue, but in the long afternoons, when His Grace is occupied with business (conducted mostly on horseback, or in the fields with his gun), there is a deal too much silence in Yorkshire. It makes Lavinia stupid, as she sits, inert, by the fire, with no lines to get, no rush for a chair to the theatre, no callers to put off or entertain, no pamphlets, however unpleasant, to remind her that she exists by showing her Polly's latest exploits in smudgy ink. The silence is damp and creeping, enveloping her in the chilly mist of suppressed resentment which, she realises, will be the air she has to learn to breathe. It is painfully clear that she will never belong here.

Lavinia knows how to behave like a lady; after all, she has imitated them long enough. The Reverend Joseph Warton will say of her, 'She was very accomplished, was a most agreeable companion, had much wit and strong sense and a chaste taste in polite literature. Her person was agreeable and well made, though she could not be called a beauty. I have had the pleasure of being at table with her, when her conversation was much admired by the first characters of the age, particularly old Lord Bathurst and Lord Granville.'[4] Since Lavinia has at present not been introduced to these gentlemen, there is no one at Bolton Hall to admire her accomplishments except the Duke, who is currently less concerned with her choice of reading than with the less virtuous charms of her person. (Perhaps Lavinia will read *Pamela* in 1734, and smile that she has made such a superior bargain for her own virtue than its heroine, who does no better than a country squire.)

What alarms Lavinia is the sheer quantity of leisure the Duke has bestowed upon her. London ladies, so far as she knows, take tea and pay calls, attend the theatre and the opera and the drawing room, visit their dressmakers and their milliners and the shops along the Strand, bustle from their chairs to concert halls and assembly rooms, pile their coaches with parcels, gossip, take lovers, read the latest scandals, dine, quarrel, attend their dancing masters and their hairdressers and are busy enough living without even the trouble of having to earn one. Being a lady is work of a sort, but in Yorkshire there are no shops to speak of, nor concerts, nor plays. No one calls on Lavinia as, being the kept woman of an adulterer, however grand, means she is no more fit for company than a sixpenny whore from Seven Dials. Lord Bathurst may well come to like her, but he will never introduce her to his wife. Reverend Warton will kindly emphasise the virtue of her taste in reading matter, but she will never exchange novels from the circulating library with the rector's daughters. Lavinia knows that the world will stand upon its dignity on this point, even if she lives twenty years with the Duke. 'Honour, especially in women, can admit of no compromise with dishonour, no approaches from one to the other must be suffered; the boundary between them must be considered impassable; the line by which they are divided is the Rubicon of female virtue.'[5]

So Lavinia has no visits to pay, or letters to write; no parties to arrange, nothing to do but dress and eat and walk and eat again and dress again and wait for her lover to attend her to supper. The cold creeps into her, dulling her blood; the rain falls on the avenue, the hours crawl by.

## MISTRESS PEACHUM'S PLEASURE

Nothing breeds discontent so quickly as contentment. Even dressing has been a swift and independent business – gowns slipped on quickly in the half-dark, laces snatched professionally between your teeth, garters snapped, shoes slipped on with an ear for your cue, and then back out to the stage – but now there is a quiet woman to lace you and hand you your handkerchief, and you chafe, frustrated at the unnecessary slowness of it, then regret, sitting neatly alone, that it does not take longer. Someone said that Mr Gay, who does not advertise his London beginnings as a silk merchant's apprentice, knew how to recite a whole list of silk mercers' wares: Genoa velvets, paduasoys, tabbies watered and unwatered, figured and striped lutestrings, ducapes, mantuas, sarsnets, Persians, half-silks as English and Turkey burdets, cherry-derries, figured and striped donjars. You think of your mother, of the pleasure she would take in your silks and your Kashmir shawl, and vicious, childish, you want to spill your tea and spoil your frock so that you must ring the bell and start the whole performance over again.

You have never in your life possessed such an overabundance of time. You have not ever been an ambitious artist, with a talent that clamours for display. Your motivation has been the pragmatism of acquiring comfort, spurred by the fear of failure and the terrible con-sequences of the poverty incumbent upon it. Freezing in Bolton Hall is infinitely preferable to freezing in a cellar in the Old Bailey. You can picture the alternative vividly, you have lived in London all your life, and you have seen, you know. See it now.

First, your room. It would not be dirty, your garret or third-floor back, because you wouldn't have it so, but sparse: bed, chair, candle, washstand, hook for gowns, chest. In the daytime your mother could sit on the chair in front of the grate and at night she would lie next to you in the bed, the slow rot of her insides panting softly on your face until you want to smother her. You would hope that if she needs to piss she will wake you to haul her on to the pot and not let it run from her, soaking you and the mattress in a horrible, infantile stream. But where to put old Mrs Fenton when you require your bed to work? You giggle at the thought of her, hung round discreetly with a bit of velvet curtain in the corner of your room, the bedsprings not quite drowning her laments about how if you'd taken her advice about the first gentleman it would never have come to this and what use were all those French lessons now?

'Take care, miss, or you will show your money!' A gaggle of gawping apprentices make a poor girl's face burn as she stands on a ladder to wash the windows of her master's shop. 'Money' is one term they use for it. You would have to prise apart the gummed lips of your money, inhale the smell off yourself, squatted over the basin, warm water if you're not too tired and there's money for coal to clean your money, but more likely cold, because having got the money you have to dress again and go outside to fetch the fuel and light the fire and wait for it to warm, and all the time the stuff all over your money, carrying God knows what.

It might not necessarily have come to that, of course. The town would not have let its Polly starve: for a season or two, at least, there would have been other parts. Mr Gay, it is said, is already preparing a sequel to his smash hit, entitled simply *Polly*, and for sure you would have had the principal role. And you would have had a choice of protectors, for a time, but you know the limits of your talent, and your beauty, no Kitty Fisher you. And it would happen slowly, the progress from the lodgings in St James's, and thence to Bloomsbury; Covent Garden next, a year or two older and shabbier every time, and your mother more trouble-some and demanding and succumbing to the lure of the gin bottle. Back in a slow circuit towards Charing Cross, with the bills unpaid and St Giles waiting beyond to swallow you up. Better safety, better security, and you have made the best bargain you could of it, even if the days in Yorkshire are so very long.

There was another story about Polly Peachum's tower. So passionately did Lavinia love her duke, it was said, that she could not bear to stay immured in the hall while he went about the estate, and begged him to indulge her in building a tower high enough for her to sit there with her sewing and glance down, every now and again, to comfort herself with a sight of her beloved. Since the tower was built by the first Duke before Lavinia was born, there is nothing but nonsense in the suggestion that it had anything to do with Polly Peachum at all. Indeed, despite the claims of her biographers, there is nothing to suggest that Lavinia was ever actually in Yorkshire. The only evidence for her presence is that the Paulets, who loathed her, so vehemently denied it, as they would, if possible, have denied her whole existence.

More enjoyable than the idea of Bolton Hall, in Lavinia's eyes, were the annual visits she and Bolton took to Bath. Their first season, Mr Gay was also at the spa, flush with his London triumph, but there is no record of Lavinia having seen him there, although she must have been aware of his presence, and it would be surprising, given the small society and regular routines of the resort, if they did not meet in the Pump Room or at a ball. The restrictions Lavinia experienced in Yorkshire due to her dubious status seemed to apply less rigidly in the more cosmopolitan setting of Bath, as Elizabeth Montague reported that the Duke of Bolton visited openly with 'Mrs Beswick'. Like her mother, Lavinia seems to have adopted the name again in times of need, as a kind of talisman of legitimacy, although maybe her reason was more practical: a wish to dissociate herself from the famous Miss Fenton, who would undoubtedly have attracted attention in 1728. Did Lavinia feel a certain wistfulness about her new, ambiguous anonymity? As Miss Fenton she had been not only superlatively successful, but an independent, self-possessed, individual. The second 'Mrs Beswick', though a considerably more accomplished adventuress than the first, was still nothing but a fallen woman.

Like many visitors to Bath, the Duke of Bolton was suffering from little more than the effects of aristocratic overindulgence. According to Dr Oliver (the inventor of the famous biscuit), the versatile Bath waters cured gout, rheumatism, palsies, convulsions, lameness, colic, consumption, asthma, jaundice, scurvy, the itch, scab, leprosy, scrofula, coldness and pain in the head, most diseases of the eyes, epilepsies, deafness and noise in the ears, heart palpitations, sharpness of urine, wounds, ulcers, piles and infertility. The Duchess of Bolton had, of course, tried the waters in her hopeless quest for an heir, and James II's wife, Maria Beatrice, had indeed successfully conceived the Old Pretender there, but the waters, as so much else, failed the Stuarts in the end, and did nothing for Queen Anne. The cause of much infertility in women was the pox, passed on by husbands who consorted with whores, and at Bath, one was apparently as likely to contract venereal disease as to cure it. At the Cross Bath were 'perform'd all the wanton dalliances imaginable, celebrated Beauties, panting breasts, and curious shapes almost expos'd to public view; languishing eyes darting killing glances, tempting amorous postures, attended by soft musick, enough to provoke a vestal to hidden pleasure',[6] as one commentator suggestively put it. Elizabeth Montague was less enamoured of the female company available, dismissing it as a combination of 'laughing Hoydens, simpering dames', and a few respectable housewives who were 'exceeding ugly'.[7] Nevertheless, this serious intellectual was infected by the spa's taste for racy gossip, reporting to a correspondent that one Mrs Lyttleton had begun a lesbian affair with a mysterious Miss R.

Society and scandal were the real reasons for visiting Bath, whose elegant terraces and parades were devoted almost entirely to the pleasures of the elite. 'You that live in the country have no deception of our doings at Bath,' malaprops the rapturously unsophisticated Mrs Jenkins in Smollett's *Humphrey Clinker*. 'Here is such dressing, and fiddling and dancing and courting and plotting.' In Bath, if one could afford it, the full panoply of the delights of the consuming classes could be enjoyed. It was vogueish to deride the trappings of society in London – 'How horrid is the life of people of fashion . . . one might imagine they forget they had souls,'[8] as one lady wrote – but in Bath, no one could be bothered to pretend that they had anything better to do. Gambling, horse-racing, balls, concerts, dinners, masquerades and receptions, card parties, shopping and visiting: all the activities which would have been denied to Lavinia in Yorkshire were available here, at least by proxy. She loved to dance, perhaps the more so now that she was no longer required to do so professionally, and when the Duke was agreeable it must have been a delight to free her limbs from their long months of cold constriction and take a turn at a public ball, even if private dances, where she might mix with decent married women, were still barred to her.

Still, the choice of Bath for their first public destination as a couple was a kindness on the Duke's part. Lavinia would be less remarked here than if he had attempted to take her on the round of country house visits, race meetings and assize balls that formed the common summer programme of the upper classes. Despite its claims to social exclusivity, Bath, like other spa towns of the Georgian period, was part of a growing mass industry that depended on a far more diverse group of consumers than it affected. As Smollett noted, 'A very considerable proportion of genteel people are lost in a mob of impudent plebeians, who have neither understanding nor judgement, nor the least idea of propriety and decorum; and seem to enjoy nothing so much as insulting their betters.' Which side was Lavinia on? Did her position as the Duke's companion confer 'gentility' upon her, or could her very presence be construed as insulting to her 'betters'? At least in the social scramble of Bath the question was less obvious, and the fact that the town bells rang out to announce the arrival of a great peer like the Duke of Bolton could not have failed to be a secret satisfaction, however much Lavinia craved discretion.

Assemblies were a new fashion which also offered a degree of social life. Since coffee houses and taverns were considered unsuitable for 'nice' women (hence the barb in Lady Mary Wortley Montagu's insult that Lavinia had been bred in an 'ale house'), assemblies met the need for regulated mingling of the sexes beyond private houses. Unlike pleasure gardens such as Vauxhall or Ranelagh which, although popular with the wealthy, were also, like the theatres, the haunt of whores and criminals, assemblies were organised by subscriptions of up to a guinea a time, expensive enough to keep out the riff-raff, or servants swanking in their masters' borrowed clothes. Tea-drinking, cards, conversation and music, with perhaps dancing, made up the entertainments, and though Lavinia was never invited to private receptions, the Duke's status was sufficient that at such semi-public gatherings the dubious moral condition of 'Mrs Beswick' could be politely glossed over, particularly as the object of the assembly was the preservation of a certain equality among those who attended. 'All ranks are mingled together without distinction. The nobility and the merchants, the gentry and the traders, are all upon an equal footing, without anybody's having a right to be informed who you are, or whence you came, so long as you behave with that decorum which is ever necessary in genteel company,'[9] was the comment on an assembly at Tunbridge. In theory, at least, the assembly offered a respite from the stifling gradations of class that permeated other forms of social interaction.

Lavinia was to spend a good deal of time in Bath, as well as other spa towns, during her years with the Duke, and she was able to watch the development of the city which was to become so emblematic of her time and culture as it grew into the capital of mid-eighteenth-century fashion. On her first visit, she saw the foundations of John Wood senior's Queen Square, completed between 1729 and 1736, and attended the Assembly Room built by the same architect in 1728. Dr Oliver's hospital was completed in 1742, the Pump Room finished by Wood junior in 1751 and the Playhouse the same year. As she returned, season after season, Lavinia watched what had initially been a rackety speculation solidify into one of the most beautiful, elegant and permanent architectural landscapes of the century.

Effectively, since her departure from the stage, Lavinia Fenton has more or less ceased to exist. The *Life of Lavinia Beswick, alias Fenton, alias Polly Peachum* was printed anonymously in May 1728, as though the hack author had a premonition that Polly would soon be dead to the world. Advertisements were still appearing over the summer for the cards, fans, figurines and prints that featured her famous face – 'not a print shop or fan shop but exhibited her handsome figure in her Polly's costume'[10] – but Lavinia had no control over, or any means to make a profit from this sale of her image, even though the press, ever unkind, were keen to suggest that she had done so.

> Whereas the Town having been imposed on by Pamphlets published in the Name of Polly Peachum; this is to inform the Publick that I never knew of any Pamphlet made Publick, save my Opera and my Life, which were wrote by a Person that perform'd in the B— O—; and in Justice to the Author and Myself, am obliged to make this Publication, in hopes to put an end to all scandal rais'd by those who are unacquainted with the Life and Character of Polly Peachum.
> P.S. Both of which Pamphlets are to be had at all Pamphlet Shops in London and Westminster, and hope those who buy my Life will judge without Partiality.

This letter in the *Craftsman*, purporting to be from Lavinia herself and having a laugh at her expense, was presumably placed by the author of the largely fictitious 'Life' to mock his subject's supposedly hypocritical desire for privacy while plugging his own work. Next to the letter ran a large advertisement which offered for sale 'a Beggar's Opera Screen ... on which is curiously engrav'd in Copper Plates, the principal Captives of the All Conquering Polly, plainly describ'd by Hieroglyphicks; and on the Reverse their Amorous Letters and Declarations to that Cele-brated Warbler of Ribaldry'. Since in the spring no one had known which of her admirers had finally carried Lavinia off, the Duke was spared the embarrassment of seeing himself depicted in 'Hiero-glyphicks', but it must have been strange for Lavinia to see Polly remain so profitably public while the actress who had created her was existing in semi-retirement.

## LAVINIA AND GRUB STREET

The commercialisation of Lavinia Fenton's fame placed her, in one sense, in a sympathetic relationship with the scurrilous writers who so plagued her reputation. Literature, like other art forms, had entered the world of commerce, and while Grub Street might be ridiculed by Pope as the seat of Dullness, it was Grub Street that fed a hungry public with the scandalous morsels of gossip which made Lavinia famous on a scale previously unknown.

The 'hack', along with the highwayman and the whore, is one of the century's representative types. Dr Johnson, in his *Rambler* essay on journalists, misquoted Shakespeare's *Henry IV* in speaking of writers 'hackneyed in the ways of men', and the writer-for-hire was a product of the descent of literature from a world populated largely – though obviously not entirely – by gentlemen amateurs to the marketplace. Johnson's essay punningly describes such writers in industrialised terms as 'the drudges of the pen, the manufacturers of literature, who have set up for authors ... and like other artificers, have no other care than to deliver their tale of wares at the stated time'. The caricaturist Thomas Rowlandson created a typical image of the skinny, penurious scribbler, his anxious forehead balding and wigless, his clothes shabby, his pockets empty but for bundles of papers. Life for a hack was hard, since 'they seldom have any claim to the trade of writing but that they have tried some other without success',[11] and the wages were distinctly meagre, adding up, in the middle of the century, to just over sixpence a page.

The status of author, autonomously controlling an original body of work, was denied to the hacks. Richard Savage, the gentleman journeyman of words immortalised in Johnson's 'Life', confessed to plagiarism and fraudulence wherever it paid. 'Sometimes I was Mr John Gay, at others Burnet or Addison; I abridged histories and travels, translated . . . what they never wrote, I was the Plutarch of the notorious thief.'[12] Hack work was often produced in a similar fashion to the production-line paintings of the studios of popular masters, where one apprentice would work on the background, another on draperies, another on hands or feet, with publishers farming out introductions to some, quotations to others, to produce books that were the work of many hands and over which their respective writers had very little influence or responsibility. Like Lavinia, who had no possibility of obtaining an income from the reproduction of her image for profit, or any control over where it was used, the hack writer had no rights to his work once it was in the publisher's hands. Nor could the subjects of the hacks' outpourings demand any recompense for slander.

Johnson's essay is relatively sympathetic to the plight of the hack, claiming that they deserved understanding, if not admiration, since their obscurity and indigence was a consequence of the fact that 'their usefulness is less obvious to vulgar apprehensions'. Like actors, hack writers were exposed to insult and censure, and their ambiguous social position was easy to attack. Their writings might have been untruthful, cruel and motivated by avarice, but their lives were frequently mean and hard: they 'live unrewarded and die unpitied'. Lavinia's lack of self-defence, her silence in the face of the inaccuracies hawked about at her expense, suggests, in addition to a certain dignified restraint, an acceptance, if not an understanding, that her success had come at the price of public defamation, the conundrum of a simultaneous need and contempt for publicity that was part of the mechanics of success.

However, now that Lavinia was determined to dispense with her previous incarnation as Polly, the incursions of the pamphleteers were a threatening reminder of her still precarious position. Was this why she hoped that the glasses of mineral water she consumed, unnecessarily but dutifully, at the Duke's side, might work their magic upon her? A child would provide not only additional security, but company and occupation, both of which she desperately needed. The season at Bath successfully provided the final development in this most extraordinary year of Lavinia's life. From being a little-known actress, she had become the greatest star of the London stage, from her lodgings with her family in the depressing precincts of the Old Bailey she was now mistress to a Duke, and finally she was to become a mother. None of the grubbing pamphleteers who had maligned her so shamelessly could have invented quite such a romantically implausible future for Polly Peachum, and it is unsurprising that one of her earliest biographers succumbed to the penny-novel temptation to entitle his story *Coffee House to Coronet*.

## 12

# $\mathscr{T}$WENTY-THREE $\mathscr{Y}$EARS $\mathscr{B}$EFORE $\mathscr{M}$ARRIAGE

$\mathscr{I}$n the decade that followed her departure from the stage, Lavinia gave Charles three sons, Charles, Percy and the rather romantically named Horatio Armand. The birth of the children consolidated the security of her position, insofar as, from the time of Charles's birth, she and the Duke effectively lived as man and wife. Since Lavinia apparently disliked the north of England, or the Paulets disliked her presence there, she and her sons spent most of their time at Hackwood, the Duke's property in Hampshire which had now reverted to Paulet use, or at Westcombe Park, Greenwich, a house which the Duke had taken for his new family.

The status of illegitimate children, or 'children of the mist', as the delicate euphemism went, was not necessarily dubious in aristocratic circles. Charles himself, after all, was connected by his own father's third marriage to the illegitimate daughter of the illegitimate son of Charles II, while his grandmother Mary had also been the child of a mistress rather than a legal wife. Of the minuscule number of Englishmen whom Charles could count as his social equals, five dukes, Buccleuch, Cleveland, Richmond, Grafton and St Albans, were also descended from the Merry Monarch's dozen or so bastards, St Albans having the blood of the actress Nell Gwynn mingled with the pure strain of Stuart. Charles made it clear that he expected his sons to have a proper role in society by giving them his own name, Paulet, to the fury of his relations. It must have been particularly frustrating for the Duke that the son he so desperately needed had been provided not by his unsatisfactory and obstinately living wife Anne, but by his mistress, since although he could assure the boys of a degree of money and influence, none of them would be able to inherit his title or estates in the event of his death.

Unless, of course, Anne were to die. As boy followed boy, Lavinia began to hope that if Charles were free, he might marry her and attempt to legitimise his children. The Duke's own wealth was due in part to the fact that his ancestor Lord Scrope had left a considerable fortune to his illegitimate daughter Mary, Bolton's grandmother. Furthermore, two of Louis XIV's children by his mistress Madame de Montespan, the Duc du Maine and the Comte de Toulouse, were still living in the 1730s, and where a French king had set a precedent, surely an English duke might follow? If Lavinia could become the second Duchess of Bolton, then her own son Charles could well expect to be the fourth Duke. Was this a ridiculous ambition? Within the aristocracy, marital equality was seen as being part of the natural order, and endogamy was the norm. It was relatively common for impoverished but well-born gentlemen to take the daughters of wealthy merchants as wives, since the status of the woman was respectably elevated to that of her husband, but in a woman's case, an alliance with someone from an inferior class was considered demeaning. In his diary, Samuel Pepys recorded that Lord Sandwich quarrelled with his wife over their daughter Jemima's prospects, 'my lady saying she would have a good merchant for her daughter Jem and he answered that he would rather see her with a pedlar's pack at her back so she married a gentleman rather than that she should marry a citizen'. Was it conceivable that the Duke of Bolton should stoop to marry an actress, particularly one who had been so notorious?

Though such a marriage would flout the rigid social hierarchy, a few men, with sufficient wealth and power, could succeed in doing so. Daniel Defoe, in *The Compleat English Gentleman*, had attempted to compile a list of men of 'rank and dignity' who had married 'inferior' ladies. The second Duke of Chandos was to create an uproar in the ranks of the aristocracy by marrying a chambermaid. Not only was the woman ill-bred, but Chandos had discovered her in an inn yard at Newbury, where he and his companions had heard a commotion and discovered that a wife sale was taking place. The inn's ostler, the worse for drink, was attempting to sell his poor wife, who stood quietly in the yard with a rope around her neck. Chandos gallantly purchased her and made her a duchess.

Lavinia was acquainted with Chandos through her relationship with John Gay. Handel had worked for two years at Chandos's country seat, Canons, where he had written his first English oratorio, *Esther*. Pepusch, who wrote the music for *The Beggar's Opera*, was kapellmeister for the Duke's extravagant private orchestra. In 1721, Gay had also been at the house, where he and Handel worked upon the first of their collaborations, *Acis and Galatea*, which was considered by the 1740s to be the only enduringly popular English opera. Pope, though he was indifferent to, if not actively irritated by music, contributed one song, 'Not Showers to Larks', though having been Chandos's guest he was subsequently rather ungraciously rude about him in his 'Epistle to Lord Burlington'.

The Duke of Ancaster married Mary Panton, daughter of a racehorse trainer at Newmarket, and the Earl of Salisbury one Miss Keate, whose father was a barber with a sideline in showing tourists round the tombs at Canterbury. But none of these women, however poor and insignificant, was tainted by having had a career on the stage. Lord Peterborough (who is depicted offering a fortune to Cuzzoni in *The Bad Taste of the Town*) did marry a singer, Anastasia Robinson, having removed her first to a convenient love nest in Parson's Green, but Robinson, who perhaps had studied her *Pamela*, had wisely held on to her final favour until 'a wasting illness and the triumph of her devout Christian principle brought him to his senses'.[1]

The low status of the acting profession was not confined to women. When Lady Susan Fox Strangways, daughter of the Earl of Ilchester, married a player in 1764, her family sent her into exile in America for the disgrace. Ever ready with the latest scandal, Horace Walpole reported: 'A melancholy affair has happened to Lord Ilchester. His eldest daughter, Lady Susan, a very pleasing girl though not handsome, married herself two days ago at Covent Garden Church to O'Brien, a handsome young actor. Lord Ilchester doted on her and was the most indulgent of fathers. 'Tis a cruel blow!' Her 'doting' father wrote that Susan had 'deliberately ruined herself, disgraced her family, acted a cruel part towards her sisters and broke her father's and mother's heart by matching herself with a scoundrel of so vile a profession that there are no possible means left to retrieve her'.[2]

In Hogarth's paintings of *The Beggar's Opera*, one of the group on the stage is Lord Gage, whose wife consulted Lady Mary Wortley Montagu about a theatrical scandal while both ladies were resident at Bath. Lady Gage had been approached by a priest who had been requested to conduct a marriage ceremony between Lady Harriet Herbert, daughter of the Earl of Waldegrave, and a Mr John Beard, currently appearing at Drury Lane. The priest had refused, and asked Lady Gage for advice; she turned it over to the worldly Lady Mary. The latter's kind opinion was that 'if the lady was capable of such amours I did not doubt if this was broke off she would bestow her person and fortune on some hackney coachman or chairman, and that I really saw no method of saving her from ruin and her family from dishonour but by poisoning her', which task Lady Mary offered to be so good as to perform at her own tea table, and even to bear the expense of the arsenic if Lady Gage would bring the unfortunate Harriet to call.

It seemed impossible at the time that acting would ever be regarded as a respectable profession. With the release in 1731 of Hogarth's *Harlot's Progress* series, Lavinia was reminded of the strength of the connection between her own reputation and the common assumption that actresses were whores. The story of poor Moll Hackabout who, in six plates, proceeds from seduction into prostitution, portrayed variously as a successful kept woman, a Drury Lane drab, a prisoner in Bridewell, in sickness and in an undignified death, emblematised the popular conception of a fallen woman's life. There was no room, or sympathy, in the popular imagination for the contented courtesan or the comfortable mistress, and yet the complex ambiguities of Hogarth's paintings suggest that the artist, if not all of his public, was prepared to lay the blame for Moll's unhappy end at society's door. As Moll tumbles her pathetic way through the ever-seedier interiors of the pictures, neglect of duty and religion, lust, avarice and luxury are suggested through Hogarth's imagery and the characters who play their roles in her demise. One such is Mother Needham, the well-known procuress, who chucks Moll under her chin with a sinister maternalism as the fresh young girl descends from the country carrier's cart, watched by Colonel Charteris, one of her most notorious customers. Needham had died in September 1730, three days after being pelted by a crowd in the pillory, where she was finally being punished for her long career as a bawd. A mock 'obituary' was quickly rushed out by the hacks. 'Mother Needham's Elegy Who Died 31 September 1730: Containing an Account of Mother Needham's

Life and Death, manner of Lying in State, her Funeral and Epitaph; also
P—y P—'s Lamentation for Her old Acquaintance . . . If we may credit
Fame, she has helped Col. Ch—r to above 100 Country Maidenheads,
which she picked up at the Carriers. But tho' there were thousands whom
she deluded, we don't hear that any came to preferment unless P—y
P—m who we understand is to be chief Mourner when her Body is
removed from the State in which it now lies.'[3]

It seemed that however quietly Lavinia lived, however good a mother
she was, or however irreproachably faithful to the Duke, she would
never escape the feeling that she was no more than a whore made
good. There was a rigidity in the attitude applied to her which took no
qualifying account of her individual circumstances, of her success in a
difficult career, of her independence, or of the absurdity of the system
that prevented the Duke from divorcing his Duchess, regardless of
whether they both desired it. It was in becoming an actress, not a
mistress, that Lavinia had originally placed herself beyond the social
pale, and she was never, it appeared, to be allowed to forget it.

At least the material circumstances of her life were reassuringly comfortable. As her sons grew up, Lavinia spent much of her time at
Westcombe, but she loved the long visits she and the Duke made to
Hackwood in Hampshire. In the seventeenth century, Daniel Defoe
had described Hampshire as a 'pleasant, fertile country, enclosed and
cultivated', and Hackwood as a 'very handsome beautiful palace, and
the gardens not only very exact but very finely situate, the prospect and
vistas noble and the whole very well kept'.[4] Set, according to Shaw's
later *Tour to the West of England*, in 'a vast expanse of arable lands and
open downs', Hackwood had been built by the first Duke of Bolton
between 1683 and 1687, developed around what had originally been a
hunting box (Hawkwood), for Basing House a mile and a half away.
The single large room which had formed the earlier building became
the hall of the new house, thirty feet by forty, with a twenty-foot ceiling,
wainscoted in varnished oak with carvings by Grinling Gibbons. The
surrounding country was excellent for shooting, and Lavinia would wait
for Charles by the great fire in the hall as he crashed in with his dogs
from a day's sport. Hackwood was not palatial, rather it was a pretty,
modern house, with two curving, colonnaded wings flowing from the
central structure, in one of which Lavinia had her own apartments,

furnished with pieces Charles had commissioned for her in 1733. Shaw comments on many features of the house as Lavinia would have known it, including several portraits of the Paulet family such as the loyal Marquis and his wife, who also scowled at Lavinia when she attended church with the Duke at Old Basing. The Paulets never seemed to have much luck as far as their spouses' appearances were concerned, as the Marchioness is notable for the 'stiffness and unmannerly awkwardness' of her arms, which Shaw gallantly attributes to poor restoration. More to his taste are two jolly ladies of Charles II's time, 'sweet and unknown', whose saucy eyes and careless draperies might have cheered Lavinia up amid the forbidding disapproval of the Paulets glaring from the walls.

Lavinia particularly loved the park at Hackwood, which though large, at six miles in circumference, was less threateningly natural than the wild landscapes of Yorkshire. 'Charming' and 'judiciously ornamented' are descriptions which accord more with her tastes. The garden had been laid out in 1720 by James Gibbs, in the style of Le Notre, and to the south-east was a picturesque farm, landscaped by Pope's friend and patron Lord Bathurst. Hackwood presented lovely views over Hampshire and Berkshire, but Lavinia's favourite spot was the spring wood, which in season was a lake of bluebells.

Lavinia Fenton's sons were not the only illegitimate Bolton children to live at Hackwood. In the late eighteenth century, the house was occupied by Thomas Orde, a gentleman from Northumbria who had married an illegitimate daughter of the fifth Duke in 1778. In 1795 Mrs Orde inherited a portion of the great Bolton estates and her husband took the name: he was created first Baron Bolton in 1799. The Boltons had the house remodelled by the architect Lewis Wyatt in the early nineteenth century, but the improvements which most struck one of their neighbours, the Reverend Mr Austen, were Lord Bolton's splendid pigsties, which he apparently visited early every morning. Mr Austen's daughter Jane was less impressed with other attempts at Bolton adornment, remarking spitefully in a letter to her sister Cassandra that Lady Bolton had failed to make herself more glamorous by the addition of an unbecoming new wig.[5] Jane Austen was generally rather impatient with the Boltons – she commented in another letter on a county ball, where she had sat out two dances 'in preference to having Lord Bolton's eldest son for my Partner, who danced too ill to be endured'.[6]

Hackwood belonged to the Paulet family until 1935, when it was sold, and the house became a hospital shortly afterwards for soldiers injured in the Second World War. The house is remembered more for its association with Lavinia than for the fact that its owners were once neighbours of the great Jane Austen. A young Canadian patient claimed to have seen the figure of a woman, dressed in grey, wandering in the bluebell woods at dusk. Inevitably, the spot became known as Polly Peachum's garden.

Until she retired from the stage, Lavinia had lived nearly all her life in enclosed spaces, cramped lodgings and crowded dressing rooms, and between them the narrow streets of the old city, so overhung with houses it was sometimes difficult to see the sky, so her delight in gardens and open views is unsurprising. The Duke seems to have selected Westcombe in Greenwich to indulge her in this particular pleasure, since it was considered 'one of the most desirable spots in England'. The original house at Westcombe (demolished in 1854) was ancient, set near the entrance gate of Greenwich Park to the east of the town. Close by, on a patch of heath known as Vanbrugh Park, the architect and playwright had constructed four houses between 1714 and 1719, one of which was Lavinia's. Another belonged to the distinguished painter Sir James Thornhill, Hogarth's father-in-law. Lavinia's home had three storeys, with a little cupola and two narrow wings, and a large central pedimented window from which it was possible to see all the way across the river and the city to Highgate and Hampstead. The house stood on a wooded rise, with a terrace at the back 'the prospect [from which] was very beautiful, commanding the winding of the Thames with Shooter's hill and the intervening woodland'.[7] From her garden, Lavinia could make out the spire of the church at Limehouse, a reminder of the world she had come from, but Westcombe was noted for the perfection of its rural simplicity, enhanced by 'the multitude of cattle continually grazing on each side of the river's verdant banks'. It was a scene fit for classical poetry. Polly Peachum, the star of Mr Gay's satirical 'Newgate pastoral', had climbed from the slums of the Mint to the bright, clear air of Greenwich, to an environment charming and sentimental enough to qualify as the home of a china shepherdess.

The long years as the Duke's mistress were a tranquil contrast to the brief headiness of Lavinia's life as a star on the stage, but she was no less occupied, and there is no reason to assume any less contented, than any other well-off married woman. If the Duke's marriage to Lady Anne had been made for duty, his domestic menage with Lavinia seems to have been founded on a cosy, some might even say bourgeois, kind of love. Lavinia's harpsichord lessons finally came in useful, as though the Duke was not fond of reading, he enjoyed her playing and singing to him in the evenings, particularly the tunes from the *Opera*. One of their rare quarrels, in which the Duke flew into a sulky temper and threatened to leave her, was supposedly prettily resolved by Lavinia sinking to her knees (yet again!) and singing her famous number 'O Ponder Well'.

The lives of the Duke and his mistress were organised according to the pattern of seasonal peregrination conventionally followed by the rich. Travel in any form was a novelty to Lavinia, but it was also a lengthy and inconvenient business. Daniel Defoe had lamented the deplorable effects on trade of England's deplorable roads,[8] and very few were in good condition, with the exception of those improved since 1697 under the turnpike system. In winter, many were impassable, and country houses could be cut off for days at a time by bad weather. Nevertheless, the number of travellers was increasing, with London boasting over 2,000 private carriages and more than 1,000 for hire in 1739. On longer journeys, Lavinia and the Duke travelled in his coach, adorned with the Paulet arms, a large, stately vehicle that could hold six people comfortably and which was accompanied by liveried footmen, a coachman and postilions, or outriders, for safety. Servants and baggage trundled in a cart behind. The coach was an essential symbol of aristocratic status, though they were often lumbering and unwieldy. For shorter journeys, the Duke had a post-chaise, or 'chariot', a lighter carriage drawn by two horses, which was more convenient for London and used for informal visits in the country. The Duke enjoyed driving himself, and would often take Lavinia out for an airing in Hackwood Park, managing the reins without a servant.

Summers were traditionally spent in the countryside, paying or receiving long visits, and this was the loneliest time for Lavinia, since she was never received, as a mistress, by married women, and therefore precluded from any family parties. In September, with the start of the shooting season, she could expect to receive (male) guests, who began blasting away at partridges in the first week of the month and continued with pheasant, then woodcock, until January. Foxhunting continued into the spring, so although Parliament began sitting in November, many MPs and peers preferred to remain out of town until after Christmas. From January to June, the London season ran and, as the *Gentleman's Magazine* commented in 1738, the exodus to the city was a relief for many women. 'I consider January the general Gaol-Delivery of the fair sex: then they come to town, flushed with the health, and irritated with the confinement of the country ... Every fine woman who comes to Town in January comes heavily tired of the country and her husband. The happy pair have been yawning at one another at least ever since Michalemas.'

Pope, in his 'Epistle to Miss Blount on her Leaving Town' of 1727, spoke for many country wives when he made the 'attractions' of the country drearily apparent.

> She went, to plain-work, and to purling brooks,
> Old-fashioned halls, dull aunts, and croaking rooks,
> She went from Op'ra, Park, assembly Play,
> To morning walks and pray'rs three hours a day;
> To pass her time 'twixt reading and Bohea,
> To muse, and spill her solitary Tea,
> Or o'er cold Coffee trifle with the spoon,
> Count the slow clock, and dine exact at noon,
> Divert her eyes with pictures in the fire,
> Hum half a tune, tell stories to the squire,
> Up to her godly garret after sev'n,
> There starve and pray, for that's the way to heav'n.

With the substitution of 'duke' for 'squire', this might well serve as a description of the early part of Lavinia's country existence, although coffee, cold or not, brought back no wistful memories for her. Yet as Lavinia accustomed herself to her radically changed life, she found that though it might be lonely, it was far from necessarily idle. Whether at Westcombe or Hackwood, she began to develop a routine which shaped her days. Lavinia liked to rise late, perhaps recalling the theatre hours of her early life, but in this she was not exceptional, as many women of the upper class rarely appeared 'downstairs' during the morning in the countryside. Breakfast was usually taken between nine and eleven, and sometimes this was a social occasion, for the benefit of male guests who would be abroad early with the grooms and gamekeepers in the coverts. Lavinia would remain in her dressing room, playing with the children, answering letters and speaking to the upper servants, until the elaborate process of dressing for dinner began.

Dinner times became later and later as the eighteenth century progressed, from two or three until as late as eight o'clock, requiring the invention of an informal meal known as 'nunch' eventually formalised as luncheon. At Hackwood, dinner was served between three and five o'clock, and Lavinia would retire afterwards to leave the men to continue drinking. Tea-drinking, with Lavinia presiding, theoretically followed, though whether the Duke was often in a condition to appreciate this nicety is doubtful, and supper, a lighter meal of fewer dishes, would be served at nine or ten o'clock.

Within this placid timetable, Lavinia found she had a great many duties to attend to. Although she and Bolton lived relatively quietly, as they were unable, even had the Duke been so inclined, to entertain on a large scale, the efficient running of a country house was an absorbing task, particularly for a woman with no experience of it. In general, housekeeping in the eighteenth century was changing. Previously it was thought necessary for even grand country ladies to be capable of managing their households, overseeing not only cleaning and cookery but work in the dairy and brewhouse and taking a personal hand in pickling and preserving and the preparation of medicines and remedies for the family. Some fashionable ladies enjoyed playing at rustic activities, like Lady Mansfield and Lady Southampton, who competed in their dairies at Hampstead over who made the best butter, and in the north of England these practices apparently continued rather longer, but gradually the work which had been supervised and participated in by the mistress became the province of the servants.

Lavinia was typical of a new generation of women whose education had been ornamental rather than practical and, curiously, she was thereby at one with those of her adopted class who were criticised by conservative voices for being too fine to manage their families in the old-fashioned way. Educated women like Lady Mary Wortley Montagu were vociferous in their denunciation of the inadequacies of a ladylike training, and she was joined by many commentators who insisted that 'the girls from such schools are totally undomesticated. And undomesticated women have houses without order, servants without discipline, children without instruction.'[9] Given her education, Lavinia, like many of her peers, preferred more 'elegant' pursuits and welcomed the fact that 'As living grew more gracious and refined emotions were cultivated, the lady's role as domestic quartermistress, as commissar of the laundry and purveyor of pickles, preserves and poultices devolved upon the shoulders of the proverbially fierce, key-jangling housekeeper.'[10]

Nevertheless, the Duke took a large and well-run household for granted and, as well as her children, Lavinia had to concern herself at Hackwood with over fifty servants, though the number at Westcombe was far smaller. Upper servants, such as the Duke's valet, Lavinia's maid, the butler and housekeeper, usually travelled with their employers, but at each home there were also footmen, a cook and kitchen staff, grooms, an endless hierarchy of maids, gardeners and male labourers not to mention the women who were brought in for tasks such as mangling, weeding and seasonal cleaning. Although the Duke was not an inspired or particularly committed landowner, his property was extensive enough to necessitate a steward, with whom he worked sporadically on business issues such as accounts, repairs and leases to tenants (a monument in the thirteenth-century church at Old Basing commemorates the long service of John Brasier, senior steward to a later Duke of Bolton), but Lavinia had to involve herself in the running of what was effectively a small self-contained village, which can only have been bewildering for a woman whose home economics had previously been practised in a few cramped rooms in London, with the convenience of the cookshop nearby.

Examples of Lavinia's exact duties are sparse, but typically she would have been responsible, with the housekeeper's help, for the supervision of the servants and the ordering of provisions. The latter was in itself a tremendous task, given the numbers of people to be fed each day, with the average week's consumption for a large country house in 1748 being enumerated at 23 lbs of beef, 13 lbs of mutton, 6 lbs of veal, 10 lbs of lamb, half a side of bacon, 5 turkeys, 3 geese, 10 ducks, 46 fowl, 1 hare, 12 rabbits, 50 lbs 8 oz of butter, 10 cheeses, 170 eggs, 40 gallons of strong beer, 27 gallons of ale and 108 gallons of small beer, not counting staples such as flour, sugar and lard and luxuries like tea, coffee, chocolate and wine. Hackwood Farm house still exists (though in a later structure), and evidence of farming implements at Westcombe suggests that both establishments produced a great deal of their own food. Landowners expected to eat their own fruit, vegetables, fish, cheese and game, with baskets often being sent from country to town in the season. Male cooks were popular in large kitchens, but women were also common, and cheaper.

London grocers such as Tolson and Lewis of New Bond Street supplied foodstuffs that could not be obtained locally, but this required planning, as transport was a lengthy process. Lavinia had also to order plenty of claret, brandy and port for her lover and his guests, which would be delivered in barrels and bottled at home. Other provisions included candles, of various grades according to where they were to be used, starch and bluing for the laundry, lead for blacking the grates and ranges, fabrics of all sorts, for everything from cleaning cloths to pinafores and aprons for the maids, and soap (this latter a pleasant reminder of how far Lavinia had travelled from her family's old lodgings against the Cowplants factory walls).

Lavinia was also busy with the education of her children. Tutors were hired for the boys as they grew up, and Charles at least showed more academic ability than his father, going on to take his university degree, but while they were small, Lavinia was able to spend a good deal of time with them. Professional nannies and governesses were not yet the norm for the children of the wealthy, who were generally taken care of by maids, though there was a growing concern that too much exposure to the ordinary servants would have damaging effects. 'Peasantry is a disease (like the plague) easily caught,'[11] observed pamphleteer William Darrell cruelly. Nevertheless, Lavinia's children were brought up by the house servants, and the boys, unusually, spent a good deal of time with their father, in the stables or the woods. Certainly the Duke's affection for his sons was obvious enough to be remarked upon by his contemporaries, rather thoughtlessly, given that many of them knew the estranged Lady Anne. The Duke genuinely enjoyed their company, and in this respect, too, he and Lavinia were an example of the developing inclination towards 'companionate' marriage that was beginning to emerge as the century progressed.

Indeed, the relationship between the Duke of Bolton and Lavinia

Fenton, though it may have begun as the cliché of an aristocrat taking an actress into keeping, was evidence of an interesting diversion in the social current. Bolton's relationship with his first wife has been characterised by one historian as 'patriarchal', that is, adhering to the conditions of the ruling class, while his experience with Lavinia is described as 'domestic'. Lawrence Stone[12] suggests that aristocratic power balances shifted in the eighteenth century from 'kinship' networks, whereby political loyalties and financial power were gathered between extended families, to a 'domestic' model, whereby, since primary loyalty to the state reduced and fragmented the power of kinship functions, the aristocratic home (supported by Protestantism's celebration of the hearth as source of support and affection), relocated aristocratic state allegiance as smaller, more uxorious nucleii.

'Affective individualism', in which the selection of a marriage partner was influenced more by personal choice and less by considerations of a family's general social and economic standing, is seen by some writers as an important sociological development across the century. The extent of this change should certainly not be overestimated, but Lavinia and the Duke of Bolton's extramarital menage might be seen, in its duration and constancy, as an indication of the trend.

So Lavinia was occupied by her lover and her children, her music, her servants, the running of her house. Like other women of the class to which she now, by proxy, belonged, she involved herself in charity, and indeed supported her stepfather to the end of his life. (Mrs Fenton, who had the potential to be an embarrassment, was carried off conveniently early, perhaps by the raptures of her daughter's success.) When Lavinia was alone she read and sewed, and occasionally she and the Duke entertained (male) friends to dinners and card parties. As the Reverend Warton observed, she was a charming and popular hostess, noted for the simple elegance of her arrangements and the cultivation of her conversation. It is rather unfortunate that one of those who praised her should have chosen to do so thus: 'Notwithstanding her Wit and Skill she is the most humble, the most affable and the least conceited of any woman that is both wise and beautiful in the King's Dominions. Nor will she bear to hear encomiums on herself, it being a greater Affront to praise her before her Face, and she resents it more than if she were to be publicly called Gilt, Coquet, or even Common Whore or Strumpet.'[13]

The Duke was proud of Lavinia, and treated her with far more respect and consideration than he ever had his legal wife.

Life with Lavinia changed Bolton. Although he continued to drink and gamble, he gave up haunting the brothels of Covent Garden, contented and occupied with the woman he loved. Betting, however, remained a passion. As well as field sports, the Duke, in keeping with family tradition, spent a good deal of time and money on the Bolton stud, which was one of the most significant in the country. Cuthbert Roth's *Early Records of the Thoroughbred Horse* (1694–1752) mentions several of his horses, including Whistlejacket, purchased in 1739 from the Earl of Godolphin and immortalised in a painting by George Stubbs, Camilla, Starling and Bonny Lass. The Duke's most famous runner was perhaps Bay Bolton, out of a horse known as the Vintner Mare, whose lineage was as romantic a story of exile as any cavalier's. She was bred out of an Arabian mare by the Duke's horse Rockwood, a son of Helmsley Turk. Helmsley Turk had belonged to a Mr Curwen, an exiled Catholic supporter of James II, who (unlike the Paulets) had not turned his coat at the Glorious Revolution, but fled with his King to the court of Louis XIV, where he was given the stallion by the Duc du Maine and the Comte de Toulouse, the King's two horse-mad sons by his mistress, the glamorous Marquise de Montespan. Vintner Mare's son, Bay Bolton, sired numerous successful racehorses, including Godolphin Whitefoot, who won 200 guineas for the Duke against Somerset Cinnamon in the year of his succession to the title. Bay Bolton's bloodline continued longer than the dukedom for which he was named: his descendants were still racing in 1899, which one would like to fancy would have been a source of some satisfaction to the departed Mr Curwen that loyalty will out in the end.

When he was not occupied with his country pursuits, the Duke's public life continued, though despite the innumerable opportunities open to him through his rank and fortune, he does not seem to have made much more than a token success of it. He retained his governorship of the Isle of Wight until 1733, though there is no mention of Lavinia having travelled with him on official business there. Perhaps he thought it indelicate, or perhaps she preferred to remain in the country, at Hackwood or Greenwich, with the children. The Duke was still a colonel in the Horse Guards, Lord Lieutenant of Hampshire and Warden of the

New Forest until the same year, but he, like John Gay, eventually fell foul of Walpole.

For all his advantages, wrote Lord Hervey in a summation of his career, 'the Duke of Bolton was not satisfied, for being as proud as if he had any consequence besides what his employment made him, as vain as if he had some merit and as necessitous as if he had no estate, so he was troublesome at Court, hated in the country and scandalous in his regiment. The dirty tricks played (in the last reign) to cheat the Government of men, or his men of half a Crown, were things unknown to any Colonel but His Grace, no griping Scotsman excepted. As to his interest in parliament, by the members he nominally made there, these were all virtually made by the Court.'[14]

Hervey's charges seem harsh, and not all of them were true. In keeping with his family's capacity for allying themselves with the winning side, the Duke had declared himself a Whig even before the death of Queen Anne, as Swift had disparagingly reported in a letter of 1711, recalling an incident at court in which 'a parcel of drunken Whiggish Lords ... who come into chocolate houses and rail about the Tories, and have challenges sent them, and the next morning come and beg pardon. General Ross was likely to swinge the [then] Marquis of Winchester for this trick t'other day.'[15]

Yet despite being associated with the ruling party, the Duke remained very much a part of the independent-minded aristocracy, as opposed to the 'Robinocracy' which had grown up around Walpole. The two had quarrelled in 1733 as a consequence of the Duke's refusal to back the Prime Minister's abolition of the land tax, which at the time was four shillings in the pound. Walpole aimed to reduce this to one shilling in the pound, which would purportedly relieve the burden on country gentlemen who had largely underpinned the state with their taxes since the institution of the national debt following the Revolution. However, in counting on the political capital to be gained from such a move, Walpole and his advisers underestimated first the extent to which the old-fashioned concept of paternalistic duty to one's inferiors was supported by many landowners, and secondly the fact that Walpole was so unpopular that some MPs would vote against their own interests just for spite. Moreover, Walpole planned to finance the reduction by introducing excise duties on wine and tobacco, converting them into inland revenue duties, an idea that outraged the city of London, which presented a petition of formal protest. The atmosphere in the capital was so tense that Walpole withdrew his excise proposal the following day, a judgement justified by the sight of the celebrating crowds that promptly burned him and Queen Caroline in effigy in the streets, along with images of the murderess Sarah Malcom, suggesting once again that an association of lowlife crime with high political corruption had penetrated the popular mind.

As a peer with a vote in the House of Lords, Bolton's objection to what became known as the 'excise crisis' was influential. Walpole's scheme, it was commonly believed, would have assisted the wealthy at the expense of the poor, and Bolton, along with the Dukes of Argyll and Montrose, very decently voted against a bill which would have led to a very substantial increase in his own income. Walpole connived to have Bolton deprived of his public posts, and Hervey, a passionate partisan of the Prime Minister, is here attempting to gloss this vindictiveness as self-inflicted, as the story was put about that Bolton had resigned.

As to his financial status, the Duke wistfully entertained Lavinia with the story of the Basing House treasure. During the civil wars, the Marquess of Winchester had supposedly hidden a great store of gold, melted into animal shapes to disguise it, in the grounds of Basing, to preserve it from Cromwellian marauding. The sum was claimed to be about £200,000, though the Marquess never bothered to dig it up. The treasure legend could also have had its source in the silver plate brought over from France and hidden by Catholic priests, seven of whom had sheltered and were killed there. The treasure, had it existed, might have been useful, since though the Duke was in no conceivable manner poor, he was, like many aristocrats, beset by debt. Lady Sunderland, writing to her son, warned him that an imprudent marriage might mean that his children would 'come to London behind coaches, as the Duke of Bolton's did, to get shoes and stockings from their aunts'.[16] Charles, Percy and Armand had no aunts on Lavinia's side, and the Paulets wouldn't speak to them, so unless it is to be believed that they went barefoot, then Lady Sunderland is exaggerating, but one explanation for Lavinia's low-key existence, especially during the decade when the Duke was deprived of his posts, is that they were forced to live quietly as much for the sake of economy as anything else. The Duke's health, which declined dramatically in the course of his relationship with Lavinia, also benefited from more regular, less self-indulgent habits.

The Duke, however, was still immensely wealthy by the standards of the day. Aside from the sinecures of public positions, his income was derived largely from land and also from real-estate holdings in London, from which many of his aristocratic contemporaries, such as the Earls of Oxford, Southampton and Burlington, made fortunes. During the 1720s, the Duke had lived in newly fashionable Hanover Square, one of thirteen aristocratic residents among a total of twenty-five (the others included the Dukes of Roxburgh and Montrose, the Earls of Essex and Pontefract and Lords Hilsborough and Londonderry). After the separation from Anne, he had acquired property in Mayfair and built a new house in Kensington, then still in the pleasant outskirts of London. Gregory King's survey of tax returns had put the total average income of a 'temporal lord' at £2,800 in 1694, in comparison with which the Duke of Kingston had an income of £19,000 in 1731. Bolton's outgoings, again like those of his contemporaries who maintained several large establishments, were high, but his income was more than sufficient to keep Lavinia in a luxury unimaginable to a woman who grew up in a coffee house.

Bolton was in any case reinstated in those posts he had lost under Walpole after the latter's resignation, during the time of the last Jacobite rebellion in 1745. He obviously commanded some degree of respect, for not only was he returned to all his former positions, but he was promoted, too, to Captain of Gentleman Pensioners and lieutenant-general in the army. However, although he raised a regiment for the '45, he did not ride into the field to see the last Jacobite hope dissolve in carnage. Ostensibly this was because of his age, although perhaps, in true Paulet style, he was hanging back to see what the outcome would be, ready to turn his coat if Prince Charlie rode south triumphant. Indeed, his absence did give rise to some unpleasant rumours that his military interest was cowardly profiteering.

> Now Bolton comes with beat of drums
> Though fighting be his loathing
> He much dislikes both guns and pikes
> But relishes the clothing.[17]

The 'clothing' referred to is the payment Bolton supposedly took from brokering commissions for army officers, hence Hervey's reference to 'dirty tricks'. Given the activities of his ancestors, this would have been a sad but entirely typical way for a Paulet to behave. (The family reputation for cowardice was upheld by the sixth Duke, who was appointed to the command of a gunship but court-martialled for deserting the fleet as a result of a false alarm he had spread concerning the safety of the ship's sternpost. Known ever after as Captain Sternpost, he was promoted out of trouble to the rank of admiral, but never sailed beneath the standard again.) But the Duke's behaviour must also be considered in the light of the very different attitude of his age towards service. Conceptions of society's duty to the individual were based upon a reciprocal paternalism, and the Duke's military arrogance exemplified a code in which human beings – wives, servants, apprentices – were legitimately regarded as possessions. So a colonel's belief that his regiment was his own property was quite usual.

Though Bolton might not have made much of a mark as a public figure in England in terms of the opportunities his position afforded him, his romance with Lavinia Fenton immortalised him in the New World. Benning Wentworth, who was governor of New Hampshire from 1741 to 1766, had also scandalised society through his relationship with a social inferior, in his case by marrying a chambermaid named Martha Hilton. The Duke of Bolton had already had a town in Vermont named after him in 1738, as a tribute to his services on the British Colonial Council, but when *The Beggar's Opera* came to America in the 1760s, Benning was so enchanted, not only by the play but by the love story of its first principal actress, that at his instigation the town of Peacham, Vermont was named for her. (Winchester in New Hampshire and Pawlet in Vermont also have connections with the Bolton family, though they were named for the fifth Duke.)

Although Lavinia lived such an unfashionably quiet life with her Duke, she was hardly, in Bath or Tunbridge, cut off from the world. She could follow the scandal of the repression of 'Polly', read Mr Pope's welcome attacks on Bolton's enemy Lord Hervey, hear of the latest extravagances at John Rich's new theatre in Covent Garden. It was here, in February 1733, that Lavinia watched John Gay's tragedy *Achilles*, which was performed before 'a crouded and splendid audience',[18] including Alexander Pope and the Queensberrys, but sadly not Gay himself.

John Gay, 'the Orpheus of highwaymen', had died aged forty-seven on 4 December 1732, at the London house of his patrons, the Queensberrys, attended by his old friend Dr Arbuthnot. Like Polly Peachum, whose 'Life' had been sold while Lavinia was very much living, he became the subject of profit-seeking Grub Street pamphleteers almost before his corpse was cold. According to an account rushed out by the publisher Edmund Curll, his funeral, which took place at Westminster Abbey on 23 December, was a tremendous affair, featuring 'a Hearse trimmed with Plumes of Black and White Feathers, attended with three mourning Coaches and six Horses'.[19] Four of the six pallbearers were members of the aristocracy, the last a poor, weeping Alexander Pope. Gay's play had made Lavinia famous, and her personification of his character had helped to establish the career which was deemed to merit such a grand send-off, well beyond what might have been expected for a former silk mercer's apprentice. Both had ascended far higher than the positions their society had prescribed for them. Another account of the funeral remarked that 'the celebrated Polly Peachum'[20] was among the distinguished mourners. Of all the apocryphal stories about Lavinia Fenton, it would be most pleasant to believe that this one were true.

Alexander Pope grieved acutely for the death of his dear friend. His biographer comments: 'After Arbuthnot's death [in 1735], only Swift and himself remained of the group of like-minded friends who in 1713–14 had nursed high hopes for themselves and each other, and for the future of letters in England in their time.'[21] The ambitions of the Scriblerians were certainly not defeated artistically, but as instruments of change they had failed. Twickenham, and its bright, hopeful summer gardens, seemed another world. Dr Swift was far away in Dublin, 'entombed ... like a defeated Titan',[22] and Pope felt that an age had passed, that he was the last representative of those sharply brilliant writers who had so gracefully made a political weapon of wit. Lavinia, too, remained a living emblem of that time, but what little contact she had had with Pope had dissolved over the years.

She was, however, better equipped than Dr Johnson to understand the epitaph Gay left for himself. Famously, he had written to Pope that his last comment on the world was to be:

Life is a jest
And all things show it.
I thought so once
But now I know it.[23]

Pope fulfilled his friend's request that he place the epitaph on the tomb, and added a few lines of his own, declaring that Gay's best monument would remain the memories in the hearts of his friends:

Of Manners gentle, of Affections mild,
In Wit a Man; Simplicity a Child . . .
These are Thy Honours! Not that here thy Bust
Is mix'd with Heroes, or with Kings thy dust;
But that the Worthy and the Good shall say,
Striking their pensive bosoms – *Here* lies GAY!

Dr Johnson was clearly not among the pensive. In a letter to the *Gentleman's Magazine* in 1738, Johnson was disparaging about *The Beggar's Opera* and with plodding logic observed that the epitaph was a blasphemy for a true Christian and nonsensical in an atheist. The epitaph might 'have preserved his [Gay's] reputation had it, instead of being engraved on a monument at Westminster, been scribbled in its proper place, the window of a brothel'. Johnson carefully elucidated the 'species of wit appropriate to particular persons and places' without seeming to grasp that it had been in the reversal of such conventions that Gay's genius had shone brightest. He would doubtless have confined Lavinia, too, to her 'proper' place, in a brothel, but then Dr Johnson, who never quite shook off the wide-eyed amazement of the provincial, maintained that Charing Cross, the site of Fenton's coffee house, contained all the diversion that life had to offer. Lavinia's life, since her first resistance to her mother's scheming, had always shared some of the defiance that Gay's epitaph displays. In her heart, as in his, was a refusal to accept the limiting dictations of position.

# 13

## WIFE AND WIDOW

The Reverend Joseph Warton, who was so polite about Lavinia's correct taste in literature, is a friend of the great painter Reynolds, the great actor Garrick, the great scholar Johnson and the great poet Pope. He is the author of an exceedingly dull poem, *The Enthusiast, or, The Lover of Nature*, which will nonetheless make claims to greatness in being yet another literary contender for the title of precursor to that Romantic movement in literature whose practical applications so disappointed Lavinia Fenton in Yorkshire. At present, kicking his heels in the dusty swelter of Aix-en-Provence in August, the Reverend Warton is greatly irritated. He is irritated to find himself in the company of the Duke of Bolton and his mistress Lavinia Fenton, who rudely emphasise his inferior social status over the respect due to him as a clergyman by living together quite openly before him, forcing him to sanction their sin by his presence. He is irritated that they are still trundling about among the baking nonentities of the French provinces, instead of having crossed the Alps, as he had hoped they would do, to explore the magnificences of Italy. He is irritated because the Duke, a man of few inner resources, is gouty and temperamental away from his English food and his English comforts, particularly as at this time of year there are few beasts in Provence which the Duke deems worthy of killing. He is irritated that, since he is the recipient of one of the Duke's many advowsons, he cannot dismiss the aristocrat's boorishness, but must try to placate him as his patron and only hope of advancement. He is irritated because he misses his wife and children. Most of all, he is irritated because Anne, Duchess of Bolton, obstinately refuses to die.

Lady Anne had fallen ill in the spring of 1751, and the Duke, distastefully anxious that he should marry his heart's desire as soon as the breath had decently left his wife's body, proposed that he and Lavinia, accompanied by the Reverend Joseph, should start immediately for France. With a system of couriers arranged to gallop the news of the Duchess's demise across Europe as soon as it was confirmed, the Duke and Lavinia could be united in matrimony by the Reverend as soon as they saw a sweating horse steaming up the road to their lodgings. They duly departed in April, not without some misgivings on the Reverend's part concerning the unpleasant circumstances under which his presence was courted. It was evident, however, 'that he could not refuse, without in some measure destroying his future expectations in that quarter, and the straitened income of his small living made an abandonment of his hopes of preferment hardly to be expected'.[1] Despite the promptings of the Reverend's conscience, it was fixed that Lavinia should come into possession of the living of Bolton just as soon as the present incumbent was out of the way.

It is now almost September, and Lady Anne shows no sign as yet of giving satisfaction to the woman she will refer to in her will as 'my husband's whore'. The Reverend Warton is tired of his commission, and he is tired of minding Lavinia's youngest brat while she bowls about the dusty countryside in an attempt to amuse the Duke. The Reverend is of the cynical opinion that she has insisted on the presence of the child (properly a young and discontented man) as a sentimental reminder lest the Duke be tempted at the last minute to go back on the long-awaited fulfilment of his promise. But Mrs Warton's letters grow plaintive, and he really thinks it's time to take his leave.

Just as he recovers his parish, in October 1751, the Duchess of Bolton's reserves of stubbornness finally run out, and she expires in London. The *General Advertiser* of 8 October reports: 'Yesterday the corpse of her Grace the Duchess of Bolton was carried out of Town to be privately interred in the Family Vault belonging to her noble ancestors in Leanvinhanghl Church in the County of Camarthen; which church was built by Her Grace's great grandfather John, Lord Vaughan, Earl of Carbery. This good and excellent lady was the daughter and sole heiress of the Right Hon. John Lord Vaughan, Baron of Mollingart, Earl of Carbery in Ireland, and Baron Emlyn in the County of Camarthen. She was married to His Grace Charles, Duke of Bolton in 1713, by whom she had no issue. Her Grace has left Golden Grove with the several Lordships and Manors adjoining and belonging, with all the rest of her real together with her personal Estate, to her Heir-at-Law, the Hon. John Vaughan Esq. Member of Parliament for the County of Camarthen etc. etc.' The *Advertiser* discreetly omits to mention that Her Grace has insisted that none of her property should fall into the hands of her husband's whore.

Meanwhile, Her Grace the Duchess of Bolton, stepdaughter of Mr Fenton, formerly of Fenton's Coffee Shop, Charing Cross, was enjoying her honeymoon in the pretty French market town of Montauban, near Toulouse.[2] The Duke was far too impatient to wait for the return of Mr Warton, so when the announcement of Anne's death reached him in Aix-en-Provence, Mr Pevisme, the chaplain from the English Embassy at Turin, was fetched across the border to do the honours. The bride was forty-three, the groom a laughable sixty-six, but when news of the marriage reached London, such had been the length of their liaison, and so obscure the life of Lady Anne, that it hardly caused a ripple. 'You desire news from England – then a roundabout truly,' wrote one Mrs Delaney to her friend Mrs Davies, barely two months after the wedding. 'All I know, you shall, though it may be as old as Queen Elizabeth's death by the time it reaches you, or at least as old as the Duke of Bolton's marriage with Polly.'[3] The honeymoon in the warm autumn of southern France was unremarkable, and since they were travelling anonymously, the Duke and Duchess of Bolton were hardly noticed by their hosts in Montauban as they sat beside the river or walked among the town's narrow, pink-bricked streets to take their coffee in the shady colonnaded square.

Surprisingly, when they returned to England, Lavinia was not presented at court, a privilege to which she was entitled in her new rank and which indeed was expected of a duchess. Whatever was said about her past, there could be no strict offence to protocol now that she was legitimately the Duke's wife, but as her sons were by this time almost grown up, and still not legitimised, perhaps the Duke refrained from insisting upon his Duchess's presence at St James's for reasons of delicacy. The retiring way in which they lived might also have been the reason why Lavinia did not wish to impose her new status on the world that had snubbed her for so long, but even if she had had any ambitions towards a more social, fashionable existence in town, she was prevented from realising them by the state of Charles's health.

(One historian cheerfully asserts that the real reason for Lavinia not being presented at court was the animosity of Robert Walpole, who bore a grudge against her for the part she had played in *The Beggar's Opera* and therefore created an 'insuperable barrier' to her introduction to fashionable society.[4] This would be exciting if it were true, but since Walpole tendered his resignation in 1742 and Lavinia did not become a duchess until 1751, it is impossible.)

Charles and Lavinia had been together for nearly a quarter of a century, and the Duke was now an old man. For the three years following their marriage, Lavinia continued in the role she had been playing for some time, that of nursemaid rather than lover, as they made their way from spa to spa in pursuit of some relief from his ailments. The sparkle of the ducal coronet must have seemed a little tarnished as Lavinia supported her tottering old husband along the walks at Tunbridge Wells, waited out the long afternoons while he snored cantankerously in his chair, dosed him and dressed him, and bore his cursing when his refusal to give up the bottle brought on the acute pain of his gout. If her devotion was a burden to her, she was gentle enough or clever enough not to let Charles see it. Curiously, she was almost in a more vulnerable position as Duchess of Bolton than she had been as the Duke of Bolton's mistress, for as Charles's strength declined the Paulets, so long ignored, began to circle around him.

For the family, the great anxiety was that Charles would attempt to leave his title and fortune to his eldest son by Lavinia, rather than to his brother Harry, currently styled the Marquess of Winchester, who was next in line to inherit since Charles and Anne had had no children. Lord Harry had made a decent career for himself, first in the diplomatic service in Portugal and subsequently as a Whig MP for Hampshire. He had a rather more successful time at court than his brother, serving as gentleman of the bedchamber to the Prince of Wales and achieving the status of a Lord of the Admiralty, Lieutenant of the Tower of London at the time of Charles's marriage. His own marriage had been no more successful than his brother's, and he and his wife Catherine, daughter of Charles Parry, who had been envoy to Portugal, had no children. This meant that in the event of Harry's death – and he was now aged sixty himself – the title would pass to his younger half-brother Charles (the second Duke's son by his third wife), who was in his early thirties. Thus both the Marquess of Winchester and Lord Charles Paulet had powerful reasons to hate and fear the new Duchess for the influence she might exert over their brother at their expense. They made their hostility apparent by continuing to refuse to receive Lavinia or have anything to do with her children. Lavinia was aware that though she would hardly be left destitute in the event of her husband's death, the brothers had the power to make things very difficult for her. The marriage, which had appeared to cap her ambitions for security, now seemed to be cruelly undermining them.

Elizabeth Montague had written wearily after a season at Bath that the only thing one could do tomorrow that one had not done the day before was die.[5] Having spent years in spa towns, the Duke of Bolton eventually essayed this final distraction, and expired aged sixty-eight at Tunbridge, three years after his wedding to Lavinia, on 26 August 1754. He was buried in the old church at Basing three weeks later. It is not certain whether his wife insisted on her right to attend the interment in the Paulet family vault, although Charles had specified in his will that the burial was to be at her discretion. The will was reassuring. Charles clearly loved Lavinia to the end, respecting her fidelity and her care of him, as the testament of 'Charles, Duke of Bolton, Knight of the Most Noble Order of the Garter', makes clear. 'All my estates,' Charles had dictated, 'real and personal whatsoever . . . I give unto my dear and well beloved wife Lavinia Duchess of Bolton and her heirs forever . . . I appoint her, the said Duchess of Bolton my said wife, whole and sole executrix.' There was no time for either grief or gratitude. Lavinia had to prove the will on the very day of Charles's death, as she knew that the instruction that his estates be left to her and her heirs in perpetuity would immediately be contested.

She could be sure of her widow's jointure, the sum of £5,000, which would revert to the next Duke on her death as it was attached to the title. She could also be secure in her ownership of Westcombe House in Greenwich. Harry immediately became the fourth Duke of Bolton, which Charles could do nothing to prevent, but he had been concerned to leave no more than he was obliged to his brother in order to provide for his three illegitimate sons. It was this injunction that the Paulets now hoped to defeat. A particular source of contention was the London property that Lavinia now owned, this being the family house, Bolton Court (now covered by subsequent buildings known as the Boltons, and still one of

London's smartest addresses) and leases in Bolton Street near Piccadilly Circus. As well as being a prestigious part of the family holdings, the properties were valuable, and the Paulets' first reaction was to try to disprove the will. As there was no doubt either of the legitimacy of Lavinia's marriage or of the third Duke's instructions, there was in fact little they could do, and they had to content themselves with a new London property in Grosvenor Square, on the site of what is now the American Embassy. Nevertheless, they refused to forgive the woman whom the 'real' Duchess of Bolton had termed a whore, and Lavinia's period of mourning for her husband was sadly entangled with the legal wranglings over his estate.

Not that the Paulets themselves were paragons of virtue. That their family titles derived from civil rather than soldierly service was all too evident in consideration of the shoddy military records of the men, and apparently the women were not entirely immune to the type of illicit attachments for which the family had once condemned Lavinia Fenton. In June 1808, the *Morning Post* reported that 'another elopement has taken place in high life. A Noble Viscount, Lord S, has gone off with a Mrs P, the wife of a relative of a noble marquis.' A note the next week informed the public that the precise location of Mrs P.'s indiscretion had been an inn near Winchester. Jane Austen was disturbed by the fact that she had taken communion at the same church as Mrs Paulet (for it was she), a short time before the scandal, writing: 'This is a sad thing about Mrs Powlett. I should not have suspected her of such a thing.'[6] (Given the date of the elopement, it is tempting to imagine that 'Mrs P.' was the wife of the son of Lord Bolton who had some years before proved to be such an intolerably bad dancer, and that Lord S. had trodden less upon her feet.)

Whether or not Lavinia had attended her husband on his last journey into Hampshire, Hackwood was now closed to her, and she spent most of her time at Westcombe, though she continued to visit the spas she had frequented with Charles, which suggests that what acquaintance she had formed she preferred to see there, rather than in the potentially more compromising Paulet territory of London. (Since she was now a duchess, it would be interesting to know whether her new neighbour, the same Earl of Chesterfield who had such contempt for actors, paid her a neighbourly call. He had purchased the nearby Ranger's House at Blackheath in 1753.) Lavinia was no longer a young woman, but she was a wealthy and titled widow, and it is surprising that so little mention of her social activities has survived. If her life continued to be quiet, it was not necessarily because she was still frowned upon by society, for society had, in some degree, changed.

Jane Austen might, at the beginning of the nineteenth century, have been disgusted by the reckless activities of Mrs Paulet, but in the period between her departure from the stage and her widowhood, Lavinia had lived through a subtle but significant shift in the moral climate. Economic endeavour had been embraced as a virtue early in the century, and a concomitant emphasis on personal fulfilment in other spheres had been, albeit cautiously, adopted. 'For many, living in Enlightenment England afforded a relaxed, emotionally frank breathing space after the strait-laced patriarchal solemnities of the world of their parents or grandparents – a brief interlude, perhaps, before the doubt, anxiety and muscular stridency characteristic of the probity-conscious Victorians.'[7] Queen Caroline herself was praised by Walpole for tolerating the presence of her husband's mistress, and even the future Bishop of London, according to Horace Walpole, was the 'natural' son of Archbishop Blackburn by his own mistress, Mrs Cruwys.[8]

For Lavinia, though, this relaxation of the hypocritical morality that had made her an outcast came almost too late. For four years she took no advantage of her new freedom, though she apparently indulged herself at the dressmaker's, since one London shop advertised its superior quality by citing 'Her Grace the Duchess of Bolton' among its clients. Polly Peachum's patronage had once meant a great deal more, but Lavinia preferred not to advertise her past as, despite the more relaxed social environment, her dubious status as a former actress might still have compromised her children's chances of advancement.

Although there is no evidence that Lavinia spent time at Hackwood Park after the Duke's death, one of her grandchildren, at least, lived there until the 1790s, though she herself never knew him. Lavinia's second son, Percy Paulet, had become a lieutenant in the Royal Navy, just like his unreliable grandpa Beswick, and proved equally undependable in the matter of returning from his last voyage, though with the decent excuse that he died. His son, Charles (1764–1834), was adopted by Lavinia's eldest boy, who had studied for the Church and become rector of Itchen in Hampshire. Little Charles also became a clergyman, although he had not graduated from university, and also held the living of Itchen, as well as that of nearby Winslade. In 1790, there was still strength enough in his family connections for him to be appointed chaplain to the Prince of Wales, who was prepared to overlook the matter of his lack of a degree. Young Charles had grown up at Hackwood and, despite being short and rather badly built, he was clever (a trait which was presumably inherited from Lavinia's side of the family) and attractive enough for Jane Austen to overlook an attempt to kiss her during a Christmas party in 1796. But blood will out, and the expensive habits with which his great-grandmother had undone Fenton's coffee house eventually undid the royal chaplain. Charles married a lady given to pricey and revealing fashions, 'everything the Neighbourhood could wish her, silly and cross as well as extravagant', as Jane Austen remarked,[9] and eventually the couple were obliged to retire to the Continent for reasons of economy. In one biography of Jane Austen they are rather charmingly pictured as rackety ex-pats, 'figures in a Thackeray novel, living on remittances in a Brussels boarding house, and sometimes surprising new guests with reminiscences of parish life on the one hand, and the Prince of Wales, dancing at Hackwood, and "the Duke my grandfather" on the other'.[10] Charles had a son, named Armand for family tradition, who was rather a dashing character. He served in the Crimean War and left an eyewitness account of the Charge of the Light Brigade.

Lavinia's third son, the first Armand in the family, also pursued a career in the Army, and his descendants became respectable members of the landed gentry at Thorpe Hall near Peterborough, though this hardly compared with the grandeur of Bolton Hall or Hackwood. So although Lavinia's boys were never to enjoy the secure, elevated public positions their uncles accepted as their birthright, they were all three moderately successful. Lavinia does not seem to have been greedy on her sons' behalf: they were gentlemen, their mother was a duchess, and if the rector of Itchen would never sit in the House of Lords, nor would he serve coffee in Charing Cross. Whatever their disappointed hopes, the Paulet boys and their descendants were undeniably respectable, which is a great deal more than Lavinia might have hoped for had Mrs Beswick had her way early on.

Did Lavinia ever regret the abandonment of her career? Her marriage to Bolton was successful, and perhaps in its way set a precedent, for another member of her profession, Harriet Mellon, was to marry the Duke of St Albans in the early nineteenth century. Miss Mellon had no doubts about the disadvantageous difference between the freedom she had enjoyed as an actress and the boredom of life as a fashionable lady, recalling that 'the society in which I formerly moved was all cheerfulness, all high spirits – all fun, frolic and vivacity; they cared for nothing, thought of nothing, beyond the pleasures of the present hour, and to those they gave themselves up with the utmost relish'.[11] By contrast, she referred to her married existence as a 'treadmill', claiming that the pleasures of aristocratic life were a dreary form of repetitive work, an emptiness which John Gay had satirised in his early work *The Toilette*. Polly Peachum is mocked for her desire to imitate such a degree of refined boredom, but Lavinia never showed that she mourned the exchange of the excitements of the stage for the tranquillity of the tea table.

Lavinia had never availed herself of those 'pleasures' of which Miss Mellon spoke so wistfully: her short life in the theatre had been one of hard work and prudence. Whether or not she agreed that society was merely a 'stupid, monotonous round', she certainly had not participated in it with much enthusiasm during the years preceding her marriage, nor did she choose to do so as a widow. The quietness and taste for domesticity that had maintained the Duke's attraction to her were genuinely part of her temperament, if her behaviour after his death is an indication of her sincerity. Almost.

# 14

# THE FATE OF POLLY PEACHUM

After the 1728 success of *The Beggar's Opera*, imitators hurried to cash in. Henry Carey's 1715 play *The Contrivances* was performed as a ballad opera in 1729 and Chetwoode's *The Lover's Opera* at Drury Lane the same year, swiftly followed by *The Wedding*, *The Village Opera* and *The Statesman's Opera* by various forgotten authors. Henry Fielding made an attempt at the style with his own *Lottery* and *Welsh Opera*. Newgate and 'lowlife' continued as popular themes, with Christopher Bullock's *Match in Newgate* appearing at Lincoln's Inn in 1729 along with Brome's *Merry Beggars*. Even the sneering Colley Cibber made an unsuccessful gambit, which he discussed bombastically in his memoirs, claiming that it was the celebration of vice that had made Gay's work so popular. 'I was so stupid as to attempt something of the kind, upon quite a different foundation, that of recommending virtue and innocence, which I ignorantly thought might not have a less pretence to favour, than setting greatness and authority in a contemptible, and the most vulgar vice and wickedness, in an amiable, light.' Cibber's moralistic toadying did not produce the hoped-for returns at the box office, but he was made Poet Laureate in 1730, to the fury, if not the surprise, of the Scriblerians, who expected nothing better from the philistine at Buckingham Palace.

The actress Kitty Clive left a recollection of the first night of Cibber's *Love in a Riddle* in which Lavinia's role in saving the first performance of *The Beggar's Opera* is commemorated. 'I remember the first night of "Love in a Riddle" (which was murdered the same year), a Pastoral Opera wrote by the Laureat, which the Hydra-headed multitude resolv'd to worry without hearing, a Custom with authors of Merit. When Miss Rafton came on in the part of Phillida, the monstrous Roar subsided. A person in the Stage-Box ... called out in the following elegant style "'Zounds Tom! Take care, or this charming little Devil will save all!'".[1] Long after Lavinia's retirement, the moment at which she captured the hearts of London audiences remained emblematic.

The rivalry between Faustina and Cuzzoni, which Gay had used as the basis for the relationship between Polly Peachum and Lucy Lockit in the *Opera*, was repeated in a quarrel between Mrs Cibber and Mrs Clive as to who should play Polly in a production of 1736. This quarrel in turn spawned a new piece, *The Beggar's Pantomime, or, The Contending Columbines*, which mocked their squabbling over the part. Whatever Colley Cibber thought of the play, the women in his family seemed to like it, as his daughter, Charlotte Charke, also played in the *Opera* – as Macheath in Roman dress at Drury Lane in 1734.

Gay himself had been equally anxious to make a profit from a sequel to his play, and it is notable that he named the second piece *Polly* after the most popular character in the first. However, by the time *Polly* was ready for production, Walpole, who had been forced to tolerate the scornful inferences of audiences of *The Beggar's Opera*, was ready to act. Previously, no direct censorship had been enacted on the theatre by the state, except through heavy taxation after the passing of the Stamp Act in 1712. Now, Walpole insisted that *Polly* be inspected by the Lord Chamberlain before permission was given to perform it. Lord Hervey reported that Walpole 'resolved rather than suffer himself to be produced for thirty nights together upon the stage in the person of a highwayman, to make use of his friend the Duke of Grafton's authority as Lord Chamberlain to put a stop to the representation of it. Accordingly, this theatrical "Craftsman" was prohibited at evey playhouse.'[2] This was the introduction of what eventually became a serious piece of legislation for the theatre, the passing in 1737 of a bill decreeing that all plays must pass through the Lord Chamberlain's office before they were performed. At the same time, Walpole briefly moved to close down all playhouses with the exception of Drury lane and Covent Garden, a measure managers cunningly avoided by giving 'concerts' with plays as the 'intermission piece'. *The Beggar's Opera* was consequently influential in one of the first formal attempts by the state to gain control of artistic expression.

The Licensing Act had far-reaching repercussions for the London theatre, and also upon the companies of travelling actors who had capitalised on the popularity of drama to build unlicensed theatres of their own in provincial towns including Bath, Bristol, York and Ipswich. Though the required patents were subsequently achieved, and those theatres remained open, the most enduring legacy of the Act was to stifle attempts at dramatic originality for fear of censure, a consequence that seriously affected both the nature and quality of writing for the stage in England for over one hundred years. Satirical comedy, with the exception of fewer than ten plays written by Oliver Goldsmith and Richard Brinsley Sheridan, died an abrupt death, inaugurating a period of sentimental dullness in drama that lasted until the last decades of the nineteenth century. The fame of actors such as Garrick and Macklin in the second half of the eighteenth century should not detract from the fact that though the roles they played were tremendous, they were almost entirely gathered from the pre-1737 repertoire. Posterity might well thank Walpole (and indirectly Gay and Lavinia), for forcing Henry Fielding to give up comedy and try his hand at novels, but *The Beggar's Opera* maintained its unique position to some extent by default, having effectively destroyed, by the power of its attack on the mores of its time, the possibility of future competition.

(According to the *Craftsman*, Colley Cibber was also instrumental in the suppression of *Polly*, having slandered it in a coffee house without having read it. That Gay was aware of the laureate's spite is suggested in his later piece *The Rehearsal at Goatham*, in which a puppet show is to be performed at one inn, kept by Broach (Rich) but envied by another innkeeper, Cackle (Cibber), who does his best to prevent the presentation.)

It was undoubtedly to Gay's advantage, though, that the Lord Chamberlain, as was expected, refused permission for *Polly* before it was staged. Like many sequels, it is a poor shadow of the original, and Gay made more from its notoriety as a censored text than he ever would have done from a production. The drama is set in the West Indies, where Polly follows Macheath, who has disguised himself as a pirate, having escaped England after a robbery. Through various adventures and betrayals, Polly eventually comes face to face with her runaway husband, but does not recognise him with his blackened face, and discovers his identity only after he dies. Gay then marries her off to an Indian chief.

The play is a sentimental and rather obvious comparison of Old World cynicism with New World innocence, and compared to *The Beggar's Opera*, it is a sorry thing, but its suppression was a joy to the gossips and pamphleteers of London. Banning it betrayed an uncharacteristic lack of acuity on Walpole's part, for in doing so he created a scandal which equalled that of the original production.

Gay's champion, the Duchess of Queensberry, was so incensed by the refusal of the government to sanction the play that she attempted to get up a subscription for the text at court, going so far as to ask the King and Queen (at the time entirely guided by Walpole, who was punishing Gay if not for the *Opera* itself then for the opposition's use of it) to contribute. As a consequence, she was punished by being barred from court. She responded to the notice of her dismissal with a letter explaining: 'The Duchess of Queensberry is surprised and well pleased that the King has given her so agreeable a command as to stay away from Court, where she never came for diversion, but to bestow a civility on the King and Queen. She hopes that by such an unprecedented order as this that the King will see as few as he wishes at his Court, particularly such as dare to think or speak the truth.'[3] The Duchess's impertinence was such that her husband was obliged to resign his post as Admiral of Scotland. She, however, remained unrepentant, and Gay made a fortune of £1,200 from the subscription to 10,000 copies of *Polly*.

Dr Arbuthnot wrote teasingly to Swift on 19 March 1729: 'The inoffensive John Gay is now become one of the obstructions to the peace of Europe, the terror of the ministers, the chief author of the "Craftsman", and all the seditious pamphlets which have been published against the government . . . He is the darling of the City . . . I hope he will get a good deal of money by printing his play, but I really believe he would get more by showing his person, and I can assure you that this is the very identical John Gay whom you formerly knew and lodged with in Whitehall two years ago.'[4] The subscription list to *Polly* became a register of declaration for Walpole's opponents, and included Lords Bathurst, Bolingbroke and Oxford as well as the Duchess of Marlborough. His Grace the Duke of Bolton naturally also subscribed.

Until the end of the century, Gay's smash hit remained the single most popular production in the theatrical repertoire. As well as being performed, the text was printed in forty-five runs and thirteen editions.

The popularity of *The Beggar's Opera* had transformed it into a source of allusion as well known as the characters of Shakespeare's plays. Even *Polly* eventually got an airing, in 1777, with a very elderly Duchess of Queensberry sitting triumphantly in the audience. The London diarist Anna Larpent touchingly recorded that 'she heard it with delight. She sang all the airs after the actors, she told me a story about every song, how Gay wrote it such a night after supper . . . how he wanted a rhyme, that she helped him.' The Duchess's loyalty was especially charming, given what a dull play *Polly* is.

## SOME MISFORTUNES ARISING OUT OF THE PERFORMANCE OF *THE BEGGAR'S OPERA* . . . AND A CHARMING STORY

While the Paulet family were scandalised by the Duke of Bolton's liaison with an actress, they were not alone in experiencing some distressing consequences of the fame of *The Beggar's Opera*. In 1732, one Signora Volante brought a troupe of rope-dancing Irish youths to perform a version of *The Beggar's Opera* at the Little Theatre, Hay, featuring the celebrated Peg Woffington as Macheath, Mrs Peachum and Diana Trapes – no mean feat even for an actress of her talents. The Signora's novel interpretation was reportedly a disaster, with the young acrobats entangling themselves like so many clumsy spiders, and Mrs Woffington withdrew from the production in disgust.

The next year, the *Opera* was performed by a travelling company in Jamaica. On the first night, they earned 370 pistoles, but unfortunately their prudence was not equal to their profits. 'Had the Company been more blessed with the Virtue of Sobriety, they might, perhaps, have liv'd to carry home the liberality of those generous Islanders,' sniffed Chetwoode in *Some Account of the English Stage*. As it was, a combination of distemper and rum punch saw to three Pollies in as many months and eventually all that remained of Macheath, Peachum and their gang was one old man, one woman and a little boy. This trio gamely embarked for Carolina to join another company at Charleston, but drowned en route in a shipwreck. Nonetheless, when Lewis Hallam prepared his company for a tour of the New World in 1752, *The Beggar's Opera* was one of only three plays included which had not been in repertory before 1728, so clearly its popularity surmounted the traditional superstition of the acting profession. It went on to earn great acclaim in the colonies.

In 1777, a dissenting version of the *Opera* was produced by a Captain Thomson, who aimed to correct the shocking morals of fifty years before. Macheath finishes in the convicts' hulks, where he is visited by Lucy and Polly. The highwayman weeps with gratitude at being let off so lightly and a good deal of mutual repentance is shared out all round. Needless to say, the production was a desperate flop.

In 1782, the *Gentleman's Magazine* reported that two sensitive ladies fell into hysterical laughter when one Mr Bannister appeared as a transvestite Polly Peachum in a rather progressive production. They were removed from their seats, but continued to be so overwhelmed with mirth that, the magazine explained, some days later they both 'expir'd as martyrs to the comic spirit'.

It has been suggested that *The Beggar's Opera* killed off the vogue for Italian opera itself, which, though its frenzied popularity certainly declined, still continued to draw crowds. Later commentators, however, have accused John Gay of being personally responsible for the horrors of the modern musical. 'Notwithstanding all the merits of this piece, it is much to be wished that it had never been written, as its success has entailed on us, from that time to this, those bastard comedies ... most of which have been miserably inferior to the prototype, and many of them little more than mere vehicles for the songs.'[5]

Gay also succeeded in giving another obscure woman a little niche in history. In 1725, during one of their tours around England, Gay, Swift and Pope had stayed at an inn, the Rose in Wokingham, where they wrote a jolly verse in praise of the landlord's pretty daughter, which was subsequently published in *Mist's Weekly Journal* in response to a challenge from the editor for poems including words ending in 'Og'. The poem is a frippery:

> The schoolboy's desire is play day,
> The schoolmaster's joy is to flog;
> The milk-maid's delight is on May-day,
> But mine is on sweet Molly Mog.

But the merest association with the famous writers was enough to merit an obituary for Molly in the *Dublin Gazette* when she died in 1766. There is still a pub on the Charing Cross Road in London which is named for her.

# 15

## ℐN ℋONOURABLE ℰXCHANGE

ℐhree years after the Duke of Bolton ran away with Polly Peachum, Lord Hervey commented upon the proposed marriage between the Duchess of Cleveland and one 'pink-cheeked' Philip South-cote: 'Such an exploit will make Her Grace's name ... proverbial for idiocy. The selling herself once to a fool with a great title and a great estate was a common, and consequently excusable, prostitution, but to buy a fool without either title or estate, and deprive her age of the comforts for which she sacrificed her youth, is a madness, a weakness, and an infamy which nobody can forgive her.'[1] Hervey here shows himself perfectly *au fait* with the ways of his world. Certain 'pros-titutions' are acceptable, and certain are not. Lavinia Fenton had cer-tainly sold herself dear to her Duke, but as mistress and wife she had remained entirely faithful to her side of the bargain. As for Mr Kelly the Irish surgeon, she was not so far gone in 'madness and weakness' that she attempted to marry him seventeen years after the Duchess of Cleveland's moment of folly, but she loved him for all that.

For George Kelly, the Duchess of Bolton was a splendid catch. Grad-ations of rank were still important within the medical profession, and surgeons were considered lower in status than physicians, having received their apprenticeship during a seven-year indenture rather than a degree from one of the universities. Some surgeons, like John Ranby, the son of an innkeeper who was elected to the Royal Society in 1724 and became principal sergeant-surgeon to George II in 1743, estab-lished profitable practices with many high-society patients, but for the practitioners who hung about flourishing spa towns like Bath, Tun-bridge and Weymouth, medical skill was not the only necessary quality for getting ahead. 'The tendency of ladies in search of social diversion and sexual dalliance to discover an urgent need for a visit to the "waters" was a well-established joke.'[2] The inter-class mingling that occurred in watering places meant that men like Kelly, who in London would never have been sent for to wait upon a duchess, had access to clients well beyond their usual social sphere, and Kelly had himself already established something of a reputation as a fortune-hunter at Tunbridge. If Lavinia knew this, she clearly didn't care, taking Kelly with her to Westcombe when she left Tunbridge. So George Kelly was with her to the end, whether or not it was because he wanted to ensure that the Duchess would not change her mind. Horace Walpole's letter describing the events gives the impression that Lavinia died at Tunbridge, but the fact that the lawyer Kelly sent for in her last days, who refused to draw up the will, was replaced by an advocate from the London Court of Chancery, confirms that her death took place at her London home, and that the relationship with Kelly had lasted two years.

Nevertheless, as a resident of Tunbridge, it was to Canterbury that Kelly travelled, two weeks after his lover's death, to prove her will. It was duly ratified by the Prerogative Court on 7 February 1760. The testament of the Most Noble Lavinia Duchess Dowager of Bolton, widow and relict of Charles late Duke of Bolton, declared:

> The money in South Sea annuities . . . is to be for the benefit of Charles Paulet and his two brothers Percy and Horatio Armand Paulet. The settlement of my house and lands at Westcombe Co. Kent, I confirm and I bequeath all the furniture and farming utensils to said Charles. I have the personal advowsons of the churches of Sherfield upon Lodden and Itchin Abbas Co. Southampton. I will my exec. to present Charles now Rev. Charles Paulet MA to said livings the first time they become vacant. I am entitled expectant upon the decease of George Kelley of Tunbridge Wells Co. Kent to reversion of certain manors in Co. Kent. I give all my intent therein to said Geo. Kelley and heirs. To Rev. Charles Paulet one thousand pounds. To Mrs Anne Sutherland two hundred and fifty pounds. To my goddaughter Lavinia Cuddon one hundred pounds. Residue to Geo. Kelley, sole Exor.

Presumably, the Rev. Charles and his two brothers were less

delighted than Mr Kelly at this outcome of their mother's death. Perhaps their disgust at their meagre inheritance was what provoked them to offer for sale in June 1760, at the rooms of Messrs Prestage and Hobbs of Conduit Street, 'the genuine and large sideboard of wrought and other plate of the Most Noble Charles, Duke of Bolton, deceased, consisting of a large service of Gadroon dishes, and plates, tureens, dish covers, waiters, salvers, sauceboats, candlesticks, knives, forks and spoons, bread basket, cruet frame, coffee pot, saucepan etc.'. How much they obtained from this transaction is unknown, but their father's coroneted silverware was likely to be worth a good deal less than the fortune their mother had so infuriatingly bestowed upon her gigolo.

One imagines that any tears shed by handsome Mr Kelly over the demise of his once-famous mistress were swiftly mopped up with bank-notes.

While the Duchess of Bolton was enjoying her last months of happiness at Tunbridge with her unsuitable lover, the name of Lavinia Fenton was heard once again about the theatres of London. During the theatrical season of 1758–9, a revival of *The Beggar's Opera* at Covent Garden, starring a Miss Brent as Polly and John Beard (the same Mr Beard of whose first marriage Lady Mary Wortley Montagu had so violently disapproved and who would subsequently marry John Rich's daughter Charlotte) as Macheath, ran for thirty-nine performances, including benefits, with only one break. London was as wild for the opera as it had been thirty years before, much to the chagrin of Mr Garrick who, despite his best efforts as Ranger and Benedict, despite the distinction of his Hamlet and his Lear, was forced to admit that this year the public was interested in nothing but English ballads and the eternal, irritating Polly Peachum. Thomas Davies's *Life of Garrick* emphasised its subject's frustration at the continued success of the *Opera*. 'Of all the entertainments of the stage, none has been so properly serviceable to the players as *The Beggar's Opera*. A new Polly or a new Macheath has successfully given such spirit and lustre to that humorous dramatic satire that the public has often run to see it for twenty or thirty nights successively. Davies added flatteringly that Miss Brent had neither the face nor the figure to represent the 'amiable simplicity' of the innocent Polly, and recalled Miss Fenton's delightfully clear rendering of the ballads.

Lavinia Fenton was a hugely talented actress, but she had not been an ambitious one. Her short period of fame has been described as 'a brief flash of summer lightning, electrifying the London stage for two magical years'.[3] She never made any attempt to revive her career, and if she continued her theatrical acquaintance after she retired from the stage she did it so discreetly, either from embarrassment or expediency, that no record can be found of it. One writer suggests that she was wise enough to resist the fleeting charm of celebrity, knowing that even success such as hers would decline in the end and that she would be left old, poor and humiliated. 'The career of Lavinia Fenton was unique, and wisely she left it to speak for itself.'[4] Perhaps the finest monument to that dazzling yet curiously modest triumph was the theatre that John Rich built from the profits of *The Beggar's Opera*. The saying that the *Opera* had 'made Gay rich and Rich gay' did not mean that the manager himself had failed to profit, and his aspirations after Lavinia's triumph were too grand to be contained by the old house at Lincoln's Inn. The new building, at Bow Street, Covent Garden, was the largest playhouse London had ever seen, with a capacity of nearly 1,400 people. Until it burned down in 1808, it stood as a monument not only to Rich's ambition and Gay's genius, but to the woman without whose talents neither of them would have succeeded so magnificently.

Meanwhile, the old theatre at Lincoln's Inn was left uninhabited, except for an old porter and his wife, who used the stage as a workshop and dried their linen in the flies. The interior looked as though it was still recovering from the aftermath of a riot, though it was in no worse a state than Drury Lane in the wake of the famous insurrection of the French dancers. The dressing rooms and the green room could still be seen, though even if anyone still remembered that Polly Peachum had played there, they were unlikely to pay the theatre a visit, especially not alone or after dark. For during the final performance of Mr Lun's *Harlequin Faustus*, the last-ever production at Lincoln's Inn itself, it was remarked that there seemed to be one dancer too many in the chorus, a dancer whose costume was even more convincingly demonic than those of his fellows. It was said that when the show ended, this 'supernumerary demon' did not retire to the wings or reappear for his bow, or, even more curiously, wait about with the other capering fiends for his pay, but flew up towards the gallery in a puff of smoke more

violent than any of Mr Rich's contriving, and disappeared through the
tiled roof, taking a good part of it with him, whereupon the company
superstitiously concluded that Lucifer himself had taken a last turn on
the doomed theatre's stage.

Given Lavinia's association by marriage with the gentleman, she
might not have been too afraid of meeting him on a nostalgic turn around
the decayed scene of her acclaim, and anyway, according to the Paulet
family, she had long since gone to the Devil. Agreeing that bad blood
would out in the end, Charles's relatives concurred that the Duchess of
Bolton was living in obscure poverty in the East End slums from which
their foolish relative had plucked her, since the London house was let.
In fact, Lavinia had returned to Greenwich, to the home she had always
preferred. The fact that the road up to Westcombe from East Greenwich
ran past the poorhouse might lend some credence to the theory that the
Paulet version was based on mere geographical inaccuracy, but it seems
far more likely to have been simple spite. Her blood was never blue
enough for her husband's family, but nor did it carry so much of the
taint of vice the pamphleteers had revelled in thirty years before. Still,
she was, after all, Lieutenant Beswick's child. After years of stifling in
sick rooms, his blood in her was roused and soothed by the lulling
proximity of the sea. Perhaps.

Or maybe the attraction of Greenwich was that it recalled other scenes
from her past. In 1665, Samuel Pepys had written of a visit 'by coach to
Greenwich Church, where a good sermon, a fine church, and a great
company of handsome women'. This was not the church that Lavinia
knew, since the building Pepys admired had fallen down in 1710, and
Nicholas Hawksmoor had been commissioned to redesign it at the
Crown's expense. St Alfege's is one and one-third times as long as it is
broad, and its height is one-third of its breadth. The new ceiling, at
seventy-nine feet, was at the time of its construction the largest suspended structure of its kind in Europe. Within, two galleries rise above
the flanks of pews, connecting opposite the altar, which is raised from
the nave, and defined by two carved columns connected by a central
arch. The woodwork is by Gibbons, recalling the fine panelling in the
hall at Hackwood. Galleries, a proscenium, a company of fine ladies . . .
The church where Lavinia Beswick, alias Fenton, alias Polly Peachum,
alias the Duchess of Bolton worshipped for the last years of her life,

and where she chose to be buried, looks, in short, very much like a theatre.

The theatre, finally, is the only place we can be sure of Lavinia. There she kneels, her gown pale as a sweep on May Day, the handkerchief clutched to her imploring face, eyes turned up pathetically to the gallery. What remains besides, mostly, is stories, stories whose plausibility is a product not necessarily of their truth, but of the confidence with which they are declared. Sometimes the untruths of a life are as revelatory as its facts. Tourists still go walking up to Capple Bank in Yorkshire to peep through the windows of Polly Peachum's tower, Polly Peachum who was Lavinia Fenton, according to some the child prostitute who rose from her knees on Rich's stage to become a duchess, who surely was a duchess and maybe never a whore, but the story is better that way.

If Lavinia Fenton represents her age, it is in the very elusiveness of her self. In Gay's play *Polly*, one character declares: 'I have a fine library of books that I never read, I have a fine stable of horses that I never ride; I build, I buy plate, jewels, pictures, or anything that is valuable or curious, as your great men do, merely out of ostentation.' The accumulation of objects about a person do not make up a life, and perhaps we should beware of 'ostentation', the assumption that the wanton heaping of facts, piled up like the glistering jumble of valuables and tat in Jonathan Wild's counting house, Clio perched gaudily atop like one of Gay's whores, makes for knowledge of a kind. We might say that Lavinia was an ordinary person who found herself living an extraordinary life, or we might say that in order to have propelled herself into such unbelievable circumstances, she must first have been extraordinary. She does not tell us. Lavinia's was an age of memoirs and letters and diaries, of an explosion of investigation of the inner life which is recognisably modern, yet she remains, for her times, uncharacteristically silent. It was also an age of masks, of disguises, of selves revealed by selves concealed. Lavinia plays teasingly with her masquerade vizard at the edge of the frame, reminding us that we have nobody's daughter's word for what really happened.

# EPILOGUE

# A SALE AT GREENWICH

If upper-classs society has despised Lavinia Fenton in life, it is certainly curious about her in death. Shortly after the Dowager Duchess of Bolton's funeral, the actress Anne Bellamy and a friend ride over to Blackheath to visit another actor, Foote, who proposes an excursion over to Westcombe to the sale of My Lady Bolton's furniture. One member of the company, a Dr Francis, is reluctant to attend the sale alongside Miss Bellamy, since there will be people of fashion there and the lady, being an actress after all, is not quite *comme il faut*. He is therefore not included in the party, though Miss Bellamy sniffily observes that he is not above accepting a free box seat from her, whatever her reputation. Instead of the prudish doctor, Miss Bellamy attends the sale with 'an author named Cleland'.[1] It is fortunate for Dr Francis that he is so distracted by the state of Miss Bellamy's character, for were he to know of Mr Cleland's, it might bring on an apoplexy. John Cleland is the author of *Memoirs of a Woman of Pleasure*, the creator of Fanny Hill, the harlot whose salacious autobiography earned more than £10,000 for her publisher, and ended far more happily than that of her poor counterpart in paint, Moll Hackabout. Mr Cleland is familiar with the world Polly Peachum inhabits, the thieves and whores and taverns and bagnios, and he has personal experience of the inside of the debtors' prison. As he squires Miss Bellamy's wounded pride between chairs and side tables, the French clock Lavinia brought back from her honeymoon, her books and her pictures, all marked with a discreet price tag, Mr Cleland smiles. A clever girl, he once wrote, may, with a care for her virtue, come to be a duchess, by and by.

# ℬIBLIOGRAPHY

ARTICLES

The *Burlington Magazine*, Vol. 90, 1948

The *Craftsman*, issues for 1728

The *Daily Journal*, April 1728

*Eighteenth Century Life*, May 1994: 'The Eighteenth Century Actress and the Construction of Gender: Lavinia Fenton and Charlotte Charke' by Cheryl Wanko

The *Gentleman's Magazine*, various issues

*The Magazine Programme*, No. 24, 'The Stage of the Past (Being Epistles in the Lives of Actors and Actresses of Other Days) (London, Westby & Co.)

*Notes and Queries*, N.S.28 (June 1981): 'The Beaux' Stratagem and The Beggar's Opera' by P. Lewis (pp. 221–4)

*PMLA (Publication of the Modern Languages Association of America)* Vol. LVIII, ed. Percy Walden Long, December 1943: 'Nature to Advantage Dressed: Eighteenth Century Acting' by Alan S. Downer

*Scientific American*, March 2001: 'French Leave' by James Burke

*Smollett's British Magazine*, 1760

*The Stage* (21 January 1960): 'Polly Peachum' by Frances Collingwood

*Studies in Philology* LII, October 1955: 'Rant, Cant and Tone on the Restoration Stage' by J.H. Wilson

*Times Literary Supplement*, No. 1734 (25 April 1935), 'The Beggar's Opera' by James Sutherland


VOLUMES

Allen, R.J.: *The Clubs of Augustan London* (Cambridge, Massachusetts, Harvard University Press, 1933)

Ashe, Geoffrey: *The Hell-Fire Clubs: A History of Anti-Morality* (London, W.H. Allen & Co., 1974)

Avery, Emmett L. (ed.): *The London Stage 1660–1800: Part 2, 1700–1729* (Carbondale, Southern Illinois University Press, 1960)

Barton Baker, H.: *History of the London Stage and Its Famous Players* (London, Routledge, 1904)

Bazin, Germain: *Baroque et Rococo* (Paris, Sari, 1994)

Bence-Jones, Mark and Montgomery Massingberd, Hugh: *The British Aristocracy* (London, Constable, 1979)

Bindman, David: *Hogarth* (London, Thames & Hudson, 1981)

Bloom, Harold (ed.): *John Gay's 'The Beggar's Opera'* (New York, Chelsea House, 1988)

Boas, Frederick S.: *An Introduction to Eighteenth Century Drama 1700–1800* (Oxford, Clarendon Press, 1953)

Bolton, W.B.: *The Amusements of London* (2 vols.) (London, John C. Nimmo, 1931)

Boswell, James: *London Journal*, ed. Pottle, F.A. (London, 1950)

Brewer, John: *The Pleasures of the Imagination: English Culture in the Eighteenth Century* (London, HarperCollins, 1997)

Burgess, C.F. (ed.): *The Letters of John Gay* (Oxford, Oxford University Press, 1966)

Cannon, John: *Aristocratic Century: The Peerage of Eighteenth Century England* (Cambridge, Cambridge University Press, 1984)

Chandler, Samuel: *The History of Basing House in Hampshire* (Basingstoke, 1858)

Chesterfield, Lord: *Lord Chesterfield, Letters to His Son* (Stanhope edition, 2 vols.) (New York, Chesterfield Press, 1917)

Cibber, Colley: *An Apology for the Life of Mr Colley Cibber*, ed. Bellchambers, Edmund (London, Simpkin & Marshall, 1822)

Craik, T.W.: *The Revels History of Drama in English: Vol. V, 1660–1750* (London, Methuen, 1976)

Day, Angelique (ed.): *Letters from Georgian Ireland: The Correspondence of Mary Delaney 1731–68* (Belfast, Friar's Bush Press, 1991)

Dillon, Patrick: *The Much Lamented Death of Madam Geneva. The Eighteenth Century Gin Craze* (London, Review, 2002)

Dobbs, Brian: *Drury Lane* (London, Cassell & Co. Ltd., 1972)

Doody, Margaret Anne: *The Daring Muse: Augustan Poetry Reconsidered* (Cambridge, Cambridge University Press, 1985)

Fenwick Gaye, Phoebe: *John Gay, His Place in the Eighteenth Century* (London, Collins, 1938)

Fielding, Henry: *The True Patriot and Related Writings*, ed. Coley, W.B. (Oxford, Clarendon Press, 1987)

Fielding, Henry: *Amelia* (Oxford, Clarendon Press, 1983)

Foucault, Michel: *Discipline and Punish: The Birth of the Prison*, trans. Sheridan, Alan (London, Peregrine Books, 1979)

Fox, Christopher: *Locke and the Scriblerians: Identity and Consciousness in Early Eighteenth Century Britain* (Los Angeles, University of California Press, 1988)

Frank, Judith: *Common Ground: Eighteenth Century Satiric Fiction and the Poor* (Stanford, Stanford University Press, 1997)

Fraser, W.R.: *Sheridan: A Biography*, Vol. 1 (London, 1896)

Gay, John: *Poetry and Prose* (2 vols.), ed. Dearing, V.A. (Oxford, Oxford University Press, 1974)

*The Beggar's Opera*, ed. Loughrey, Brian and Treadwell, O.T. (London, Penguin, 1986)

*Plays Written by Mr John Gay* (London, Strahan, Lowndes & Co., 1772)

George, M. Dorothy: *London Life in the Eighteenth Century* (London, Kegan Paul, 1951)

Goldgar, B.A.: *Walpole and the Wits: The Relation of Politics to Literature 1722–42* (Lincoln, Nebraska, University of Nebraska Press, 1976)

Gould, Robert: *Works* (2 vols.), 'The Play-House: A Satyr' (London, 1709)

Griffiths, Arthur: *Chronicles of Newgate* (London, Chapman & Hall, 1884)

Grundy, Isobel: *Lady Mary Wortley Montagu: Comet of the Enlightenment* (Oxford, Oxford University Press, 1999)

Guerinot, J.V. and Julg, R.D. (eds.): *The Beggar's Opera* (Connecticut, Archon, 1976)

Harvey, A.D.: *Sex in Georgian England* (London, Phoenix, 2001)

Hervey, Lord John: *Memoirs*, ed. Sedgwick, R. (3 vols.) (London, 1931; reprinted 1970)

Hibbert, Christopher: *The Road to Tyburn* (London, Penguin, 1957)

Hill, Aaron: *Essay on the Art of Acting* (London, 1753)

Hill, Brian W.: *Sir Robert Walpole, 'Sole and Prime Minister'* (London, Hamish Hamilton, 1989)

Hook, Michael and Ross, Walter: *The 'Forty Five* (Edinburgh, National Library of Scotland, 1995)

Howson, Gerald: *Thief Taker General, The Rise and Fall of Jonathan Wild* (London, Hutchinson, 1970)

Irving, William Henry: *John Gay, Favourite of the Wits* (North Carolina, Duke University Press, 1940)

Jenkins, Elizabeth: *Jane Austen, A Biography* (London, Victor Gollancz, 1938)

Johnson, Samuel: *The Major Works*, ed. Greene, Donald (Oxford, Oxford University Press, 1984)

Langford, Paul: *A Polite and Commercial People: England 1727–1783* (Oxford, Oxford University Press, 1989)

Lees-Milne, James: *Earls of Creation: Five Great Patrons of Eighteenth Century Art* (London, Hamish Hamilton, 1962)

Levine, J.M.: *The Battle of the Books: History and Literature in the Augustan Age* (New York, Cornell University Press, 1991)

Linebaugh, Peter: *The London Hanged: Crime and Civil Society in the Eighteenth Century* (London, Verso, 2003)

Mack, Maynard: *Alexander Pope: A Life* (New Haven, Yale University Press, 1985)

Macklin, Charles: *Memoirs*, ed. Cooke, William (London, Bible & Crown Constitution, 1804)

Martin, Joanna: *Wives and Daughters: Women and Children in the Georgian Country House* (London, Hambledon & London, 2004)

Moore, A.: *The Life of Lavinia Beswick, alias Fenton, alias Polly Peachum* (London, Schultz, 1728)

Moore, Lucy (ed.): *Con-Men and Cutpurses: Scenes from the Hogarthian Underworld* (London, Penguin, 2000)
*Amphibious Thing: The Life of Lord Hervey* (London, Viking, 2000)

Muralt, Louis de: *Letters Describing the Character and Customs of the English and French Nations* (London, T. Edlin, 1726)

Neale, R.S: *Bath 1680–1750, A Social History, or A Valley of Pleasure Yet a Sink of Iniquity* (London, Routledge & Kegan Paul, 1981)

Nokes, David: *John Gay: A Profession of Friendship* (Oxford, Oxford University Press, 1995)

O'Gorman, Frank: *The Long Eighteenth Century* (London, Hodder Headline, 2002)

Paulson, Ronald: *Hogarth: His Life, Art and Times* (New Haven, Yale University Press, 1971)

Pearce, Charles E.: *Polly Peachum and 'The Beggar's Opera'* (London, Stanley Paul & Co., 1913)

Picard, Lisa: *Dr Johnson's London* (London, Weidenfeld & Nicolson, 2000)

Porter, Roy: *English Society in the Eighteenth Century* (London, Penguin, 1982)
*Flesh in the Age of Reason* (London, Allen Lane, 2003)

Price, Cecil (ed.): *The Letters of Richard Brinsley Sheridan* (3 vols.) (Oxford, Clarendon Press, 1966)

Ribeiro, Aileen: *Dress and Morality* (Oxford, Berg, 2003)
*Dress in Eighteenth Century Europe* (New Haven, Yale University Press, 2002)

Richards, Sandra: *The Rise of the English Actress* (London, Macmillan, 1993)

Rogers, Pat: *Grub Street: Studies in a Subculture* (London, Methuen, 1972)

Rudé, George: *Hanoverian London* (Stroud, Gloucestershire, Sutton, 2003)

Sambrook, James: *The Eighteenth Century. The Intellectual and Cultural Context of English Literature 1700–1789* (New York, Longman, 1986)

Saussure, César de: *A Foreign View of England in the Reigns of George I and George II* (London, 1729)

Schultz, William Eben: *Gay's 'Beggar's Opera': Its Content, History and Influence* (Newhaven, Yale University Press, 1923)

Scouten, Arthur H. (ed.): *The London Stage 1660–1800. Part 3, 1729–1747* (Carbondale, Southern Illinois University Press, 1961)

Shaw, Stebbing: *A Tour to the West of England* (London, 1788)

Stone, Lawrence: *The Family, Sex and Marriage in England 1500–1800* (London, Penguin, 1977) and abridged edn (New York, Harper & Row, 1979)

Straub, Kristina: *Sexual Suspects: Eighteenth Century Players and Sexual Ideology* (Princeton, Princeton University Press, 1992)

Strong, Roy: *Feast: A History of Grand Eating* (London, Jonathan Cape, 2002)

Styan, J.L.: *The English Stage: A History of Drama and Performance* (Cambridge, Cambridge University Press, 1996)

Summers, Judith: *The Empress of Pleasure* (London, Viking, 2003)

Thomas, David (ed.): *Theatre in Europe: A Documentary History, Vol. 1: Restoration and Georgian England 1660–1788* (Cambridge, Cambridge University Press, 1989)

Tomalin, Claire: *Mrs Jordan's Profession* (London, Penguin, 1994)

Trumbach, Randolph: *The Rise of the Egalitarian Family: Aristocratic Kinship and Domestic Relations in Eighteenth Century England* (New York, Academic Press, 1978)

Turner, E.S.: *Amazing Grace: The Great Days of Dukes* (Stroud, Gloucestershire, Sutton, 2003)

Uglow, Jenny: *Hogarth: A Life and a World* (London, Faber & Faber, 1997)

Voltaire, *Letters Concerning the English Nation* (Oxford, Oxford University Press, 1994)

Warren, W.T.: *The History of the Great Siege of Basing House* (Winchester, Hampshire, 1920)

Waterhouse, Ellis: *Painting in Britain 1530–1790* (London, Penguin, 1953)

Wickham, Glynne: *A History of the Theatre* (2nd edn) (London, Phaidon, 1992)

Wilkes, Robert: *A General View of the Stage* (London, 1730, and J. Coote, 1759)

Willey, Basil: *The Eighteenth Century Background* (London, Routledge, 1940)

Wintoun, Calhoun: *John Gay and the London Theatre* (Lexington, University Press of Kentucky, 1993)

Woodfield, Ian: *Opera and Drama in Eighteenth Century London* (Cambridge, Cambridge University Press, 2001)

# $\mathcal{N}$OTES

INTRODUCTORY NOTE ON SOURCES
Many editions of the works of Pope, Gay and Swift are available. Those I used
for the frequent citations in this book are the one-volume version of the best
edition of Pope's works, *The Twickenham Edition of the Poems of Alexander
Pope* (11 vols.), edited by John Butt (Methuen, 1938–68), V.A. Dearing's edition
of John Gay's writing *John Gay: Poetry and Prose* (Oxford University Press,
1974) and for Swift, *The Poems of Jonathan Swift*, edited by Harold Williams
(3 vols.) (Clarendon Press, 1937) and Herbert Davies's *Swift: Prose Works* (14
vols.) (Blackwell, 1939–68). Since the latter two titles are somewhat unwieldy,
I also used the Oxford Authors edition, *Jonathan Swift: A Critical Edition of
the Major Works*, edited by Angus Ross and David Woolley (Oxford University
Press, 1984). For Gay's correspondence, C.F. Burgess's *Letters of John Gay*
(Clarendon Press, 1966) is the standard edition, while for Pope's letters I consulted George Sherburn's edition, *The Correspondence of Alexander Pope* (5
vols.) (Clarendon Press, 1956), which is the edition employed by Pope's finest
biographer, Maynard Mack. Swift's letters are quoted from *The Correspondence
of Jonathan Swift* (5 vols.), edited by Harold Williams (Clarendon Press, 1963).
*The Beggar's Opera* is also widely available, but the edition I have drawn upon
most frequently is that edited by Brian Loughey and O.T. Treadwell (Penguin,
1986), which is both accessible and portable.

Lord Hervey, Horace Walpole and Lady Mary Wortley Montagu are among
the most famous chroniclers of their period, and their commentaries were indis-
pensable in the construction of this book. For Lord Hervey, I used both the
standard edition of the *Memoirs*, which is Lord John Hervey, Marquess of
Bristol, *Memoirs of the Reign of George II*, edited by J.W. Croker (1884), as well
as the more modern abridged version of Romney Sedgwick's three-volume
edition of 1931 (Penguin, 1981). Lady Mary's writing was standardised in 1837
by her relative Lord Wharncliffe. I consulted the slightly later *Letters and Works
of Lady Mary Wortley Montagu* (Swan Sonnerschein & Co., 1893). I also used
*The Letters of Lady Mary Wortley Montagu*, edited by Robert Halsband, (3
vols.) (Clarendon Press, 1965). Walpole's œuvre, edited in forty-five volumes by
W.S. Lewis (Yale University Press, 1937–83), is frankly terrifying, but was less

daunting in the shorter version of Lewis, *Correspondence* (Penguin USA, 1998).

The only approach at a serious life of Lavinia Fenton of which I am aware is Charles E. Pearce's *Polly Peachum and 'The Beggar's Opera'* (Stanley Paul & Co., 1913), which I used eagerly, but with some reserve, as where its narrative focuses on Lavinia herself, it depends largely on the various apocryphal 'Lives' which appeared in such bewildering and inventive abundance in 1728.

## PROLOGUE: THE DUCHESS AND THE IRISH SURGEON

1. Quoted in William Henry Irving's *John Gay, Favourite of the Wits* (1940).
2. William Cooke, actor and theatrical diarist, in Charles Macklin, *Memoirs* (1804).
3. Charles Pearce, *Polly Peachum and 'The Beggar's Opera'* (1913).

## 1: A SUCCESSFUL EXECUTION

1. Maynard Mack, *Alexander Pope: A Life*, p. 361.
2. Letter to William Broome, *The Correspondence of Alexander Pope*, No. 1922.
3. Pope to Swift on Motte's *Miscellanies in Verse and Prose*, 18 February 1727, cited in *John Gay: Favourite of the Wits*, p. 227.
4. George Gilfillan, *Life of John Gay* (London, John Walker, 1851).
5. Swift, 'Description of a City Shower'.
6. Pamphlet published by London Sheriffs in 1782, quoted in Arthur Griffiths, *Chronicles of Newgate* (1884), p. 282.
7. James Boswell, *Life of Samuel Johnson* (1791).
8. William Oxberry, *A Dramatic Biography* (London, 1825).
9. H. Barton Baker, *History of the London Stage and Its Famous Players 1576–1903* (1904).
10. Ibid.
11. Quoted in *Plays Written by Mr John Gay* (1772).

## 2: THE CELEBRATED MISS FENTON

1. Lady Mary's letter is quoted in Pearce, op. cit.
2. Pearce, op. cit.
3. Ibid.
4. The 1813 print of Lavinia and accompanying (anonymous) poem are in the Heinz Archive, London.
5. A. Moore, *The Life of Lavinia Beswick, alias Fenton, alias Polly Peachum* (1728).
6. John Brewer, *The Pleasures of the Imagination: English Culture in the Eighteenth Century* (1997).
7. Quoted in David Thomas, *Theatre in Europe. A Documentary History* (1989), p. 189.
8. William Law, cleric, author of *The Absolute Unlawfulness of the Stage Enter-*

*tainment, Fully Demonstrated* (1736) and *The Players' Scourge* (1757).

9. Boswell's comment on whores is quoted in A.D. Harvey, *Sex in Georgian England* (2001).
10. Ibid.
11. Jenny Uglow, *Hogarth: A Life and a World* (1997).
12. Cecil Price, *The Letters of Richard Brinsley Sheridan* (1966), Vol. 3, p. 305.
13. Law, *The Players' Scourge*, op. cit.
14. Johnson to Garrick on actresses, quoted in Thomas Davies, *Life of Garrick* (2 vols.) (London, Longman, 1808).
15. Horace Walpole to Horace Mann, quoted in Arthur Griffiths, *Chronicles of Newgate* (1884), p. 265.
16. Griffiths, op. cit., p. 451.
17. M. Dorothy George, *London Life in the Eighteenth Century* (1951).
18. Johnson is quoted in George, op. cit.
19. Patrick Dillon, *The Much Lamented Death of Madam Geneva: The Eighteenth Century Gin Craze* (2002), p. 6.
20. Bernard de Mandeville, philosopher and satirical social commentator, whose most famous work is *The Fable of the Bees*.
21. A. Moore, op. cit.
22. The Portuguese lover is quoted in A. Moore, op. cit., and in a 1728 pamphlet, *The Original Polly Peachum*.

**3: THEATRICAL CRIMINALS**

1. Johnson's remarks are quoted in Boswell's *Life*. Johnson's prejudice against theatre actors, to which Boswell refers as a 'peculiar acrimony' is also evident in his *Life of Savage*, p. 28, and attributed to 'the licentious and dissolute manners of those engaged in that profession'.
2. Ibid. Also quoted in Davies, *Life of Garrick*.
3. Robert Wilkes, actor and writer – whose finest role, according to Colley Cibber, was Othello – in *A General View of the English Stage* (1730 and 1759).
4. Quoted in Brian Dobbs, *Drury Lane* (1972), p. 86.
5. *Letters from a Moor at London* (London, F. Noble, 1739), p. 109.

**4: SEEING IS DECEIVING**

1. *Objections to Descartes' 'Méditations Philosophiques'*, quoted in Roy Porter, *Flesh in the Age of Reason* (2003), p. 72.
2. *Lord Chesterfield: Letters to His Son* (1917).
3. Earl of Shaftesbury's private notebooks, quoted in Brewer, p. 112.
4. Brewer, op. cit., p. 69.
5. Aileen Ribeiro, *Dress in Eighteenth Century Europe* (2002).
6. *Spectator* No. 107, quoted in Judith Frank, *Common Ground: Eighteenth Century Satiric Fiction and the Poor* (1997), p. 4.

## 5: UNNATURAL TASTES AND CURIOUS DIVERSIONS

1. David Thomas, *Theatre in Europe: A Documentary History, Vol. 1: Restoration and Georgian England 1660–1788* (1989).
2. Colley Cibber, *An Apology for the Life of Mr Colley Cibber* (1822).
3. Aaron Hill, quoted in 'Nature to Advantage Dressed' by Alan S. Downer, *PMLA*, Vol. LVIII, December 1943, p. 1023.
4. Review in the *Laureat*, quoted in Dobbs, op. cit., p. 75.
5. Cibber, op. cit.
6. Quoted in Thomas, op. cit.
7. *Spectator*, 1711.
8. This description of the castrato voice is from the critic and poet Enrico Panzacchi (1840–1904), after hearing one of the last of the castrati sing in the Sistine Chapel at the end of the nineteenth century. Quoted in 'I Preziosi Mostri' by Marina Pinto in *Scienza*, March 2004 (translated from Italian by the author).
9. Sir John Hawkins, *A General History of Music* (London, 1776).
10. Quoted in Lucy Moore, *Amphibious Thing. The Life of Lord Hervey* (2000), pp. 18–19.

## 6: OPERA, WALPOLE AND THE MAKING OF THE STAR

1. Frank, op. cit., p. 3.
2. David Hume, 'Of Refinement in the Arts' (1752) in *Essays, Moral, Political, Literary*, ed. Eugene F. Miller (Liberty Fund, 1987), Library of Economics and Liberty.
3. Thomas Clayton is quoted in Thomas, op. cit.
4. Cibber, op. cit.
5. The apposite comparison between Walpole and Wild is drawn by Lucy Moore, *Amphibious Thing: The Life of Lord Hervey*.
6. David Nokes, *John Gay: A Profession of Friendship* (1995).
7. Quoted in Nokes, op. cit.
8. Griffiths, op. cit., p. 207.
9. Quoted in Nokes, op. cit.
10. Swift, *Gulliver's Travels*, Book 3, Chapter 6.
11. Quoted from an article in a Dublin newspaper by Sir John Hawkins, op. cit.
12. Pope, 'Essay on Man'.
13. Paul Langford, *A Polite and Commercial People: England 1727–1783* (1989), p. 12.
14. Quoted in Langford, op. cit., p. 22.
15. John Cannon, *Aristocratic Century: The Peerage of Eighteenth Century England* (1984).
16. Nokes, op. cit., p. 438.
17. From Pope's introduction to 'The Dunciad'.

## 7: POLLY PEACHUM'S LOVER

1. William Cobbett's remarks on the first Marquis of Winchester appear in an essay on Netley Abbey, published in 1830, the revenues from which were given by Henry VIII after the dissolution of the monasteries to 'one of his Court sycophants', William Paulet.
2. Bishop Burnet, *History of My Own Time* (2 vols.) (London, 1724 and 1734).
3. Ibid.
4. Quoted in Cannon, op. cit.
5. Lord John Hervey, Marquess of Bristol, *Memoirs of the Reign of George II*.
6. Thomas Hearne, *The Complete Peerage* (1771).
7. Quoted in M. Dorothy George, *London Life in the Eighteenth Century* (1951).
8. Quoted in George Rudé, *Hanoverian London* (2003), p. 71.
9. Quoted in Pearce, op. cit.
10. W.S. Lewis, *Correspondence* (1998).
11. Ibid.
12. Quoted in Cannon, op. cit.
13. Lewis, op. cit.
14. Quoted in Randolph Trumbach, *The Rise of the Egalitarian Family: Aristocratic Kinship and Domestic Relations in Eighteenth Century England* (1978).

## 8: PLAYING THE GENTLEMAN

1. Quoted in Griffiths, op. cit.
2. Charles Johnson, *A General History of the Lives and Adventures of the Most Famous Highwaymen* (London, 1734).
3. Ibid.
4. James Boswell, *London Journal*.
5. Boswell's *Life of Samuel Johnson*, op. cit.
6. Quoted in Roy Porter, *English Society in the Eighteenth Century* (1982), p. 95.
7. Quoted in Lucy Moore, *Con-Men and Cutpurses: Scenes from the Hogarthian Underworld* (2000).
8. The *Monthly Chronicle*, April 1728.
9. A. Moore, op. cit, corroborated by Pearce, op. cit.
10. Swift, 'A Tale of a Tub'.
11. Quoted by Pearce, op. cit., from the *Craftsman*.

## 9: THE POLITICS OF SATIRE

1. Nokes, op. cit.
2. May 1727. Quoted in Irving, op. cit., p. 231.
3. Gay's *Letters*, Nos. 65–7. Also quoted in Nokes, op. cit., p. 402.

4. Sherburn, *The Correspondence of Alexander Pope*.
5. Mrs Howard to Gay quoted in Irving, op. cit., p. 232
6. Mack, op. cit., p. 217.
7. Macklin, a well-known actor, was tried and acquitted for murder in 1735. He also quarrelled famously, though less fatally, with his fellow actor Quin.
8. Quoted in Nokes, op. cit., p. 76.

## 10: AN EXCUSABLE PROSTITUTION

1. Ronald Paulson, *Hogarth, His Life, Art and Times* (1971).
2. Pearce, op. cit.
3. Ibid.
4. A. Moore, op. cit.
5. Ibid.
6. Anonymous, 'Laura, or The Fall of Innocence, a Poem' (1787).

## 11: VALLEYS OF PLEASURE

1. Quoted in M. Girouard, *Life in the English Country House* (London, 1979).
2. Thomas Coke, Earl of Leicester, quoted in Porter, *English Life in the Eighteenth Century*, p. 60.
3. George Colman, *The Genius*, No. 5 (1761) in *Prose on Several Occasions* (London, 1787).
4. Reverend Joseph Warton, *Memoirs*, also quoted in Pearce, op. cit. For a further description of Warton who eventually became Headmaster of Winchester School and a distinguished literary critic, see 'French Leave' by James Burke in *Scientific American* (March 2001).
5. Bernard de Mandeville, *A Modest Defence of the Public Stews* (1724).
6. From a pamphlet quoted in R.S. Neale, *Bath 1680–1750, A Social History, or A Valley of Pleasure Yet a Sink of Iniquity* (1981), p. 17.
7. Elizabeth Montague was a distinguished intellectual, author and patron who was included in Richard Samuel's 1777 engraving *The Nine Living Muses of Great Britain*. She is quoted in Neale, op. cit.
8. From the journal of Anna Larpent, quoted in Brewer, op. cit., p. 70.
9. T. Benge Burr, *The History of Tunbridge Wells* (London, 1766), p. 121.
10. Macklin, op. cit.
11. Johnson, *Rambler*.
12. Ibid.

## 12: TWENTY-THREE YEARS BEFORE MARRIAGE

1. This story told in Isobel Grundy, *Lady Mary Wortley Montagu: Comet of the Enlightenment* (1999).
2. Lord Ilchester is quoted in Joanna Martin, *Wives and Daughters: Women and Children in the Georgian Country House* (2004), p. 40.

3. Quoted in Irving, op. cit.
4. Quoted in *From London to Land's End* (London, Cassell & Co., 1888).
5. R.W. Chapman, *The Letters of Jane Austen* (Oxford, Oxford University Press, 1952). Also quoted in Claire Tomalin, *Jane Austen: A Life* (London: Viking, 1997), p. 87.
6. Ibid.
7. *Hasted's History of Kent*; also Pearce, op. cit.
8. Daniel Defoe, *A Tour Thro' The Whole Island of Great Britain* (1727). (Penguin USA edition, 1978, ed. Pat Rogers.)
9. R. Polwhele, *Poems*, v. 65. Quoted in Langford, op. cit., p. 109.
10. Porter, *English Society in the Eighteenth Century*, op. cit., p. 29.
11. Quoted in Martin, op. cit.
12. Lawrence Stone, *The Family, Sex and Marriage in England 1500–1800* (1977), p. 7.
13. A. Moore, op. cit.
14. Hervey, op. cit.
15. Swift's *Journal to Stella*, Letter 41, London, 9 February 1711; *Journal to Stella* ed. Steve Thomas (Adelaide, University of Adelaide ET Collection, 2003).
16. Quoted in Trumbach, op. cit.
17. The rhyme is credited (by Hervey, and subsequently in Pearce) to Sir Charles Hanbury Williams.
18. Quoted in Pearce, op. cit.
19. 'The Life of Mr Gay', published in *The Weekly Miscellany*, 30 December 1732. The quotation is from the version published in London in February 1733, p. 72.
20. Pearce, op. cit.
21. Mack, op. cit., p. 585.
22. Ibid., p. 585.
23. Discussed and quoted in Mack, op. cit., p. 189.

## 13: WIFE AND WIDOW

1. Pearce, op. cit.
2. Lavinia's honeymoon inspired the Reverend Warton to write 'Venes Written at Montauban in France', a patriotic piece published in the April edition of the *London Magazine* in 1755. The poem contrasts the delightful climate of southern France with its political oppression, and stoutly states a preference for liberty, albeit beneath a 'colder, changeful sky'.
3. *Letters from Georgian Ireland: The Correspondence of Mary Delaney 1731–68*, ed. Angelique Day (1991).
4. Pearce, op. cit.

5. Elizabeth Montague to the Duchess of Portland, 1740, cited in Neale, op. cit., p. 12.

6. W.R. Chapman, op. cit. Also quoted in Elizabeth Jenkins, *Jane Austen, A Biography* (1938) and Tomalin, op. cit.

7. Porter, *English Society in the Eighteenth Century*, op. cit., p. 258.

8. W. S. Lewis, op. cit

9. W.R. Chapman, op. cit. Also quoted in Elizabeth Jenkins, *Jane Austen, A Biography* (1938) and Tomalin, op. cit.

10. Tomalin, op. cit.

11. Quoted in Brewer (op. cit.), pp. 341–2.

### 14: THE FATE OF POLLY PEACHUM

1. Kitty Clive's recollection is quoted in Irving, op. cit.

2. Hervey, op. cit.

3. Quoted in Hervey, op. cit.

4. Quoted in Nokes, op. cit.

5. *Plays Written By Mr John Gay*, op. cit.

### 15: AN HONOURABLE EXCHANGE

1. Lord Hervey to Stephen Fox, quoted in Martin, op. cit., p. 10.

2. Langford, op. cit.

3. Frances Collingwood, 'Polly Peachum' in *The Stage*, 21 January 1960.

4. Pearce, op. cit.

### EPILOGUE: A SALE AT GREENWICH

1. Anne Bellamy's memoirs were privately printed in London in the 1740s. Her description of the visit to Westcombe is confirmed by Pearce.

# ℐNDEX